Nature's Virtue

Other Books of Interest from St. Augustine's Press

Nature's Virtue

James F. Pontuso

ST. AUGUSTINE'S PRESS
South Bend, Indiana

Manufactured in the United States of America.

1 2 3 4 5 6   25 24 23 22 21 20 19

Library of Congress Cataloging in Publication Data
Names: Pontuso, James F., author.
Title: Nature's virtue / James F. Pontuso.
Description: 1st [edition].
South Bend, Indiana : St. Augustines Press, Inc., 2016.
Includes bibliographical references and index.
Identifiers: LCCN 2016033737
ISBN 9781587315572 (hardcover : alk. paper)
Subjects: LCSH: Virtue.
Classification: LCC BJ1521 .P66 2016
DDC 179/.9--dc23 LC record available at https://lccn.loc.gov/2016033737

∞ The paper used in this publication meets the minimum
requirements of the American National Standard for Information Sciences -
Permanence of Paper for Printed Materials, ANSI Z39.48-1984.

St. Augustine's Press
www.staugustine.net

Table of Contents

Acknowledgments

The Committee on Professional Development at Hampden-Sydney College supported this book through its summer grant program. My friend Rosalind Warfield-Brown took time from her responsibilities as director of various English language programs in the Middle East and Asia to lend her expert eye to the manuscript. My thanks to Helen Freeh and Bruce Fingerhut at St. Augustine's Press. Chapter 1 of this book was published as "Can the Free Market Work Without Virtue?" *Perspectives on Political Science* 44 (Spring 2015): 65–76. Various other parts were published in quite different form as "Being, Time, and Art: Solzhenitsyn's Reflections on Heidegger's Question," *Society* 51:2 (Spring 2014): 156–68. "Why Hollywood Hates Business: Immanuel Kant's Role in *Avatar*; Movie Reviewed by Adam Smith," *Philosophy Study* 3:6 (June 2013): 470–480. "Aristophanes as the Founder of Postmodernism Rightly Understood," *Perspectives on Political Science* 45 (Fall 2007): 215–221.

Introduction

I have not seen a person who loved virtue, or one who hated
what was not virtuous. Confucius[1]

Virtue is not what it used to be. It has lost its reputation and even its good
name. "The word 'virtue,'" explains Bernard Williams, "has for the most
part acquired comic or otherwise undesirable associations, and few now use
it except philosophers."[2] If virtue were a television show, it would garner
low ratings and promptly be cancelled. If it were a politician, it would have
been voted out of office long ago. If virtue were running for president, it
would fare poorly in the Iowa caucuses and would drop out of the race after
a weak showing in the New Hampshire primary.

Virtue is not taken seriously nowadays because it is considered unnatural. Virtue is not seen as perverse, just as not natural. Most people do not
use the word virtue at all. In common parlance, people discuss morality,
although it too has a vaguely negative connotation. Morality is often associated with hidebound bigots and religious fanatics who are intent on forc-
ing their narrow views on others. Academic institutions offer courses in
ethics, usually with a modifier: medical ethics, leadership ethics, business
ethics, or criminology and ethics. What is most often heard when people
make judgments is the word values. Since each person has his or her own
values, the idea fits nicely into our egalitarian, tolerant, non-judgmental
culture. Occasionally, brighter college students, trying to impress the
teacher, employ the term ideology. But they have no idea what the word
means, and use it as a synonym for values. They would be distraught if
they realized that ideology was popularized by Karl Marx to undermine

---

1   Confucius, *Analects of Confucius*, trans. James Legge (New York : Paragon Book
     Reprint Corp., 1966 [1893]), VI:1
2   Bernard Williams, *Ethics and the Limits of Philosophy* (Cambridge, MA: Harvard
     University Press, 1985), 9.

the bourgeois life with which they are so familiar and comfortable. Moreover, students do not realize that having "values" connotes not moral rectitude, but rather the nihilistic will-to-power that marks the end of Western metaphysics and, with it, all hope of grounding judgments in anything beyond personal whim.[3]

People on the political left dislike virtue because they associate it with narrow-minded dogmatists who defended their position, prestige, and way of life with rationalizations based on traditional norms of behavior. They often point to Southerners who justified segregation by arguing that civil rights protesters were uncivil and ill-mannered.[4]

Virtue has lost its luster on the political right – or at least among Libertarians – because they see it as an infringement on personal freedom. Virtue requires that people act in certain ways, but Libertarians maintain that people should act as they please. Libertarian principles advocate freeing people to pursue their rational interests. Proponents believe no government, set of beliefs, or divine commands should interfere with personal autonomy.

Postmodernists ridicule virtue because they view it at best as a quaint convention of various historical cultures. At worst, it is a tool of oppression foisted on society to keep the lower classes orderly.

Deconstructionists see virtue as a way to disguise and rationalize the superiority of the upper class. They use literary criticism to attack the legitimacy of every hierarchical principle, since all are based on a disproportion of power.

Feminists dismiss virtue as a manifestation of male chauvinism. They point out its historical association with male dominance.[5]

Virtue has lost its good name in part because of the nature of modern communication. Many of the perceptions we have of human nature come from movies, television, newspapers, and the Internet. The media is driven by the imperative to deliver the news, which means, of course, something "new," as in novel, unexpected, and never-before-seen.[6] In order to attract

---

3 See Martin Heidegger's analysis of "values" in "The Word of Nietzsche 'God is Dead,'" in Martin Heidegger, *The Question Concerning Technology and Other Essays*, trans. William Lovitt (New York Harper & Row, 1977), 104–106.

4 Stephen L. Carter, *Civility: Manners, Morals, and the Etiquette of Democracy* (New York: Basic Books, 1988), 20–37.

5 Catharine A. MacKinnon, *Women's Lives, Men's Laws* (Cambridge, MA: Belknap Press, 2005).

6 On the role of the media and the "new" see Harvey C. Mansfield, Jr., *America's Constitutional Soul* (Baltimore: Johns Hopkins University Press, 1991), 163–76.

viewers, the media and popular culture present the out-of-the-ordinary, exceptional, and astounding, inundating viewers with stories of violence, sadism, and catastrophe. These depictions have become so widespread that they are easily taken as the norm of human conduct. The news reports war, murder, famine, and cruelty. The entertainment industry has created a genre of the murder mystery with more clever, diabolical, and sinister villains than Conan Doyle, Ian Fleming or even Edgar Allen Poe created. As the ability to communicate has advanced, more and more stories, both fictitious and real, assault us daily – meant to entertain and astound, but in reality coarsening and brutalizing many among us. With the exponential growth of the media, the extraordinary has become ordinary, and once-commonplace virtues have become outdated and ultimately discarded.

Innovations in communication and transportation have also made it possible for people to learn about cultures different from their own. The panoply of moral, religious and ethical traditions that were once distant and foreign are today still foreign but not distant. People have always known that societies different from their own existed, but modern communication and transportation make it possible for them to actually confront "otherness" instantaneously. The postmodern condition is now an experience, not a theory, a state of affairs in which various cultural practices, principles, and values are thrown together in a global stew. As Czech playwright-dissident-President Václav Havel explains:

> Today, this state of mind or of the human world is called post-modernism. For me, a symbol of that state is a Bedouin mounted on a camel and clad in traditional robes under which he is wearing jeans, with a transistor radio in his hands and an ad for Coca-Cola on the camel's back.[7]

In the past, people understood that other cultures treasured religious and ethical beliefs different from theirs, but most rejected those principles as false, even when the differences had more to do with form than substance. The record of war, struggle, and conquest indicates that the clash of cultures – one cause of which is disagreement about mores – has always been part of human history. Differences in language made the other incomprehensible and deepened fears and suspicions about anything unfamiliar.

---

7   Václav Havel, "Address to the Senate and the House of Commons of the Parliament of Canada," Parliament Hill, Ottawa, 29 April 1999, http://www.hrad.cz/.

In our age, the question is not which of the moral codes is correct, but rather, whether any valid moral codes exist. Globalization has eroded our belief in virtue because people now have a universal perspective from which to assess the differing moral principles of the world's cultures. Such a view makes relativism more forceful than in times past since there are so many conflicting, yet equally confident, claims to moral authority.

Oddly, the media's frantic response to almost-daily instances of inhumanity and carnage shows that notions of proper behavior still exist somewhere. In fact, it might even be possible to maintain that we live in a moralistic age. Any hint of corruption, self-serving behavior, or cruelty is swiftly condemned in the public arena. Even the appearance of a conflict of interest can result in accusations of misuse of power. Unintended impoliteness toward an oppressed race or gender has become grounds for formal rebuke.[8] Some people go so far as to extend moral imperatives to our treatment of animals.[9] We live in a highly moralistic age that does not believe in morals.

Is everyday life actually as dramatic and violent as it is presented? In most places in the world, ordinary life is quite ordinary. What accounts for these normal, even kindly, relationships between people? Why are they peaceful, law abiding, and decent? If, as some insist, there is no foundation for virtue, or people act only out of self-interest, how can we explain why so many people are good to each other?

This returns us to the topic of this book, virtue. So many volumes have been written about virtue – or its close relatives, morality and ethics – that a number of questions come to mind. Can any book comprehensively cover the subject? The answer in the present case is no. Only an encyclopedia could encompass even a fraction of the works dedicated to the idea and practice of virtue. I have consulted a variety of texts and have tried to present ideas that are both interesting in the current discourse and essential in understanding the issues. Moreover, a manuscript that tries to present all the secondary literature on this subject risks becoming tedious, more erudite than informative.

Is another book on a well-worn topic really needed? Obviously, I think it is. Perhaps each generation needs to revisit the subject of virtue and vice,

8   John McWhorter, "'Microaggression' Is the New Racism on Campus," *Time*, March 21, 2014, http://time.com/32618/microaggression-is-the-new-racism-on-campus/.

9   Alasdair C. MacIntyre, *Dependent Rational Animals: Why Human Beings Need the Virtues* (Chicago: Open Court, 1999).

if for no other reason than to place the topic in a contemporary setting and to remind ourselves of the complexity of the issues. My reflections began in my studies of two dissidents, Aleksandr Solzhenitsyn and Havel. Both men tenaciously opposed tyranny, believing that the actions of their governments were evil. They were steadfast in exhibiting the most highly regarded virtue of the ancient world – courage. In order to justify their civil disobedience they explored how people come to know what is right. In pondering the problem, both men confronted what is sometimes called the crisis of the West – the loss of belief in principles that guide and explain our lives. Both addressed the issue in speeches at Harvard University, one of the centers of Western learning.[10]

My own position is also influenced by James Q. Wilson's commonsense view of morality. Wilson begins with an obvious yet intriguing question: Why do people do good? If humans are always and everywhere self-interested, or if there are no unquestioned standards of proper human conduct, how can so many acts of good behavior and virtue be explained? Of course, some individuals are antisocial and amoral, and for them, force or threat of force might be the only means to subdue their aggressive behavior. But most people do not abuse their parents, beat their children, steal from their local grocery store, wantonly destroy public property, or kick their pets.[11]

Wilson indicates that claims of moral relativity are overstated. Most ethical systems decry the same onerous acts and promote similar responsibilities. Moral codes are more alike than dissimilar. Perhaps the differences between cultures stand out because they are so rare and therefore noticeable.[12]

The defect of Wilson's analysis is that it mentions, but does not confront, the anti-foundationalist argument.[13] If there is no foundation for truth, it is impossible to claim any validity for morals, as Wilson does. Therefore, a defense of virtue turns on the question of whether there is a metaphysical ground to existence.

The loss of belief is not simply a result of instantaneous communication

---

10 Aleksandr Solzhenitsyn, "Harvard Address," in *The Solzhenitsyn Reader: New and Essential Writings 1947–2005*, eds. Edward E. Ericson, Jr. and Daniel J. Mahoney (Wilmington, Del.: ISI Books, 2006), 561–575; Václav Havel, Speech at Harvard University, 8 June 1995, http://www.vaclavhavel.cz/showtrans. php?cat=projevy&val=190_aj_projevy.html&typ=HTML.

11 James Q. Wilson, *The Moral Sense* (New York: The Free Press, 1993), 1–26.

12 Wilson, *Moral Sense*, 199.

13 Wilson, *Moral Sense*, 4, 6, 8.

and quicker travel times. Relativism has also become pervasive thanks to a sophisticated set of ideas trumpeted by some of the world's leading thinkers.

The anti-foundationalist school of thought does not deny the loss of belief; it revels in it. Postmodernism and deconstruction – pervasive today in philosophy, the arts, and academia – argue that traditional values serve not to humanize people but to stifle creativity and oppress the disenfranchised.[14]

Because of the morass into which anti-foundationalist thought has cast philosophy, economic theorists, most notably Ludwig Von Mises, have posited the theory that metaphysical ideas are inconsequential, and only action is important. Mises' principles are the basis of the Libertarian school of economic theory. Libertarians maintain that we need not worry about virtue because calculation of economic interest harmonizes people's behavior.

What, then, is an argument for virtue? We live in an odd time. Much of the world enjoys unprecedented peace and prosperity. Wherever the Western model of liberal democracy reigns, people enjoy longer, more secure lives than ever in history. On the other hand, anxiety is the hallmark modern affliction. People feel unconnected, displaced, and unsure. "'Alienation' has become a prominent, even common, theme in current appraisals of man's situation," writes David Easton.[15] Many traditional principles that were primarily based on religion have come under attack – or, more accurately, have been dismissed and discarded. The once-common argument that good societies rest on a strong sense of personal virtue, seems to be contradicted by our "anything goes" culture and our hodge-podge of beliefs.

No one understands the dichotomy of our time better than two flawed geniuses of the last two centuries, Friedrich Nietzsche and Martin Heidegger, to whose ideas much of this book is devoted. Both thinkers objected to the easy resolution of social and political strife inherent in Immanuel Kant's metaphysics and Georg Hegel's philosophy of history. They agreed that creation of a more peaceful world might be possible, but they declared that the price for tranquility is to strip people of spirit and to deny them a purpose for life.

---

14 Georg Lukács, "Existentialism," *Marxism and Human Liberation: Essays on History, Culture and Revolution*, trans. Henry F. Mins (New York: Dell Publishing Co., 1973), http://www.marxists.org/archive/lukacs/works/1949/existentialism.htm; Leslie Paul Thiele, *Thinking Politics: Perspectives in Ancient, Modern, and Postmodern Political Theory* (Chatham, New Jersey: Chatham House, 1997), 82–83.

15 Loyd D. Easton, "Alienation and History in the Early Marx," *Philosophy and Phenomenological Research* 22, no. 2 (Dec. 1961): 193.

In *The Genealogy of Morals*, Nietzsche makes a frontal assault on the humanitarian morality of Kant and Hegel. He attempts to restore the ethos of virtue as excellence and distinction. Even these principles, Heidegger claims, are chimerical, as are all judgments about virtue. Virtue is a metaphysical concept, he says, and all metaphysical speculation is unsound. Metaphysics is no more than a fond hope for redemption in an unknowing and uncaring universe. It has been so since the first people looked to the sky and wished that something in the heavens would save them. As his multi-volume study of Nietzsche shows, Heidegger maintains that the foundational principles of Western Civilization have culminated in a blind alley – or as Nietzsche put it, God is dead.

It is in taking up the challenge of anti-foundationalism that I hope this book will contribute to the on-going dialogue about the place of virtue in human life. It will attempt to define virtue in the course of a discussion of its friends and adversaries.

I have made every effort not to use the complex idioms of Heidegger and his followers. Heidegger's language is often impenetrable, but he repeats himself often enough to make his points clear. His interpreters are sometimes more obscure and less poetic than Heidegger, making the explanations more difficult to comprehend than the original.[16] Heidegger adopted this language because the terms and ideas of philosophy had become encrusted by centuries of interpretation and therefore petrified into patterns of thought that obscure instead of illuminate. "Tradition thus becomes master," Heidegger explains of the historical development of the search for wisdom. "Tradition takes what has come down to us and delivers it over to self-evidence...blocks our access to...original concepts....makes us forget that they had an...origin."[17] He claimed that, "Making itself intelligible is suicide for philosophy."[18]

---

16 See for example William McNeill, *The Glance of the Eye: Heidegger, Aristotle, and the Ends of Theory* (Albany, NY: State University of New York Press, 1999); Jerry Weinberger, "But Which Gods Will Save Us? The Political Legacy of Nietzsche and Heidegger," *Political Science Reviewer* 16 no. 1 (1986): 353–412; Julian Young, *Heidegger's Later Philosophy*, (Cambridge, UK: Cambridge University Press, 2002); Jacques Derrida, *Of Spirit: Heidegger and the Question,* trans. Geoffery Bennington and Rachel Bowlby (Chicago: University of Chicago Press, 1989).

17 Martin Heidegger, *Being and Time*, trans. John MacQuarrie and Edward Robinson (London: SCM Press, 1962), 43.

18 Martin Heidegger, *Contributions to Philosophy (From Enowning),* trans. Parvis Emad and Kenneth Maly (Bloomington: Indiana University Press, 1999), 307.

Scholars familiar with Heidegger's work will likely find my account simplistic (though I hope not suicidally so) and therefore inexact. Perhaps my choice of language is the result of having taught undergraduates for my entire career. I have found that students understand difficult concepts best when given everyday examples to illustrate them. The experience has made me an unreconstructed admirer of Socrates' use of the language of the marketplace.[19]

This book attempts to respond to the challenge posed by anti-foundationalism by restating Plato's theory of the forms or ideas. My method is not to undertake a close examination of one or two texts from the Platonic corpus, but to give a general account and defense of Plato's position. I have tried to make the ideas accessible. Gains in clarity may have resulted in a loss of profundity, but I hope have not descended to level of banality.

19   Plato, *Apology*, 17c.

Chapter One
Can the Free Market Work Without Virtue?

We discuss matters which concern us more, and of which it is
harmful to be in ignorance – whether wealth or virtue makes
men happy, whether self-interest or uprightness leads us to
friendship, what is the nature of the good and what is its highest
form. Horace[1]

Libertarianism, or free-market economics, has grown in popularity and political strength over the last two decades.[2] Ted Cruz (R-TX) has brought
free-market principles to the forefront of the political debate. The Tea Party
and the Republican majority in the House of Representatives are expressions of its vigor. Senator Rand Paul (R-KY) was a strong contender for
the 2016 Republican Presidential Nomination. *Reason Magazine*, the Institute for Humane Studies, and the Austrian School of Economics at
George Mason University have provided the movement with academic
credibility.[3] John Stossel's television program is a showcase for Libertarian
ideas. The works of Libertarianism's founders, Ludwig Von Mises, Murray

1   Horace, *Satires, Epistles, and Ars Poetica*, trans. H. Rushton Fairclough (Cam-
    bridge, MA: Harvard University Press, 1970), 216.
2   Nate Silver, "Poll Finds a Shift Toward More Libertarian Views," FiveThirtyEight,
    New York Times, 20 June 2011, http://fivethirtyeight.blogs.
    nytimes.com/2011/06/20/poll-finds-a-shift-toward-more-libertarian-views/; James
    Antle, "Thanks to Rand Paul, libertarian politics is more popular than ever," *The
    Guardian*, 18 March 2013, http://www.guardian.co.uk/commentisfree/2013/
    mar/18/rand-paul-2016-libertairan-best-chance.
3   Von Mises Institute, http://mises.org/; *Reason Magazine*, http://reason.com/; Insti-
    tute for Humane Studies, http://www.theihs.org/.
4   Friedrich Hayek, *The Constitution of Liberty* (Chicago: University of Chicago Press,
    1960); Murray N. Rothbard, *The Ethics of Liberty* (New York: New York University
    Press, 1998); Robert Nozick, *State, Anarchy, and Utopia* (Oxford, UK: Blackwell,
    1974); Ludwig Von Mises, *Human Action: A Treatise on Economics*, 4th Revised

N. Rothbard, Robert Nozick, Friedrich Hayek, and Ayn Rand, are available online and are widely read.[4] While Libertarianism has never become a dominant public philosophy in the United States and enjoys even less support in Europe, the assumptions of free-market economics underpin strategies adopted in many countries and have fueled broad economic exchanges on a global scale.

Free-market ideas have challenged the neo-Keynesian consensus that reigned after World War II, and the political effect of these dueling economic approaches is apparent in the policy deadlock plaguing America's political institutions at the beginning of the 21st Century.[5]

After the near monetary collapse of 2008, much public outcry blamed the failures of bankers, traders, and real estate investors. The media and many others laid the crisis squarely at the feet of the greedy rich. Their lack of virtue, it was reported, had brought the global economy to the brink of collapse. The Occupy Wall Street Movement was the most visible symbol of the widespread loathing of unregulated financial institutions.

In response to these attacks, Libertarians have promoted free-market principles ever more vigorously. In fact, they propose that applying Libertarian ideas can solve almost all social, financial and even personal problems.[6]

In order to assess Libertarians' claims, it is appropriate to examine the theoretical roots of the philosophy because a group's principles are often best comprehended by exploring their origin. A discussion of the foundational ideas of Libertarianism is warranted because, as James Buchanan points out, "The economist rarely examines the presuppositions of the

Edition (San Francisco: Fox & Wilkes, 1996). See also Jennifer Burns, *Goddess of the Market: Ayn Rand and the American Right* (Oxford: Oxford University Press, 2011; Anne C. Heller, *Ayn Rand and the World She Made* (New York: Nan A. Talese, 2009); Ayn Rand, *Atlas Shrugged* (New York: Random House,1957); Ayn Rand, *The Fountainhead*, (Indianapolis, IN: The Bobbs-Merrill Company, 1943); Friedrich Hayek, *The Road to Serfdom: Text and Documents – The Definitive Edition*, ed. Bruce Caldwell (Chicago: University of Chicago Press 2007).

5   For a historical account of the battle of ideas see Daniel Stedman Jones, *Masters of the Universe: Hayek, Friedman, and the Birth of Neoliberal Politics* (Princeton, NJ: Princeton University Press, 2012); Angus Burgin, *The Great Persuasion: Reinventing Free Markets since the Depression* (Cambridge MA: Harvard University Press, 2012).

6   Peter J. Boettke, *Living Economics: Yesterday, Today, and Tomorrow* (Oakland, CA: The Independent Institute, 2012).

models with which he works. The economist simply commences with individuals as evaluating, choosing, and acting units."[7]

What are Libertarianism's views of social organization, political authority, and human nature? Do those notions accurately reflect the complexity of the human condition? Is their "rational actor" model of individual behavior accurate? Was the theoretical model of free markets ever true in practice? Do societies that organize themselves in ways other than as predicted by Libertarian models contradict the theoretical basis of free-market principles?

What do Libertarians think about virtue and morality? Is it true, as they claim, that something like virtue is so commonplace that it hardly merits study? Do efforts to comprehend and apply ethical principles interfere with mutually advantageous exchanges? Does the quest to find a theoretical foundation of virtue obstruct the practice of virtue?[8]

Action Instead of Metaphysics

Libertarianism is an offshoot of classical liberalism, a movement rooted in John Locke's political philosophy and Adam Smith's economic analysis. It is a reassertion of those principles intended to counter political and theoretical disillusionment with classical economics.

The most influential critic of classical economics is Karl Marx, who virtually demonized the free market, likening it to "dead labor, that, vampire-like, only lives by sucking living labor, and lives the more."[9] Marx's critique was accepted by a substantial portion of the intellectual elite and became a transcendent rallying-point for progressive change in the last two centuries.

Less radical and more commonly accepted theories sought to mitigate the perceived inequality, dislocation, and unfairness created by markets. The welfare state, as it came to be called, attempted to establish a social safety net, shielding people from – in Franklin Roosevelt's words – "fear and want."[10]

---

7   James M. Buchanan Jr., "The Constitution of Economic Policy," Nobel Prize Lecture, December 8, 1986, http://www.nobelprize.org/nobel_prizes/economic-sciences/laureates/1986/buchanan-lecture.html.

8   Christopher J. Coyne, *Doing Bad by Doing Good: When Humanitarian Action Fails* (Stanford, CA: Stanford University Press, 2013).

9   Karl Marx. *Capital*, vol. 1, trans. Samuel Moore and Edward Aveling (Moscow, Progress Publishers, 1924) Marx and Engels Internet Library, http://www.marxists.org/archive/marx/works/1867-c1/ch10.htm#4.

10   Franklin D. Roosevelt, 1941 State of the Union Address, "The Four Freedoms," (6 January 1941), http://millercenter.org/president/speeches/detail/3320.

Libertarianism is a protest against Marxist-inspired central planning and the growth of the welfare state. It assails the inefficiencies of managed economies and the loss of freedom that centralized bureaucratic decision-making entails.

Libertarianism is, however, more than a criticism of super-sized government; its goals are more ambitious than making the economy work more efficiently. The philosophy of Libertarianism claims to make human existence more fulfilling both communally and personally. It is a doctrine of advocacy, prescribing what should happen and how people should strive to achieve well being. Libertarians claim their philosophy is value-free: people should choose whatever way of life pleases them. Yet, Libertarianism also insists that people should dedicate themselves above all to personal autonomy and individual choice. As Nozick makes clear, the Libertarian philosophy not only describes the "truth"; it prescribes behavior.[11] In that sense, Libertarianism is similar to metaphysics in explaining what reality is and how we ought to behave. Perhaps it is more accurate to say that Libertarianism is an effort to replace or rescue metaphysics from the morass of relativism and nihilism that, as Friedrich Nietzsche and Martin Heidegger dramatically point out, undermines its suppositions.[12] Mises explains:

> The radicalism of this wholesale condemnation of economics was very soon surpassed by a still more universal nihilism.... [which] questions not only economics and praxeology but all other human knowledge and human reasoning in general.[13]

Hayek too decries the loss of belief in Western thought. He writes:

> In the struggle for the moral support of the people of the world, the lack of firm beliefs puts the West at a great disadvantage. The mood of its intellectual leaders has long been characterized by disillusionment with its principles, disparagement of its achievements, and exclusive concern with the creation of "better worlds."[14]

11 Nozick, *State, Anarchy, and Utopia*, Preface.
12 Nietzsche, *The Birth of Tragedy and the Genealogy of Morals*, trans. Francis Golfing (Garden City, NY: Doubleday, 1956); Heidegger, *Being and Time*.
13 Mises, *Human Action*, 4–5.
14 Hayek, *Constitution of Liberty*; Murray N. Rothbard, *Ethics of Liberty* (New York: New York University Press, 1998), 2.

If the metaphysics that supported the West is no longer valid, Libertarians argue, at least the behavior of people can be known; hence, the title of Mises' most influential work, *Human Action.*

While philosophers bemoan the lack of unifying principles that explains existence and provide some guidance about how to behave, Mises embraces uncertainty and diversity. Uncertainty allows for innovation, adaptation, and change. Diversity fosters competition, ingenuity, and distinction. It allows people to decide what they want and how they should obtain it. While Western thought might be moribund, Mises insists, people's actions can be studied, understood, and calculated.[15]

Libertarians deny the existence of a single, unifying truth. People are free to choose whatever pleases, gratifies, and fulfills them. Libertarians then apply the concept of marginal advantage to all human conduct: people weigh the advantages and disadvantages of pursuing what they desire. This tenet might be called metaphysical and ethical consumer sovereignty. No one can explain *what* people will desire, but it is true always and everywhere that they will seek to fulfill *some* desire. The role of economics is to understand and explain how people go about getting what they want. "Economics," writes Mises,

> does not assume or postulate that men aim only or first of all at what is called material well-being. Economics, as a branch of the more general theory of human action, deals with…man's purposive aiming at the attainment of ends chosen, whatever these ends may be. We may furthermore say that it is perfectly neutral with regard to all judgments of value, as it refers always to means and never to the choice of ultimate ends.[16]

---

15 Mises, *Human Action*, 1–9.

16 Mises, *Human Action*, 884–5. See also Mises' statement of the manner in which economics overcomes the problem of relativistic values:

> Modern subjective economics starts with the solution of the apparent paradox of value. It neither limits its theorems to the actions of businessmen alone nor deals with a fictitious homo oeconomicus. It treats the inexorable categories of everybody's action. Its theorems concerning commodity prices, wage rates, and interest rates refer to all these phenomena without any regard to the motives causing people to buy or to sell or to abstain from buying or selling. It is time to discard entirely any reference to the abortive attempt to justify the shortcoming of older economists through the appeal to the homo oeconomicus phantom.

While Rothbard criticizes Mises for his values-free economics, he does so only because Mises does not consider free-market economics to be *the* human value. All Libertarians agree with Mises that individual choice should be sacrosanct. Freedom is the predominant good of individual and social life.[17] Walter Williams makes the point even more forcefully. Free markets are morally superior, he maintains, because they respect individual dignity. He writes:

> All too often defenders of free-market capitalism base their defense on the demonstration that capitalism is more efficient in terms of resource allocation and, hence, leads to a larger bundle of goods than socialism and other forms of statism. However...the intellectual defense of free-market capitalism should focus on its moral superiority. In other words, even if free enterprise were not more efficient than other forms of human organization, it is morally superior because it is rooted in voluntary relationships rather than force and coercion, and it respects the sanctity of the individual.[18]

The Practice of Economic Liberty

John Maynard Keynes wrote, "The political problem of mankind is to combine three things: Economic Efficiency, Social Justice, and Individual Liberty."[19] Libertarians would probably agree. However, they would add that economic efficiency and social justice are the inevitable consequences of individual liberty and therefore need not be pursued as political goals. Libertarians take Adam Smith's principle of the invisible hand seriously.[20]

---

17 Rothbard, *Ethics of Liberty*, 206–14.
18 Walter E. Williams, "The Argument for Free Markets: Morality v. Efficiency," *Cato Journal* 15:2–3 (Fall/Winter 1995/1996): 182.
19 John Maynard Keynes, *Essays in Persuasion* (New York: The Norton Library, 1963), 344.
20 Adam Smith, *The Wealth of Nations* (New York: Modern Library, 1776, 1994), 484–85. Smith explains that a person:

> intends only his own security; and by directing that industry in such a manner as its produce may be of the greatest value, he intends only his own gain, and he is in this, as in many other cases, led by an invisible hand to promote an end which was no part of his intention. Nor is it always the worse for the society that it was not part of it. By pursuing his own interest he frequently promotes that of the society more effectually than when he

If people are free to acquire, use, and dispose of property, they will make choices that not only serve to further their own interests, but will also increase the common stock of goods available to everyone. Libertarians celebrate autonomous individuals who in pursuing their interests, raise the standard of living by improving their property and skills. Every human activity will be enhanced by allowing individuals to freely choose what is best for themselves. Libertarians argue that market exchanges are moral – indeed, one of the highest types of morality – because they leave people free to choose where to live, what work to do, and what to buy and sell. Individuals gain dignity since they determine their own destiny.

Libertarians allege that the free market produces the highest possible quality goods and services at the lowest possible prices, while at the same time paying laborers the highest possible wages. "Possible" here is defined as the price at which people's efforts are rewarded by a mutually agreeable compensation. Every business wants to maximize its profits by getting the most return for its investment, but there are only a limited number of methods available for making more money. Companies can, of course, raise prices. But higher prices are no guarantee of larger profits. Consumers may switch to another brand or forego a product entirely. Companies are driven by their own interest to reduce the cost of production and invest in innovations that will yield a greater market share.

Businesses are compelled to compete in order to attract customers seeking the best goods at the lowest price. Companies that attempt to maintain a market share with tried-and-true products and fabrication techniques are always in danger of being overtaken by more appealing items and more efficient manufacturing methods. The best and most efficient always wins out on a level playing field. Mises explains:

> A characteristic feature of the unhampered market society is that it is no respecter of vested interests. Past achievements do not count if they are obstacles to further improvement. The advocates of security are therefore quite correct in blaming capitalism for insecurity. But they distort the facts in implying that the selfish interests of capitalists and entrepreneurs are responsible. What harms the vested interests is

> really intends to promote it. I have never known much good done by those who affected to trade for the public good. It is an affectation, indeed, not very common among merchants, and very few words need be employed in dissuading them from it.

}15{

the urge of the consumers for the best possible satisfaction of their needs. Not the greed of the wealthy few, but the propensity of everyone to take advantage of any opportunity offered for an improvement of his own well-being makes for producer insecurity.[21]

Libertarians envision a labor market in almost the same way they picture capital and production markets. Free people will seek the most lucrative professions and train themselves to become skilled in those jobs. When people are responsible for their own well-being, they will pursue that goal with an eye to their long-term prosperity and advancement.[22] They will improve their condition by doing work that best suits their skills, training themselves to perform tasks that will enhance their earning capacity. They will also change professions and locations from arenas where jobs are scarce to places where they are plentiful.

Upheaval and change are characteristics of free-market economies, but such uncertainty is beneficial because it forces suppliers to acknowledge consumer preferences and provide better, less-expensive goods and services. Workers may be uprooted from their communities, but they will move to places where their labor can be most efficiently used and highly rewarded.[23]

It is difficult to deny that micro-economic theory has the power of prediction. When food is cheap relative to income, people get fat. When high-paying jobs emerge, people move into those professions. When a cheaper or better product appears on store shelves, people buy it.

On the other hand, Libertarians suggest, managed economies distort, although they do not destroy, this naturally occurring desire for self-improvement. People living in state-managed economies seek to gratify their interests in ways not conducive to the advancement of the common good.

For example, in centrally planned communist-era economies, mechanisms of distribution were particularly inefficient. Communist countries produced goods, but they had trouble distributing them rationally. Consumer preferences were not adequately registered because there was no pricing mechanism to tell producers what people wanted. The production of goods was planned years in advance, as was their retail price. When styles or technology changed, communist industries could not adapt. Just as Libertarian

---

21 Mises, *Human Action*, 852.
22 Hayek, *Constitution of Liberty*; Murray N. Rothbard, *Ethics of Liberty*, 598–99; Hayek, *Constitution of Liberty*, 118–32.
23 Mises, *Human Action*, 852.

theory predicts, centrally planned economies had little incentive to maximize profits. The system rewarded managers who met state-set production targets and showed growth over the previous year's figures. The "best" managers were those who could secure and stockpile the often-scarce raw materials required for production.

Just one example among thousands illustrates the inefficiencies of planning. When the U.S.-based company Otis bought a controlling share in the Czech elevator company Tanza, it had to dispose of an entire trainload of rusty, useless raw materials. Former managers had stored the supplies on the site of the Breclav factory to insure that components were available. Such practices meant that communist-era industries often sold goods at prices above the cost of manufacture. Otis managers with an eye to the bottom-line, introduced the less expensive, more efficient just-in-time method of raw material supply.[24]

Communist-era managers also had to employ and retain the skilled labor necessary to meet production targets, often monopolizing and under-utilizing experienced workers who might have been better employed in other jobs. In short, managers had no incentive to consider the cost of production, the quality of goods, or the need for technological innovation.

Because no price mechanism existed in the labor market – all people were paid pretty much the same – absenteeism was a major problem in communist countries. Most workers felt very little commitment to their employer. Moreover, a strong work ethic was incompatible with the communist practice of full employment, where workers were paid whether they worked hard or not. The catch phrase became, "They pretend to pay us, and we pretend to work."

Many workers preferred jobs in the "second economy" where they did not have to pay taxes. They supplemented their salaries with second jobs, which meant that fatigue was often a cause of absence.

Communist Party bureaucrats tried to strike a bargain with the workers: the Party would insure a social safety net for citizens if they remained quiescent. But the deal unraveled when the centralized planned economies with over-capitalized industries failed to provide a high standard of living. While huge sums were expended to build large-scale factories employing thousands of workers, these super conglomerates could not adapt to changes in technology and public taste.[25] They were too expensive to replace and too

---

24 Saul Estrin, Kristy Hughes, and Sarah Todd, *Foreign Direct Investment in Central and Eastern Europe: Multinationals in Transition* (London: Pinter, 1997), 89, 121.

25 Minton Goldman, *Revolution and Change in Central and Eastern Europe* (Armonk, NY: M.E Sharpe, 1997), 157–60.

big to fail since they provided most people's livelihood. "The overall result of these half measures and systematic rigidities," Joseph Rothschild argues, "was to transform both the Soviet Union and east Central Europe into a single 'Greater European Co-Stagnation Sphere.'"[26]

Libertarians, most notably Hayek, predicted all of these disastrous outcomes. He also surmised that planned economies would lead to serfdom; political liberty would be lost along with economic freedom. One could argue that the whole experiment in Marxist economics failed exactly because of the inefficiencies of planning and the bureaucratization of communal life.

The Libertarian critique of government intervention in economic activity does not end with communism. According to Libertarians, democratic nations that attempt to foster growth through an industrial policy or establish a social safety net also jeopardize prosperity. Government programs cause what Theodore Lowi calls "policy triangles." Recipients of government largesse use those funds to lobby governments to keep and expand programs that benefit them. Legislators respond to narrow but intense and financially lucrative incentives by maintaining and expanding those programs – giving both lobbyists and recipients even greater leverage in furthering their interests.[27] Interest groups pressure political leaders to make promises beyond the capacity of countries to meet them; government programs become expensive, intrusive, and inefficient.[28]

---

26 Joseph Rothschild, *Return to Diversity* (Oxford: Oxford University Press, 1993), 219.

27 Theodore Lowi, *The End of Liberalism: The Second Republic of the United States* 2nd ed. (New York: W.W. Norton, 2009).

28 Mises, *Human Action*, 847–848, Mises's 1949 comments on Social Security and government debt:

> Paul in the year 1940 saves by paying one hundred dollars to the national social security institution. He receives in exchange a claim which is virtually an unconditional government IOU. If the government spends the hundred dollars for current expenditures, no additional capital comes into existence and no increase in the productivity of labor results. The government's IOU is a check drawn upon the future taxpayer. In 1970 a certain Peter may have to fulfill the government's promise although he himself does not derive any benefit from the fact that Paul in 1940 saved one hundred dollars.... The trumpery argument that the public debt is no burden because 'we owe it to ourselves' is delusive. The Pauls of 1940 do not owe it to themselves. It is the Peters of 1970 who owe it to the Pauls of 1940.... The statesmen of 1940 solve their problems by shifting them to the statesmen of 1970. On that date the statesmen of 1940 will be either dead or elder statesmen glorying in their wonderful achievement, social security.

Libertarians insist that welfare-state programs create a moral hazard: recipients come to rely on assistance. This dependence is as true for businesses as for individuals.[29] Moreover, when monetary intervention by central banks, under pressure from public officials to maintain constant growth, causes over exuberance in various sectors of the economy, the excessively stimulated bubble bursts. Mises is particularly critical of governmental intervention in business cycles, which he insists intensifies the size and effect of both booms and busts.[30]

Libertarians are wary of experts who claim to know what is good for people better than people know themselves. They deny that *real* interests differ from what people *believe* to be in their interest.[31] They argue that no one has enough information to decide what is best for the economy or for the individuals in it. Although people might make the wrong choice for themselves in some instances, in the long run, Libertarians believe, no one can manage his/her life better than an individual acting for him/herself. Moreover, the millions of personal decisions made by people can never be fully comprehended even by the most complex calculations. What cannot be understood cannot be managed, they say. Thus, it is better to leave people free to choose, a policy that will increase their well-being and, by extension, the general good.[32]

Finally, Libertarians argue that efforts to equalize social conditions actually hurt the poor. Government taxation moves money away from wealthy people who might invest in productive new industries. Such businesses need labor to grow and thrive, employing at least some of those at the lower end of the social hierarchy. Industry, business, trade, and commerce raise all people's standard of living. The productive forces of society increase wealth, whereas government programs merely distribute it. So long as people are left free to decide their destiny, they will labor to improve their own well-being, and at the same time create more goods and services for the common use of all. In a growing economy, wealth is not a zero sum game.

Theory or Advocacy?

While Libertarianism might be a sound economic theory, it also claims to embody a general truth about the human condition. Freedom is the key

29 Hayek, *Constitution of Liberty*, 340–76; Mises, *Human Action*, 812–16.
30 Mises, *Human Action*, 780–93.
31 Hayek, *Constitution of Liberty*, 24–6.
32 Hayek, *Constitution of Liberty*, 24–6.

element of existence, Libertarians believe, because there is no ultimate truth; all people must decide for themselves how to live, which desires to pursue, and what to believe. However, as Nietzsche points out, all theories that deny the existence of truth must be applied to themselves. Are Libertarian principles true, or are they merely the preference of Libertarians?

As we have seen, Mises and Hayek attempt to avoid or sidestep the metaphysical quagmire of modern philosophy. Both present an alternative to the confusion of ideas by offering a description of the way people behave. They maintain that the principles of economics, especially their analysis of micro-economic incentives, can explain much of what people do and why they think as they do. Mises holds that every action can be comprehended only when a coherent theory can be found to explain it. For him, praxeology, the free-market principle of supply and demand and marginal value, is the organizing principle of all true knowledge of human action.

> History cannot teach us any general rule, principle, or law. There is no means to abstract from a historical experience *a posteriori* any theories or theorems concerning human conduct and policies. The data of history would be nothing but a clumsy accumulation of disconnected occurrences, a heap of confusion, if they could not be clarified, arranged, and interpreted by systematic praxeological knowledge.[33]

In this Libertarians are correct, of course, since people respond to incentives – most importantly, to inducements conducive to their physical well-being. But ideas also influence what people think they should do, which in turn influences their actions. Mises' statement makes this clear. Theory organizes and explains actions. Theory precedes comprehension. Facts often are made to fit a theory. This means that human action is only part of the human story. As Bernard Williams points out, if self-interest – the way people behave without prompting or education – were natural, Libertarians would not need to lecture "people who are failing to pursue their own interests."[34]

Because thought is an independent variable, any theory that attempts to explain human nature must take ideas into account. In fact, both the

---

33 Mises, *Human Action*, 41.
34 Bernard Williams, *Ethics and the Limits of Philosophy* (Cambridge, MA: Harvard University Press, 1985), 13.

variability and controversial nature of thought is evident in the field of economics. Despite its claim to scientific rigor, there is as little agreement among economists as there is among philosophers.

Two examples are sufficient to demonstrate the uncertainty of economic theory. First, although many Libertarian claims about the welfare state are accurate, there is some cross-cultural empirical evidence that social democracies have been able to combine income equality with expanding and competitive economies.[35]

Second, the 1974 Nobel Prize in economics was shared by Hayek and Gunnar Myrdal. In his prize lecture, Hayek described the dangers inherent in efforts to stimulate prosperity and growth through government macro-economic intervention. Myrdal then made the opposite argument with regard to foreign aid for developing countries.[36] Thus, it is clear that economists have not reached the level of agreement of, say, physical scientists about the basic tenets of their discipline. Libertarians acknowledge the power of ideas, but the way they try to account for theory's role in human action is either self-contradictory or based on unproven conjectures about human nature.

Libertarians begin with the hypothesis that human beings have rights. This is, of course, an enormous supposition. Why can we take as a given that people have rights? Why should I bother to protect other people's rights if it is not in my interest to do so?

This is exactly the problem with Robert Nozick's influential book, *Anarchy, State, and Utopia.* He begins with the premise that people have rights. From this claim, he reasons that rights are secure only where governments are limited. If rights are the first principle of existence, then government action by definition infringes on those sacrosanct principles when it compels anyone to do anything. Nozick does not try to show from where rights arise.[37] However, does not the basis of such a fundamental assumption have

35 Jonas Pontusson, *Inequality and Prosperity: Social Europe vs. Liberal America* (Ithaca, NY: Cornell University Press, 2005).

36 Compare Gunnar Myrdal, "The Equality Issue in World Development," Nobel Prize Lecture March 17, 1975, http://www.nobelprize.org/nobel_prizes/economic-sciences/laureates/1974/myrdal-lecture.html and Friedrich August von Hayek, "The Pretence of Knowledge," Nobel Prize Lecture, December 11, 1974, http://www.nobelprize.org/nobel_prizes/economic-sciences/laureates/1974/hayek-lecture.html.

37 Alan Dershowitz makes a thoughtful effort to account for the origin of rights in *Rights from Wrongs*, although in order to discover the origin of rights Dershowitz gives up on the idea that rights are natural. Alan M. Dershowitz, *Rights from Wrongs* (New York: Basic Books, 2005).

to be identified? Why have rights not been recognized during much of human history? Why did the concept of rights become the ruling public philosophy only after the Enlightenment? Many would argue that the origin of the "rights revolution" was the philosophy of the Enlightenment, most keenly expressed by political writers such as Francis Bacon, Thomas Hobbes, and John Locke.[38]

Although Rothbard criticizes Nozick for his "immaculate conception" theory of the origin of civil society, he does so only because it is not immaculate enough. Rothbard writes:

> It is highly relevant to see whether Nozick's ingenious logical construction has ever indeed occurred in historical reality: namely, whether any State, or most or all States, have in fact evolved in the Nozickian manner ...the historical evidence cuts precisely the other way: ... every State where the facts are available originated by a process of violence, conquest, and exploitation.[39]

However, this admission indicates that, unlike economics, there is not an invisible hand at work in politics. As Libertarians point out, order is a precondition of commerce.[40] Who wants to open up a shop in the middle of a battlefield? But order is not spontaneous; it is forced on people against their will.[41] So if the order that makes economic exchanges possible is not contractual but is established by compulsion, where do natural rights come from? After all, natural rights theory maintains that people consent to government only to protect their rights. Rights are those things that people have not ceded to the state, and if they *have* ceded them, they did so conditionally. Governmental powers can always be revoked.[42]

Rothbard presents his own hypothesis about the origin of rights by referencing Daniel Defoe's *Robinson Crusoe*.[43]

---

38 Peter N. Stearns, *Human Rights in World History* (London, UK: Routledge, 2012).
39 Rothbard, *Ethics of Liberty*, 231.
40 Hayek, *Constitution of Liberty*, 56.
41 Smith, *Wealth of Nations*, 440. Smith points that "by far the most important of all their effects" of "commerce and manufacture" are that "they gradually introduced order and good government and with them, the liberty and security of individuals."
42 Steven Pinker, *The Better Angels of Our Nature* (New York: Penquin Books, 2011).
43 Daniel Defoe, *The Life and Strange Surprizing Adventures of Robinson Crusoe of York, Mariner*, London, New York, Oxford University Press, [1719] 1972.

Let us consider Crusoe, who has landed on his island, and, to simplify matters, has contracted amnesia. What inescapable facts does Crusoe confront? He finds, for one thing, himself, with the primordial fact of his own consciousness and his own body. He finds, second, the natural world around him, the nature-given habitat and resources which economists sum up in the term 'land.'[44]

Rothbard's Crusoe would immediately begin to acquire the necessities of life from the resources available. If other people came along – say, Friday – he would enlist them in his project in order to fulfill his desires and theirs. Crusoe would become the perfectly rational actor, as nature intended him to be.

But Rothbard's claim that humans are naturally rational actors is not historically accurate, nor is it a proper account of human conduct. Why does Crusoe remember only what Rothbard wants him to? If Crusoe truly had amnesia, would he know how to hunt, fish, or build a hut? Would he not have learned all the skills of survival from other people?[45] Evidence suggests that youngsters not trained by their parents, teachers, peers, or society in general have almost no ability to solve complex problems or think rationally beyond their immediate bodily needs. Does this not prove that humans are more than isolated individuals? As Jean-Jacques Rousseau points out, the notion of autonomous individualism is implausible.[46]

Because Hayek and Mises were not steeped in America's rights tradition and are closer to continental philosophy, they contend that natural rights developed as part of a historical process.[47] But this version of the origin of natural rights is also flawed. If natural rights developed over time, then people have changed their behavior. Rights are not natural – that is to say, intrinsic to human behavior always and everywhere. If natural rights are not natural, but rather historical, and if people have altered the way they act, then it is possible they might change again. The principles of free-market

44 Rothbard, *Ethics of Liberty*, 29.
45 Aristotle, *Politics*, 1253b24–6 where he comments that, "the city is both by nature and prior to each individual...for the individual when separated [from it] is not self-sufficient."
46 Jean-Jacques Rousseau, *The First and Second Discourses*, ed. Roger D. Masters, trans. Roger D. and Judith R. Masters (New York: St Martin's Press, 1964). See also Rousseau's notes on the capacities of feral children.
47 Hayek, *Constitution of Liberty*, 162–204; Mises, *Human Action*, 30–69.

economics may not apply to some future race of more communal human beings, just as Marx predicted.

Since the roots of natural rights are obscure, some Libertarians take a different tack. They argue that personal freedom is preferable to any other objective in life because it works to produce prosperity and well-being. Freedom may not be natural, but it is valuable. Mises explains of the individual:

> Whatever the future may have in store for him, he cannot withdraw from the necessities of the actual hour. As long as a man lives, he cannot help obeying the cardinal impulse, the *elan vital*. It is man's innate nature that he seeks to preserve and to strengthen his life, that he is discontented and aims at removing uneasiness, that he is in search of what may be called happiness.[48]

However true this may be, it is not a defense of free-market economics. What makes people happy is a complex question. As Dennis C. Rasmussen points out, happiness is not the same as "bettering one's condition." The quest to satisfy bodily desires is a never-ending task, hardly conducive to the repose of a contented person. Moreover, commercial societies create a sense of vanity in people who seek to "keep up with the Joneses" and perhaps even surpass them. The constant struggle for advancement and superiority can lead people to fear and worry about their place on the social hierarchy or how others view them. Although some possessions are needed to lead a happy life, property can also become a burden. Even wealthy folks fret about losing their fortune.[49]

To take the point further, some people enjoy conquest – or violence – more than peace and prosperity. Theft and confiscation of another's possessions are time-honored means of bettering one's condition. Moreover, since the origin of human society is uncertain, it is possible warrior nobles established political order to control the violent impulses of their tribesmen and commerce and trade commenced after security was established. Nietzsche may be correct in declaring that civilization owes its foundation to people who were happily vicious and celebrated their victories with "the innocence of wild animals."[50]

---

48 Mises, *Human Action*, 881–2.
49 Dennis C. Rasmussen, "Does 'Bettering Our Condition' Really Make Us Better Off? Adam Smith on Progress and Happiness," *The American Political Science Review* 100 (August 2006), 309–318.
50 Nietzsche, *Genealogy*, 155.

Rothbard contends that "Libertarian goals – including immediate abolition of invasions of liberty – are 'realistic'...if enough people agreed on them, and that, if achieved, the resulting Libertarian system would be viable."[51] However, any system, including the communist state, will work if people believe in it. The question might be asked why a majority of people have never accepted Libertarianism.

If Libertarianism cannot show that economic freedom is the natural condition of human beings, then it is little more than a principle of advocacy. However, promotion of values violates one of Libertarianism's key tenets – people should be left free to choose. As Anthony Randazzo states the problem, "There is no practical, objective way for an outside observer – even a super-rational economist – to define another individual's best interest."[52]

The Rational Individual

Libertarians argue that human beings make rational choices. However, even the most cursory examination of human action shows that not all people are rational. Moreover, is it always reasonable to behave as economic rational actors? For example, suppose that people applied marginal advantage reasoning during courtship. The partners' cost-benefit analysis might sound like this: "That girl over there has better legs, but your hair is nicer." "You aren't as handsome as my last boyfriend, but your parents have more money." Or, perhaps, "I will promise to be faithful to you so long as you are young, attractive, and healthy, but if you get old, dowdy, and sick, all bets are off."

Some people might actually consider these factors in picking a mate, but if they revealed such calculations, it is unlikely the romance would survive. Love wants to be beyond calculation or interest; it reaches for a realm purer than computation. In complicated romantic relationships, being a Libertarian rational actor may be irrational.

No one would say that two-year-olds are rational. Most are not allowed to do as they please because they are not old enough. We would never let two-year-olds pursue their self-interest. Therefore, it is not self-interest that

---

51 Rothbard, *Ethics of Liberty*, 259.
52 Anthony Randazzo, "The Case Against Libertarian Paternalism," *Reason.com*, April 23, 2013, http://reason.com/archives/2013/04/23/the-case-against-libertarian-paternalism.

is the core of the rational actor model, but rather reason.[53] Children become reasonable through parental training. Children with bad parents or bad training often act irrationally. Human beings are not naturally rational unless we use Aristotle's teleological understanding of natural. But no Libertarian would agree that humans should behave in a particular way in order to become fully human, as does Aristotle.[54]

Why do parents take the time and trouble to train children? Some people might genuinely love their children, but even they might decide that there is no marginal benefit in the time, effort, and expense necessary to promote their children's interest. Rothbard explores the conflict between parental rights and duties, hoping that a baby market will solve the problem of bad rearing. He writes:

> Applying our theory to parents and children…means that a parent does not have the right to aggress against his children, *but also* that the parent should not have a *legal obligation* to feed, clothe, or educate his children, since such obligations would entail positive acts coerced upon the parent and depriving the parent of his rights. The parent therefore may not murder or mutilate his child, and the law properly outlaws a parent from doing so. But the parent should have the legal right *not* to feed the child, i.e., to allow it to die. The law, therefore, may not properly compel the parent to feed a child or to keep it alive. (Again, whether or not a parent has a moral rather than a legally enforceable obligation to keep his child alive is a completely separate question.) This rule allows us to solve such vexing questions as: should a parent have the right to allow a deformed baby to die (e.g. by not feeding it)? The answer is of course yes, following *a fortiori* from the larger right to allow any baby, whether deformed or not, to die. [In] a Libertarian society, the existence of a free baby market will bring such "neglect" down to a minimum.[55]

---

53 The difficulty of libertarian theory reconciling rights and responsibilities to children is visible in Timothy Fowler, "The Status of Child Citizens," *Politics, Philosophy & Economics* 13 (February 2014): 93–113.

54 Aristotle, *Politics* 1252a1 maintains that a "human being…when its coming into being is complete is…the nature of the thing." He adds that humans are "by nature political animal[s]" who would live "a mean sort of life" as individuals.

55 Rothbard, *Ethics of Liberty*, 100–101.

Will a society produce rational human beings if parents do not feel a responsibility to raise offspring well? Is calculation of personal interest on the part of parents sufficient to make children feel secure enough to become rational? Is not unconditional love what leads to well-adjusted children who act rationally?

There are also people whose physical or mental handicaps make them incapable of becoming rational actors. Infirmities occur by chance. Even if people take good care of themselves, old age can eventually rob them of rationality and the ability to act. How do non-rational actors figure into Libertarian principles? For Mises, at least, they do not; they are "outside" the principles of marginal advantage. He explains:

> Then there are invalids, who can perform a small quantity of work, but whose disability prevents them from earning as much as normal workers do.... These people can keep body and soul together only if other people help them. The next of kin, friends, the charity of benefactors and endowments, and communal poor relief take care of the destitute. Alms-folk do not cooperate in the social process of production; as far as the provision of the means for the satisfaction of wants is concerned, they do not act; they live because other people look after them. The problems of poor relief are problems of the arrangement of consumption, not of the arrangement of production activities. They are as such beyond the frame of a theory of human action which refers only to the provision of the means required for consumption, not to the way in which these means are consumed. Catallactic theory deals with the methods adopted for the charitable support of the destitute only as far as they can possibly affect the supply of labor.[56]

Is a society that makes no provision for the poor, weak, and incapable truly "better" than one that does? One could say that much of humanity looks at the neglect of the weak as irrationally inhumane. However, there is no principle in Libertarianism that promotes care for others – it is like other motivations, a matter of personal choice.

In a Libertarian world, people might take care of their parents, children, and neighbors if they see some marginal advantage in it. Or they may not.

56   Mises, *Human Action*, 603.

There are no social sanctions imagined by Libertarians that would establish an expectation of responsibility. In fact, Libertarians reject the long history of social obligations passed down through social norms almost unconsciously. They favor adopting practices that rationally further people's marginal advantage. Traditions rest on irrational, almost thoughtless acceptance of conventions. Customs do not fit in a world of rational actors, hence Hayek's rejection of the value of conservatism and tradition-based morality along with it.[57]

It is impossible to tell what induces people to be good parents, neighbors, and children. It could be that rational choice encourages them to behave admirably. Conversely, it could be traditions that create the expectation that they will act responsibly.

James Madison, father of the world's most successful liberal democracy, takes up the question of conservation and change in *Federalist* 49. He argues that "veneration, which time bestows on everything," is a lesson that applies to "the wisest and freest governments," as well as social mores that require discipline and self-limitation. Veneration is not rational, of course. Rather, it is unreasoned dedication to one's country and its laws; a passion that counteracts the interest of people to do only what they want and not what they should. Without veneration, countries might "not possess the requisite stability" to survive. "All governments," Madison reasons, "rest on opinion." Since not all people's opinions are rational or well thought out, no government can persuade everyone that it is natural and must be obeyed. To be effective, governments must have passion and not merely calculation supporting them. Madison explains:

> In a nation of philosophers, this consideration ought to be disregarded. A reverence for the laws would be sufficiently inculcated by the voice of an enlightened reason. But a nation of philosophers is as little to be expected as the philosophical race of kings wished for by Plato. And in every other nation, the most rational government will not find it a superfluous advantage to have the prejudices of the community on its side.[58]

Madison rejects the rational actor model in favor of developing a spirit of patriotism and dedication among the non-philosopher-king citizens of America.

---

57 Hayek, "Why I am not a Conservative," *Constitution of Liberty*, 397–414.
58 Alexander Hamilton, John Jay, James Madison, *The Federalist Papers*, #49 (Indianapolis, IN, Liberty Funs, Inc, 2001).

Are people rational actors? Sometimes they are, and sometimes they are not. Even if most people are rational and look to the long-term health of society to meet their needs, a few irrational people can ruin the peace and security of the rest. Political life measures numbers and intensity. The passions of a few often overwhelm the common sense of the many. We should not forget that one of the first proponents of natural rights thought that a Leviathan state would be necessary to protect the population from their own desires and certainly from those of violent outliers.[59]

As can be seen in many countries, civil societies rest on voluntary obedience to the rule of law. The rule of law is necessary for a prosperous community. Without voluntary obedience, some power, governmental or otherwise, will have to establish order. In those places without either a powerful government or a strong civil society, there is no security, no prosperity and little spontaneous order. If, as Libertarians want, governmental interferes in personal affairs as little as possible, then a civil society is essential to their project.

Are civil society and free market economics compatible? Joshua Mitchell argues that free-market economics creates tolerant, future-oriented, and self-motivated individuals, people best suited for popular rule. The free-market inculcates habits that support people who understand how to govern themselves. It also cultivates individual initiative by breaking down time-honored religious, familial, and class barriers. However, people in market-oriented societies can lose their equilibrium. They must decide every question for themselves without relying on the authority of the clergy, elites, or even elders. The influence of customs, moral prescriptions, and manners is minimized so that people can act as rational individuals.[60]

How are all these autonomous individuals to get along? Why should they consider the wellbeing of others or act for the good of the community? As Aristotle explains, politics involves ruling and being ruled. It is often the case that ruling is simpler than being ruled. To be ruled, people must accept the decisions of others with whom they disagree. Why should an autonomous individual submit to the *rule* of another?

Individualism has two seemingly incongruent consequences. First, people can become estranged, cut off from their neighbors. They gripe incessantly about how others control their fortune, but take no action to fix the

---

59   Thomas Hobbes, *Leviathan* (New York: Penguin, 1982 [1651]).
60   Joshua Mitchell, *Tocqueville in Arabia: Dilemmas in a Democratic Age* (Chicago: University of Chicago Press, 2013).

problem. On the other hand, they may seek to lessen their anxiety by creating a government that, in the words of Alexis de Tocqueville, "provide[s] for their security, foresees and supplies their necessities, facilitates their pleasures, manages their principal concerns, directs their industry, regulates the descent of property, and subdivides their inheritances."[61]

Tocqueville famously advocates intermediary institutions that draw people out of their private concerns. Participation in groups allows people to recognize the issues facing their localities, and makes them responsible for creating solutions. As Mitchell argues, free-market economics may create "delinked" individuals who feel little responsibility towards others. Often, people must move from place to place to further their careers. Their rootedness to a particular place and its people becomes ever more tenuous as the world becomes more globalized.

Without civil society's required voluntary obedience to law, it is unclear whether a society will have the requisite security to flourish. "It is easy," Havel warns,

> to destroy the complex and fragile social, cultural and economic relationships and institutions built up over centuries.... It is as easy to do that as it is to smash a piece of antique, inlaid furniture with a single blow from a hammer. But it is infinitely more difficult to restore it, or to create it directly.[62]

What is Self Interest?

This analysis of Libertarianism grew out of discussions with my free-market students. They are often very thoughtful, so their argument should be taken seriously. They claim that every action can be explained by self-interest, and there is some truth in their position. But, I ask them next: What do you mean by self-interest? Why does a soldier run away from a battle? He is self-interested, they respond. But if he stands and fights, risking and maybe sacrificing his life, why does he do that? Self-interest, they reply. If self-interest

---

61   Alexis de Tocqueville, *Democracy in America*, trans. and eds. Harvey Mansfield and Delba Winthrop, (Chicago: University of Chicago Press, 2000), 663.

62   Václav Havel, "Address at George Washington University," Washington, D.C., 22 April 1993, http://www.vaclavhavel.cz/showtrans.php?cat=projevy&val=243_aj_projevy.html&typ=HTML.

is natural, something people do spontaneously, why do not soldiers captured in war switch to the side that provides them security, food, warm beds, and new uniforms? Self-interest is the answer. Yet, some soldiers absolutely refuse to capitulate to an enemy, even enduring imprisonment, torture, and death. What is in it for them? At this point, the bright students give me a knowing, pitying smile, indicating I have not understood the complex reasoning of economic rationality.

However, a principle that explains all actions, no matter how contradictory, actually does not explain anything. "This theory," Bernard Williams argues, "finds it hard to avoid being either obviously false or else trivially vacuous...it identifies...the agent's [interest as] anything that the agent intentionally does."[63] The old fashioned categories – the soldier who runs away is a coward, and the soldier who fights is a hero – give a far better account of the phenomenon.

If there are no moral codes – as Libertarians suggest – and if Libertarianism, as the quote from Mises above states, is "perfectly neutral with regard to all judgments of value, as it refers always to means and never to the choice of ultimate ends," then what is wrong with me using the welfare state to pursue my interest?[64] I am now of retirement age. When I calculate my marginal advantage, it is obvious that the best thing for me is to accept large Social Security payments – more than I have paid into the fund – and make someone else pay for them. It is in my interest to force other people by means of state action to support my elder care. The argument that the system might collapse is irrelevant to my calculations because it will not fail in my lifetime. Why should I care about future generations?

To make matters clearer, I don't even have to worry about my offspring paying into the system for the length of their working lives but then receiving no benefits – because I don't have children. If Libertarianism is "perfectly neutral" with regard to values, there can be no complaint that my values might infringe on another's freedom. My values have less to do with other people's freedom and more to do with my government check. What do I care if in my quest for comfort, your grandchildren pay for my cruises? Why should I give a thought to the general good of society if I will be gone before the system becomes insolvent?

Libertarians seem to want to have it both ways. They want me to think beyond my immediate interest to the prosperity of the community, but they

---

63   Bernard Williams, *Ethics and the Limits of Philosophy*, 15.
64   Mises, *Human Action*, 884–85.

also want me not to impose my will on others. Given their value-neutral beliefs, can they make such demands on my values and my freedom?

If all values are "perfectly neutral," what limits my freedom? What if I decide to become violent or perverse? If the Libertarian state should not restrain me, and the free-market value system does not condemn my desires, perhaps I should satisfy my longings no matter how bizarre they may be. Mises seems to admit this will take place under a regime of freedom:

> Some kinds of work satisfy particular wishes. There are, for example, occupations which meet erotic desires – either conscious or subconscious ones. These desires may be normal or perverse. Also fetishists, homosexuals, sadists and other perverts can sometimes find in their work an opportunity to satisfy their strange appetites. There are occupations which are especially attractive to such people. Cruelty and blood-thirstiness luxuriantly thrive under various occupational cloaks.[65]

Indeed, why should not adults have sex with minors? If Libertarianism is "perfectly neutral," such behavior cannot be considered wrong. Of course, a Libertarian might insist that by such an act, I am denying another's freedom. But what if I convince the minor to submit to my desires? What if I pay him/her for the favors? Are not both partners free to choose? Would not someone have to show that the child was harmed? Harm is not easy to prove. Harmed how? Morally? Psychologically? Financially? Libertarians are "perfectly neutral" regarding morals. Anyway, why should I worry about hurting someone else? Does not Libertarianism preach that I should always seek to gratify my interests as I define them?

Economic rationality cannot account for existence or for the question of Being. We not only want to be prosperous, we want our lives to have purpose. We are finite beings who imagine the infinite. Economics deals only with the finite and the material, and therefore it never speaks to questions about the *meaning* of economic activity. Since the purpose of life is obscure, there will always be an opening for the irrational, for behavior not based on economic rationality. Passionate devotion – as during the Middle Ages or with today's religious fundamentalists – is always an alternative to the economist's view of the world.

Libertarians claim that the check on people's base, dishonest, or violent

65   Mises, *Human Action: A Treatise on Economics*, 588–89.

behavior is fear of a response from the person injured or abused. The same mechanism that supports consumer sovereignty – the interests of the other party – will restrain wrong-doers. People will behave well because they will calculate it is in their interest to do so. The will learn to obey the principle that Tocqueville calls self-interest rightly understood.

It is true, of course, that most people are apprehensive about being caught doing wrong and having to pay a penalty. However, some people are not. Thoughtless people do not evaluate the consequences of their actions, and ambitious people ignore the penalties because they think they can avoid them. There are always a few people who think they possess Plato's ring of Gyges – their superior talents exclude them from the rules of others. Tyranny is always a possibility for human beings because they are ambitious. Love of honor and glory are prevalent in the human species, although not as widespread and visible as the love of gain. Self-interest rightly understood, called consumer sovereignty, which checks selfishness with the fear of loss of business or profit, is not a check on ambition. There are two ways to comply with the demands of the market. One can satisfy consumers' demands in hopes of securing their return business and one can do an honest day's work in return for wages in hopes of keeping one's job. On the other hand, one can cheat people and not get caught. Tyrants attempt to do the latter by creating laws and sanctions behind the laws for their own benefit. They then scare people into obeying the laws. Tyranny is a kind of consumer sovereignty based on an interest – the desire not to be killed.

Great ambition is rare, but not incomprehensible in average people. Humans are aware that they will die. They want what they do to matter. They want to be recognized. They are willing to take chances – even with their safety and prosperity – to stand above the crowd. For them, risking death by seeking danger may be a better way to overcome the fear of death than taking comfort in a tranquil, prosperous existence. Publicly flirting with peril will certainly make them stand out and above the crowd. "Fame," Alexander Hamilton writes, prompts people to "plan and undertake extensive and arduous enterprises for the public benefit." The same ambitious person, however, might be "violently tempted to embrace…every personal hazard" to achieve that goal.[66]

On this point, we might ask why Adam Smith wrote two quite different books. *The Wealth of Nations* explains how self-interest promotes the common good, while *The Theory of Moral Sentiments* shows why self-interest

---

66 *Federalist Papers*, #72.

does not devolve into the war of all against all. Smith tries to account for the complexity of human action: people are often self-interested, parochial and selfish, but they can also be generous, kind, and thoughtful. Spontaneous order is possible because there seems to be a natural limit to narrow self-interest – people learn to get along. We should remember that what the human race has done to establish order is form governments.

Libertarian theory does not seem to account for the best and the worst in human beings. It lumps such motives as hate, envy, pride, courage, love, longing, and distinction in the same category as economic calculations. In an effort to achieve clarity, it narrows its perspective. It seeks to comprehend life by reducing all human action to a single cost-benefit reckoning. In so doing, however, it obscures rather than clarifies the complexity of human behavior.

Human motivation is not easy to understand. Libertarianism tries to overcome that complexity by ignoring it. Whatever people desire, they should have the freedom to seek. Libertarianism reduces all motives to self-interest. But, if self-interest were the only source of human action, would not people at all times and in every society behave in a similar fashion? Would not all political and economic arrangements be the same? The variety of economic and political systems indicates, however, that what motivates people is variable. Some people calculate a marginal advantage in their exchanges of goods and service, others seek honor, and still others foreswear any sort of physical well-being and devote their lives to a deity. Some people behave as rational actors while others are fulfilled only if they dedicate themselves to charity. We must reconcile the demands of our bodies, the competitive nature of our spirit, and the urge to stimulate our minds. These things do not go together easily. No one of them is entirely satisfying to everyone. Perhaps virtue is a compromise among these conflicting parts of our nature.

Paul Stern describes the dilemmas caused by social life and the need for government:

> The marketplace…exists, most basically, because of our mutual dependence in the satisfaction of our corporeal needs. But in the satisfaction of these needs conflict arises. Individuals are not always willing to reconcile the satisfaction of their needs with the needs of others. And so government is necessary with its council-house, courts, and other common assemblies. These rely especially on the rule of law, which, as an amalgam of reason and

coercion, implies that these differences can be controlled or minimized but not eliminated. [67]

Virtue

Libertarians attempt to reduce all human motives to self-interest. The argument makes certain sense since people do not seem to do things without reason. If I had no interest in acting a certain way, I would not do it. However, is having an interest in doing something the same as having an economic interest in doing it?

When Libertarians say that we do everything because of self-interest, what they mean is that we do everything because we make a choice, and when we make a choice, we must have a reason for choosing it. As Heidegger argues, existence presents itself as choice. He explains, "Our whole human existence everywhere sees itself challenged – now playfully and now urgently, now breathlessly now ponderously—to devote itself to the planning and calculating of everything."[68] Our lives are inevitably full of choices because our existence matters. We want to make it matter by the decisions we make. Does the fact that we must make choices mean that we always make decisions for the benefit of our interests? Choices might be made on criteria that matter to us but have very little to do with whether we personally benefit from them. We might want to become powerful or famous. We might just want to do the right thing.

Insofar as Libertarians observe that human nature or natural inclination leads to spontaneously cooperation, they are looking at people whose behavior is habituated by law, habit, custom, and the traditions of civil society. Those laws, customs, and moral codes disguise and mitigate truly selfish, self-centered behavior. If Libertarians want to get a true perspective on how economic incentives affect behavior, they will have to find a place where those cultural limitations do not exist.

Some did, and when free-market economists advised post-communist governments to create unfettered markets, they were unprepared for the scale and determination of those who sought to misuse their freedom for

---

67   Paul Stern, "The Philosophic Importance of Political Life: On the 'Digression' in Plato's *Theaetetus*" *The American Political Science Review* 96:2 (June 2002), 281.
68   Martin Heidegger, *Identity and Difference*, trans. Joan Stambaugh (Chicago: University of Chicago Press, 2002), 34–35.

their own advantage.[69] Many economists involved in the transition from managed economies mistakenly believed that once state control was eliminated, people would cooperate on the basis of rational interest. After all, as we have seen, they believe rational self-interest is natural. What they discovered, however, is that social cooperation is based on the effects of custom, law, and habit, and not on nature.

Virtue takes training, but the doctrine of natural rights insists that "natural" behavior requires no training. Parents trying to raise children recognize that teaching responsibility is more complicated than telling young people they are self-interested and free to assert their rights. But it is far from clear whether children in rights-oriented countries are happier and better adjusted than those in cultures with more circumscribed training and fewer rights. Although it seems counterintuitive, children are happier when they have a structured understanding of what is expected of them, of where the boundary-lines are.

As we have seen, Libertarians believe that natural rights that allow people to do mostly what they want should supplant traditional notions of right and wrong. People can choose where they work, who their friends are, what church to attend, what god, if any, to believe in, and what profession to pursue. They are even free to choose whatever "lifestyle" they please.

But market-oriented societies discovered that along with this freedom came a loss of community. In dynamic economies, people move around to pursue their careers, and that rootlessness undermines a sense of belonging. As Robert Putnam argues, the institutions of civic engagement have decreased in almost direct proportion to the rise of economic prosperity.[70] Free-market prosperity seems to be in direct conflict with those forms of association that encourage voluntary obedience to the rule of law – the very foundation of peaceful exchanges.

Virtue is difficult, inegalitarian, and often imposed from the outside – by a religion or community, or by social convention. Natural rights are easy and egalitarian. And yet, even in an age when natural rights predominate, we still see examples of virtue. Attributes such as courage, temperance, prudence, and justice still matter to people. People's attachment to

---

69 Michael Busch, "Jeffrey Sachs's Metamorphosis From Neoliberal Shock Trooper to Bleeding Heart Hits a Snag," *Foreign Policy Focus*, January 22, 2012, http://www.fpif.org/blog/jeffrey_sachss_metamorphosis_from _neoliberal_shock_trooper_to_bleeding_heart_hits_a_snag.

70 Robert D. Putnam, *Bowling Alone: The Collapse and Revival of American Community* (New York: Simon & Schuster, 2000).

virtue can be weakened, yet the allure of virtue seems still to have power over us.

People are virtuous not simply because they calculate their own interests and then act on them; they are virtuous for exactly the opposite reason. They understand their own interest and do not act on it.[71]

Libertarians get half of the classical conception of virtue right. Virtue means excellence or achievement. The free market produces a kind of excellence. Entrepreneurs who invent, invest, and build achieve a great deal; as do workers who are skilled at a trade.

Aristotle argues that virtue embodies both excellence and a commitment to do the right thing. Perhaps people are good to each other not because they calculate their personal interest, but because they care for others. We grow up with people who care about us. We are vulnerable and needy, and others provide security and fulfill our wants. We learn virtue from the example of those who care for us; our families, teachers, elders, coaches, clergy, and neighbors instruct us how to behave.

Libertarians contend that an unfettered market will eventually solve most human problems in a manner best for everybody. In the short run, people might suffer, but in the long run the profit motive will induce people with an entrepreneurial spirit to find a solution for all dilemmas.

Critics find Libertarianism heartless because of its insistence on doing nothing as a community and letting the market work its magic. It is here that empathy comes into play. When we see the plight of working people who have lost their jobs, old people without adequate incomes, young people without opportunities, or infirm people unable to care for themselves, it is human nature to identify with their distress. We want to solve the problem – right now, not in the long run. Modern communication has brought the plight of other people into our living rooms. When we see individuals suffering, it is natural that we "feel their pain," to paraphrase President Bill Clinton. We want to do something. We turn to the government to solve the problem because, at least formally, it represents the community.

The same sense of empathy makes people responsible to others, the law, and the community. It helps them understand why they should, in Adam Smith's words, "truck, barter, and exchange," rather than murder, rape, and

---

71 Irving Kristol, "When Virtue Loses All Her Loveliness — Some Reflections on Capitalism and the 'Free Society,'" *The Public Interest* 21 (Fall 1970), http://www.nationalaffairs.com/ doclib/20080523_197002101whenvirtue losesall-herlovelinesssomereflectionsoncapitalismandthefreesocietyirvingkristol.pdf.

plunder. The moral sense is what makes the free market possible. Without a moral sense, society could easily devolve into chaos.

It turns out that Libertarians are right about how people normally behave towards one another, but their reasoning is flawed. People do not cooperate spontaneously because a rational assessment of their marginal advantage tells them to. People get along – and therefore engage in economic transactions – because the principles of virtue and proper behavior are ubiquitous, although we sometimes fail to notice them. Perhaps, as James Q. Wilson argues, human beings *do* have a moral sense that guides judgment without calculation of marginal advantage.[72]

Free economic exchanges will not occur without social order because not all people have a sense of empathy. Social order is vulnerable without the rule of law, and the rule of law will not work unless people voluntarily submit to its dictates. People will not follow the law unless they have a sense of civic engagement and responsibility. People will not agree to be responsible unless responsible actions are seen as proper and good. Virtue is the basis of proper and good action. Libertarian principles depend on virtue.

72　Wilson, *The Moral Sense.*

Chapter Two
The Postmodern View

Absurd is that which is devoid of purpose…. Cut off from his religious, metaphysical, and transcendental roots, man is lost; all his actions become senseless, absurd, useless." Eugene Ionesco[1]

Defining Postmodernism

It is hackneyed yet hard to resist. Postmodernism can no longer be praised; the time has come time to bury it. Postmodernism sickened in 1996 when physicist Alan Sokal published an article in a leading cultural studies journal purporting to demonstrate a relation between quantum mechanics and Postmodern analysis. He later revealed the essay to be a hoax, written to expose the lack of rigor in humane studies.[2] Postmodernism went to the ICU on November 14, 1997, when Postmodernists met at the University of Chicago to ponder what should come next.[3] There is not much left for a literature professor to do once all truth and rationality have been methodically deconstructed. Postmodernism went into a coma when its most celebrated proponent, Jacques Derrida, died in 2004. And it finally expired after obituaries for Derrida ridiculed Postmodernism's most treasured belief: that language constructs reality. If speech is the true ground of Being, then declaring,

1   Eugène Ionesco, "Dans les Armes de la Ville," *Cahiers de la Compagnie Madeleine Renaud Bean-Louis Barrault*, (Paris, No. 20, October, 1957), quoted in Martin Esslin, *The Theatre of the Absurd*, (London: Eyre & Spottiswoode, 1962), 17.
2   Alan D. Sokal, "Transgressing the Boundaries: Toward a Transformative Hermeneutics of Quantum Gravity," *Social Text* 46/47 (spring/summer 1996): 217–252 and "A Physicist Experiments with Cultural Studies," *Lingua Franca* (May/June 1996): 62–64. http://www.physics.nyu.edu/faculty/sokal/#papers.
3   "Conference on After Postmodernism," University of Chicago, November 14–16, 1997, http://www.focusing.org/apm.htm.

"Jacques Derrida lives," should have brought the famous man back to life. Unfortunately, death deconstructed Derrida's existence just as it has every other being that has lived. Derrida stayed dead.[4]

Of course, Postmodernism has not expired everywhere. Scattered throughout academe are professors whose graduate education was inspired by what was then the cutting edge of literary theory. They exist as islands of outdated trendiness, archipelagos of discarded academic chic. Like other literary movements such as New Criticism, Structuralism, Post-Structuralism, Psychoanalysis, Marxist Criticism, Deconstruction, Feminism, and New Historicism, Postmodernism is a victim of its own avant-garde stance.[5] It has been replaced by Post-Colonial Studies, the object of which is to read and not just criticize books from authors around the world, some of whom are quite good writers.

Postmodernism was once the most important intellectual movement of its time. After the demise of communism and the subsequent abandonment of Marxism as a tool of analysis, progressive intellectuals adopted Postmodernism as a method for challenging the established order by uncovering the hidden power relationships in Western bourgeois society.[6] Postmodernism is not explicitly political; indeed, those who use its intellectual cousin

---

4   The London *Times* eulogized Derrida as follows:

> Can there be any certainty in the death of Jacques Derrida? The obituarists' objective attempts to place his life in a finite context are, necessarily, subject to epistemic relativism, the idea that all such scientific theories are mere "narrations" or social constructions. Surely, a Postmodernist deconstruction of their import would inevitably question the foundational conceptual categories of prior science – among them, Derrida's own existence – which become problematised and relativised. This conceptual revolution has profound implications for the content of future Postmodern and liberatory science of mortality.
>
> Quoted in "Notes & Comments," *The New Criterion* 23: 3 (November 2004) http://www.newcriterion.com/archive/23/nov04/notes.htm. See also John J. Miller & Mark Molesky, "Jacques Derrida, R.I.P.: The legacy of deconstruction," *National Review*, 13 October 2004. http://www.national-review.com/comment/miller_molesky200410130841.asp.

5   Perhaps, Solzhenitsyn suggests, Postmodernism should be replaced by "Post-Avant-Gardism." Solzhenitsyn, "Playing on the Strings of Emptiness" in *Solzhenitsyn Reader*, 585–90.

6   For the reception of *The Gulag Archipelago* in France and the subsequent destruction of the French Communist Left and its turn to Postmodernism, see Robert Horvath, "'The Solzhenitsyn Effect': East European Dissidents and the Demise of the Revolutionary Privilege," *Human Rights Quarterly* 29 (2007): 879–907.

deconstruction as a tool of literary criticism abjure direct political involvement. Yet, Postmodernism's critique of the West's literary tradition (the so-called "canon"), as well as of its metaphysics, undermines the legitimacy of every hierarchical institution, especially one based on power, such as the state.

An examination of Postmodernism is warranted because it has influenced "a wide variety of disciplines or areas of study, including art, architecture, music, film, literature, sociology, communications, fashion, and technology,"[7] according to Mary Klages. Although it is sensible to define a topic before analyzing it, there seems to be no clear definition of Postmodernism. As Klages states, "Postmodernism is a complicated term, or set of ideas, one that...is hard to define."[8] Leslie Paul Thiele explains that:

> Postmodernist thinkers are far from a unified bunch. They have been usefully described as a 'constellation' of thinkers, that is to say, a juxtaposed cluster of elements that resists reduction to a common core....[P]ostmodernists do attempt to uncover universal structures or patterns that operate according to a stable logic or scientific laws. They assume that their identities, desires, and predilections are the products of social power and therefore acknowledge that their investigations will only reveal the effects of particular relations of power as they are theorized from a particular vantage point.[9]

Postmodernism began primarily as a literary theory that reacted against New Criticism, the reigning orthodoxy of the post-World War II era. According to Warren Hedges, New Criticism held that "the 'Western tradition' is an unbroken, internally consistent set of artistic conventions and traditions going back to ancient Greece and continuing up to this day, and that good art participates in and extends these traditions." The task of the reader was to understand the "text as an *autotelic* artifact, something complete with in itself, written for its own sake, unified in its form and not dependent on its relation to the author's life or intent, history."[10] Moreover, proponents of New Criticism wanted to distinguish between high art and popular culture,

---

7   Mary Klages, "Postmodernism," http://www.willamette.edu/~rloftus/postmod.htm.
8   Klages, "Postmodernism."
9   Leslie Paul Thiele, *Thinking Politics: Perspectives in Ancient, Modern, and Postmodern Political Theory* (Chatham, New Jersey: Chatham House, 1997), 82–83.
10   Warren Hedges, "Criticism Explained," http://www.sou.edu/English/Hedges/Sodashop/RCenter/Theory/Explaind/ncritexp.htm.

upholding Western traditions and protecting them from commercialism and offensiveness.

New Criticism was itself a reaction against Modernism – although when Modernism was in fashion it did not call itself Modernism. J. L. Lemke argues states that Modernism is "defined by its belief in objective knowledge, or at least in the possibility of objective knowledge, and by its assumption that such knowledge refers directly to an objective reality which would appear in the same way to any observer."[11] Yet, Modernism emphasizes impressionism and subjectivity over objective rationality in literature and other arts – stream-of-consciousness writing is one offshoot. Modernism was eclectic rather than formal; it blurred distinctions between genres and forms and even attacked the barrier between high and low art. Modernism was self-reflexive; it self-consciously called attention to itself as a production or construction, further collapsing the barrier between author and audience.

According to Klages, Postmodernism is much like Modernism in:

> rejecting boundaries between high and low forms of art, rejecting rigid genre distinctions, emphasizing pastiche, parody, bricolage, irony, and playfulness. Postmodern art (and thought) favors reflexivity and self-consciousness, fragmentation and discontinuity (especially in narrative structures), ambiguity, simultaneity, and an emphasis on the destructured, decentered, dehumanized subject.[12]

While Modernist thinkers bewailed the loss of rationality in contemporary culture – viewing its demise as sad – Postmodern critics do not oppose fragmentation, conditionality, or incoherence, but rather celebrates the overthrow of the logo-centric dominance of Western ideas. While they argue that existence is meaningless, they embrace the lack of rationality as an opportunity to "play with nonsense."[13] As Richard Rorty explains, since Postmodernists are "unable to worship anything" and cannot pour their "hearts, souls and minds" into one great project, there is little else for them to do but play.[14]

---

11 J. L. Lemke, "Semiotics and the Deconstruction of Conceptual Learning," *Journal of Accelerative Learning and Teaching* 19 (January 1994):67–110, http://academic.brooklyn.cuny.edu/education/jlemke/papers/jsalt.htm.
12 Klages, "Postmodernism."
13 Klages, "Postmodernism."
14 Richard Rorty, *Essays on Heidegger and Others* (Cambridge: Cambridge University Press, 1991), 132.

Postmodernists insist that there is no single unitary truth, and any attempt to assert such a claim is, according to Lemke:

> a politically convenient assumption for Europe's imperial ambitions of the past, but has no firm intellectual basis. Many Postmodernists go further and point out that just as Europeans temporarily imposed their view on other cultures by force, so within European cultures, the upper social classes, and particularly middle-aged, masculinized males have dominated the natural and social sciences (as well as politics and business), and so this would-be-universal worldview is even more narrowly just the viewpoint of one dominant social caste or subculture.[15]

Postmodernist thinkers make three other claims. First, they argue that speech constructs social reality and mediates what we see and comprehend. As Derrida put it: "Il n'y a pas de hors-texte" (There is nothing except text).[16] Second, Postmodernists maintain that thought is a product of the society from which it arises. There is no objective truth, and every assertion of a claim to veracity or moral judgment is little more than a discourse, a partisan perspective revealing a person's particular class, nation, culture, or civilization. Gary Kochhar-Lindgren explains:

> Postmodernist reflection... suggests that contemporary subjectivity occurs as the subjected nexus of linguistic, familial, political, cultural, economic, and electronic grids of power that crisscross the individual at every instant. This world-system, which creates the conditions for a certain institutionalization of objectivity and subjectivity, exists in turn only because through a complex historical process the world has come to be viewed as a representation, a picture. If the world is a picture, then the subject is fixed in that picture as a wide-eyed spectator of the framed scene – apparently looking on from the outside, but

15 Lemke, "Semiotics," 67–110, http://academic.brooklyn.cuny.edu/education/jlemke/papers/jsalt.htm.

16 Quoted in "Notes & Comments," *The New Criterion* 23 no. 3 (November 2004) http://www.newcriterion.com/archive/23/nov04/notes.htm.

actually absolutely dependent upon the determinations of the system.[17]

Gonda A. H. Van Steen suggests that Postmodern interpretations should "distance" themselves "from hypotheses about (or criticisms of) the poet's... intention." She claims that "The meanings attributed by contemporaries are only tentatively objective, because they are the historicizing results and effects of modern conditions."[18]

Finally, and somewhat in contradiction to the idea that we are determined by our environment, Postmodernists delight in the idea of self-creation. They claim that once individuals become aware that social conventions influence behavior, they can break free of society's bonds and create their own persona. Perhaps the best example of the self-constructed person is Andy Warhol, whose eclectic art became a symbol of Postmodern culture. Andrew Warhola, the shy child of Ruthenian immigrant parents who frequently worshipped at St. John Chrysostom Byzantine Catholic Church, made himself into a pop icon, in many ways becoming his own artistic creation.

What does all this have to do with virtue? Postmodernists reject virtue as little more than a pretense by which privileged people maintain their power over the less fortunate, a tool of the status quo, a convention established to justify dominance.

Why is Postmodern thought so opposed to Western Culture? Before we can begin to answer that question, we should explore how Postmodernism came to be. The term Postmodern was probably first used by Arnold Toynbee who wrote, "The contest for hegemony between the Hapsburgs and the Bourbons...inaugurated the Modern age of our Western history...our own 'Post-Modern' Age has been inaugurated by the General War of 1914–1918."[19] Contemporary scholars credit Nietzsche and Heidegger as progenitors of the Postmodern turn. However, it could be argued that the principles of Postmodernism were conceived even before the advent of the modern.

---

17 Gary Kochhar-Lindgren, "The Vertiginous Frame: Václav Havel, Martin Heidegger, and Everyday Life in a Disjointed Germany," in *Picturing Cultural Values in Postmodern America*, William G. Doty, ed., (Tuscaloosa, Alabama: University of Alabama Press, 1995), 37.

18 Gonda A. H. Van Steen, *Venom on Verse: Aristophanes in Modern Greece* (Princeton: Princeton University Press, 2000), 7.

19 Arnold J. Toynbee, *The Disintegrations of Civilizations* (London: Oxford University Press, 1939), 43.

Much of what is considered Postmodern actually originated in 1806 when Hegel explained the importance of Napoleon's victory at the battle of Jena. Hegel recognized that Napoleon was a strange admixture of military genius and technological innovator, of old-fashioned tyrant and enlightened ruler, and of patriotic Frenchman (his adopted country) and universal lawgiver. Napoleon was a throwback to an earlier time when martial prowess was the supreme virtue. He was also the champion of a new age, bringing Enlightenment ideas and ideals to places he conquered. Napoleon kept the form of the *ancien regime,* but he forever destroyed its substance. The eclectic nature of the Napoleonic phenomenon indicated to Hegel that Western culture and history had reached an end.

Hegel did not mean that passing of time had ceased, but rather that the principles on which Western culture had been built had reached their logical conclusion by coming into being. History arrived at a culmination exactly because Hegel was able to comprehend and proclaim that a new Moment, as he called it, was at hand. By a "Moment" he meant the religious, philosophic, social, legal, political, technological, artistic, and architectural practices and principles that attempt to explain and express being or existence. The various principles that had been postulated about the best way of life, ideas over which people had vigorously disagreed and fought, were, for the first time, seen to be imperfect, or incomplete. All ideas and principles were true for their time and place, but, Hegel reasoned, were not true in all places at all times, as they had been thought to be. Once it was accepted that concepts were relative, Hegel believed, traditional ideas would lose their hold over the human mind. People would be less likely to fight and die for principles that were no more "true" than another person's or culture's views. While loss of belief might be seen as a disaster for humankind, Hegel insisted that without parochial dogmas, people would become more tolerant, willing to accept what had been feared and persecuted as "the other."

At the root of the movement of History, Hegel reasoned, is a struggle for recognition, the desire to be considered interesting, funny, important, powerful, attractive, and all the other things that humans aspire to be. The longing to be seen as distinctive is so strong that people are willing to fight, even to risk death, in order to make others acknowledge their importance. As a result of these contests, some people come to dominate while others submit, acknowledging the superiority of the more powerful.

Hegel calls this the battle between master and slave. The outcome of the contest has manifested itself historically in the various regimes that have represented particular class interests and in the diverse national cultures into which people have organized themselves. For example, European feudal lords created an elaborate social, political, religious, and philosophic defense of their superior position, all of which maintained and justified their rightful place as rulers. The aristocrats were not cynically feigning dedication to their beliefs to maintain their status. They, along with almost everyone else, accepted that the ideas of their age were ordained by nature or God. In essence, the aristocrats were "recognized" while everyone else was not.

During the Enlightenment, however, individual rights gained sway. Hegel reasoned that relativism would culminate in the final victory of human rights. If all philosophic, social, and political doctrines are of equal merit – that is, equally incomplete – then all people are equal as well. Since no person or group can justify any particular distinction, all are equally deserving of recognition. For Hegel, Napoleon embodied History's absolute moment. He was the synthesis of the old and the new, combining the fighting spirit of past generations with a recognition of the universal rights of man.

In Hegel's view, at the end of History all humans would lead genuinely fulfilling lives. The laws, made by and equally applicable to all, would accord dignity to the uniqueness of every person. There would be freedom with responsibility, individuality with community, transcendence with imminence, autonomy with order, God with man. Hegel's vision is so striking in its scope and promise that most philosophy in the West, including that of Nietzsche and Heidegger, has been a reaction either for or against it. Postmodernism is the latest attempt to defy Hegel's announcement of the end of History.

Language, Being, and Diversity

If, as Hegel argues, the truth is relative to a particular time and place, how do people come to understand the truths of their era? According to Heidegger, people gain their understanding of existence through their culture, which explains the meaning of the phenomena. Put more simply, we learn about the world from "them," our parents, teachers, the media, and other people in general. Heidegger claimed that being reveals itself within culture. Since cognition is primarily grasped through the medium of language, Heidegger called language "the house of Being."

Here arises a difficulty, however. If language constructs the meaning of events, and languages differ, then people of different linguistic groups understand the world differently. Since most people favor what is familiar to them, societies, nations, ethnic and even racial groups organize themselves around these common linguistic traditions. Because all people form communities but the interests of these communities sometimes differ, quarrels are predictable.

While linguistic theory leads to diversity, modern bourgeois principles, which aims to treat all people in a similar fashion, regardless of race, sex, ethnicity, or language, results in conformity. For many, if not all, Postmodernists, the heterogeneity of languages ought to be – and usually is – represented in the diversity of cultures. Postmodernists employ the tools of literary deconstruction to undermine the stultifying sameness of modern bourgeois life. They claim that the "truth" as understood by the dominant culture is merely one discourse among many. The effort to conserve and perpetuate Western rationalism is indicative not of intellectual taste, but of fear of losing power. Paul de Man explains that:

> more than any other mode of inquiry, including economics, the linguistics of literariness is a powerful and indispensable tool in the unmasking of ideological aberrations, as well as a determining factor in accounting for their occurrence. Those who reproach literary theory for being oblivious to social and historical (that is to say ideological) reality are merely stating their fear at having their own ideological mystifications exposed by the tool they are trying to discredit.[20]

Postmodernism and multiculturalism are closely connected. According to Postmodernism, the West has fostered the false notion (if "false" is an appropriate concept) that there is but one truth, one proper way of thinking, one metaphysics. Linguistic analysis indicates that there is not just one way to comprehend reality, but many. The principles of the West are responsible, therefore, for its imperialistic attitude towards other cultures and other modes of cognition. It has enforced its monistic vision of reality, not by its compelling ideals, but by its powerful arms. It has repressed and subjugated all who have resisted its logo-centrism. The Postmodern response to the cultural, military, and political dominance of the West (Euro-centrism) is to celebrate those people, ideas, and cultures that had been traditionally

---

20 Paul De Man, *The Resistance to Theory* (Minneapolis, MN: University of Minnesota Press, 1986), 11.

excluded from the mainstream. Multiculturalism favors the discourses of the downtrodden, the dispossessed, and victims of Eurocentric oppression. It raises "the other" to the status of an equal, even a superior, for in its philosophy and application, the voices of those so long excluded are finally heard. Indeed, the discourses of the victims of the West's domination – women, homosexuals, non-Western people, and persons of color – can demonstrate the diverse character of reality. The traditional canon that promotes virtue is seen as both antiquated and oppressive.

We have, then, two views of social life. Postmodernism's analysis of the human condition raises the question of whether the gulf between people of one linguistic culture and "the other" is surmountable. If there is always "the other," what does this imply about the possibility of a universally valid principle of conduct, of the brotherhood and rights of man, of Hegel's assessment of the end of history? The Postmodern account seems to suggest that different peoples will remain distinct. Conversely, the Hegelian world view posits that under the influence of mass communication, differences between people, religions, cultures and traditions will cease to matter.

Which is the more accurate portrayal of the human condition? Are human beings moving towards a common humanity in which all will be recognized and valued, and there will be no "other"? Or are we forever to be divided by the insurmountable gulf of cultural and linguistic diversity? Perhaps, more importantly, which vision of human destiny *ought* to prevail?

If the particular and the parochial are to be overcome, there must be some mechanisms for inculcating a universal perspective. Hegel foresaw that both the material and ideal worlds would combine to make the human race more homogeneous. Science and technology would liberate people from the grinding poverty of the pre-industrial age. Not only would their lives become easier, but new inventions would afford them enough free time to become educated. With literacy would come independence from the priests and feudal lords who ruled for centuries by keeping the masses in a perpetual state of ignorance. Once superstition, prejudice, and benighted folly were overcome, people would act on the basis of rational self-interest. They would turn their attention to the conquest of the material world rather than to the slaughter of each other. Peace and prosperity would replace war and poverty.

Technology would make communication easier. People from remote parts of the earth would become participants in the world-wide movement toward homogeneity. The differences between people would diminish, too, as various cultural customs and traditions became less strange, better understood, and more accepted.

In addition to the material basis for universal brotherhood, Hegel says a philosophic or ideal principle must exist as a rallying point for the transformation of the old hierarchical order. This he sees in the doctrines of the Enlightenment. Its ideals appeal to human beings not on the basis of their rank, religion, or culture, but rather on the grounds of their humanity. The Enlightenment displaced the intricate web of feudal social arrangements with a simple but universal message, perhaps best expressed in Jefferson's resounding phrase that "all men are equal." Hegel was well aware that people in his day were not equal. But, he maintained that practices follow principles and actions follow ideas. Once an idea such as equality becomes embedded as an accepted fact or a worthy goal, every institution or activity standing in its way will be swept aside.

Hegel believed that the Enlightenment's egalitarian ideals would eventually lead all nations to adopt some form of democracy, or at the very least a mixed regime with a strong popular element. Under such governments, every individual would be recognized as essentially equal before the law. The state would be constructed to protect human rights. All citizens would vote and thereby have a hand in determining their own destinies. Furthermore, ruling institutions would become rational.

His noted follower Max Weber best explains what Hegel meant. Weber argued that in order for people to be treated fairly and equitably, the arbitrary or charismatic leaders of previous ages would have to be replaced by bureaucracies. Bureaucratic organizations do not depend on the whim of those who direct them; rather, they act in accordance with a fixed set of rules. They keep written records and hold employees of the bureaucracy responsible for their actions; they maintain an institutional memory so that past actions become the basis for future choices. Bureaucracy is just in two ways. Its staff is hired on the basis of some skill, not because of a family or social connection, and all those who come before the bureaucracy are treated the same; all are recognized equally.

In the Postmodern era, all ways of life are of equal merit. People come to understand that their own culture is one among many. They do not adhere to the jingoistic dictate that they must love their country or leave it. Moreover, technological advances that are so much a part of the modern era (the precursor of the Postmodern) expose the various cultural expressions to the whole world, making the distant and different familiar. Postmodernism throws many disparate forms together.

The end of history as Hegel foretold it would be quite a nice time, with people treated fairly and equitably on the basis of their abilities and without regard for their incidental traits such as religion, nationality, linguistic or cultural identity, or sex. In essence, all people would be the same. Science and technology would make it possible to create sufficient wealth so that the struggle against scarcity would be winnable. The increase in productivity would attenuate the age-old struggle between the rich and the poor. Political and social structures would not be arbitrary or capricious. Information would pass easily between borders. Differences between races and cultures, although they would not disappear, would not lead to senseless violence. The age of common humanity would be at hand.

Dilemmas at the End of History

Unfortunately, the mechanisms that Hegel dreamed would usher in this new ideal world have a darker side. First, along with technology come higher standards of living, longer life spans, population growth necessitating demands for more goods, and inevitably more pollution, waste, and conflict. Second, the forces set loose by technology and automation create an impersonal society. Production and consumption become standardized because the free market rewards those goods that can be produced most cheaply and sold most effectively to as many people as possible. Although survival is easier in an advanced industrial culture, and, of course, there are more material goods available, little direction is provided as to how to live well or what to do with the goods. As Heidegger argues, technology transforms the world into "standing reserve." Technology allows people to better manipulate the world's resources, but to what end? Indeed, there are so many material objects at hand today that people are overwhelmed by the world of objects and everyday routine. Many have become conventional and follow only the shallow behavior of the crowd. In such a society, people are deflected from the most basic human activity: confronting questions of life and death, meaning and purpose.

Since political stability in democracies depends on providing material well-being for citizens, it is inevitable that these societies will foster a spirit of scientific investigation and technological creativity. However, technology cannot be contained, and its uses are not always peaceful. Technology has been put to work not only to make life easier, but also to kill on an epic scale. As science has progressed, slaughter has increased, culminating in the mass murder of millions in the twentieth century. It does not seem to be a coincidence, then, that the most democratic nation is also the richest and has developed the most technologically advanced weapons of war.

The production of wealth also requires large corporate enterprises whose ability to manufacture goods is increased by economies of scale. These huge entities are needed to satisfy the material desires of the many. At the same time, large bureaucracies are required to administer the programs needed to provide comfortable lives. In ceding power to vast organizations as a way of having their needs met, most people lose the ability to control their own future.

People can be so organized by technological and bureaucratic organizations (hallmarks of Western culture) that they become tools rather than masters of those forces. Although the Postmodern world has eliminated most ruthless tyrants, the problem of our era is that heartless bureaucrats have the technological means to control our lives. As the Postmodernist thinker Michel Foucault has argued, the information age dictates that records be kept of every action and event in an individual's life, and revelations about America's National Security Agency cyber spying have validated his prediction.[21] This data, though innocuous in itself, provides a source of power for those who hold it, for it can be used to manipulate and control us. The same technology that brings the people of the world together is the source of control over them. The contest in the Postmodern age is between order that promises to make life peaceful, safe, and standardized but at the same time ultimately limits freedom and distinctiveness.

Alexander Kojève has written that the softening or "feminization" of the political arena may result in a kinder world, but inevitably will dispirit and enervate great deeds and bold action. There will be little to inspire people: no excitement, no desire for distinction, no need for noble sacrifice, and no cause to spur courageous actions. In one sense, the entire Postmodern movement is a reaction against the confines of the end of history.[22]

Shadia Drury suggests that Kojève is symptomatic of the Postmodern agenda. He so dislikes a world without manly and martial virtues that he

21   Compare Michel Foucault, *The Birth of the Clinic: An Archaeology of Medical Perception,* trans. A. M. Sheridan Smith (New York: Vintage Books, 1994); Michel Foucault, *Madness and Civilization: A History of Insanity in the Age of Reason,* trans. Richard Howard (New York: Vintage Books 1988); Michel Foucault, *Discipline and Punish: The Birth of the Prison,* trans. Alan Sheridan (New York: Vintage Books, 1995).

22   Alexandre Kojève, *Introduction to the Reading of Hegel,* assembled Raymond Queneau, ed. Allan Bloom, trans. James H. Nichols, Jr. (Ithaca, N.Y.: Cornell University Press, 1980).

perverts Hegel's views.[23] On the other hand, Kojève worked to bring about the Hegelian ideal both in his writing and in his professional career with the European Union. Kojève's thought is indicative of the Postmodern view. He desires all the benefits of a harmonious world order, but opposes its smothering effects. He seeks to make virtue so commonplace that people will not have to struggle to practice it. Yet he mourns the loss of individual achievement when virtue is no longer difficult.

What does one *do* in the Postmodern era? What project does one undertake at the end of history? Although the Arab Spring brought unrest to the Middle East and parts of Africa are in turmoil, at the beginning of the 21st Century, the Western world is in a state of relative peace and prosperity. There are great conflicts elsewhere, but Postmodern principles hardly seek martial solutions to political divisions. In the West, where virtually all Postmodern thinkers reside, invading barbarians are not a threat. There is no balance of power to maintain in Europe; almost all the countries, with the notable exception of Vladimir Putin's Russia, are allied. The era of discovery is long past, and although space remains to be explored, there is no pressing need to do so. The age of devotion has passed. It is unlikely that any artist feels strongly enough about God to paint the Sistine Chapel or build Gothic cathedrals to the glory of the Maker. True, some people still believe in God. But, in line with the natural rights doctrines of our time, the Postmodern God does not demand much. He (perhaps She) asks only that we feel good about ourselves and be nice.

The profound ideological struggles between liberal democracy and it enemies fought for the heart and soul of the human race are over. Despite the rise of terrorism, there are a few people, very few, for whom having a cause is more important than the security provided by globalization, stable societies, and economic interdependence. As Hegel foretold, the principles, if not the practices of liberal democracy have triumphed. The vast majority of human accept the scientific revolution and the kind of open society that supports it.

There are no great projects in the Postmodern era because there are no principles for which sacrifice is necessary. Kojève wondered whether, at the end of history, human beings would lack any projects to inspire them. Without spirit, people might become so content with mere animal pleasures that they would revert to a pre-conscious animal existence. They would erect

---

23   Shadia Drury, *Alexandre Kojève: The Roots of Postmodern Politics* (New York: St. Martin's Press: 1994), 24–41.

their buildings the way birds construct their nests and make music as do cicadas and frogs.

On a visit to Japan in 1953, however, he discovered snobbery as an alternative to the pleasure-seeking principle. When action has no substance, the form or rituals become all important. In a footnote to the *Introduction to the Reading of Hegel,* Kojève relates an example of an activity appropriate to the Postmodern age: the traditional Japanese tea ceremony. The tea is presented beautifully in a complex, stylized, intricate manner. The point of the ceremony is that it has no point. It is all form with no substance. Its significance is its style and beauty; not its rational meaning.[24] In Postmodern terms, the ceremony, like life, has no deeper meaning.

Following this line of thought, Postmodernists have discovered that they should play at the end of history. Since they are "unable to worship anything" and thus cannot pour their "hearts, souls and minds" into a great project, there is little else for them to do but play.[25] But since there can be no truth to which Postmodernists can commit themselves, there is no compelling reason to favor any particular activity, no reason why one game should be preferred over another.

Postmodernists have fought a rear-guard action against the suffocating implications of the end of history. Postmodern thinkers have counterattacked by condemning all hierarchical institutions as efforts to constrain human freedom. They have sought to unmask, expose, and ultimately destroy every power relationship that hampers individual preference. Politics, social organizations, family relations, sexual roles, art, philosophy, metaphysics, thought, and, most importantly, language, have come under the blistering fire of Postmodern criticism. Postmodernists do find something to respect: multiculturalism, they believe, represents the multiplicity of "truth" because the discourses of the victims of the West reveal the oppressive character of its logo-centric power.

While most Postmodernists favor multiculturalism, none would accept one of its consequences. In the real world, diversity often leads to suspicion, separation, hatred and violence. The Postmodernists' dream that the discourses of "the other" should become the canon must be considered in light of the political effects cultural diversity has had. Nobel Prize-winning author Ivo Andri explained the source of the conflict that broke out in his native Bosnia when Archduke Franz Ferdinand was assassinated in 1914:

24 Kojève, *Introduction,* 161–62.
25 Rorty, *Essays on Heidegger and,* 132.

Adherents of the three main faiths, they hate one another from birth to death, senselessly and profoundly…often, they spent their entire lives without finding an opportunity to express that hatred in all its facets and horrors; but whenever the established order of things is shaken by some important event, and reason and law are suspended for a few hours or days, then this mob or rather a section of it, finding at last an adequate motive, over-flows into the town…and, like a flame which has sought and has found fuel, these long-kept hatreds and hidden desires for de-struction and violence take over the town, lapping, sputtering, and swallowing everything, until some force larger than them-selves suppresses them, or until they burn themselves out and tire of their own rage.[26]

Most, if not all, Postmodernists would no doubt condemn such horrible events. In fact they argue that if all human projects become play, it will be possible to enjoy diversity as well as peace and brotherhood. As J. Hillis Miller states, "The millennium [of universal peace and justice among peo-ple] would come if all men and women became good readers in de Man's sense."[27]

If Postmodernism ushers in that particular millennium, it might also undermine multiculturalism. True, people might associate with particular cultures, but in order for those groups not to become violent factions, all individuals would have to recognize the worth of other groups. In doing so, however, they would have to acknowledge something more important than cultural identity. In fact, in the Postmodern world where only meta-dis-courses are possible, people will be forced to realize that there is nothing special about their own culture. Each culture is no more than one discourse among many. Commitment to a heritage would be equivocal since people would see beyond the horizon of their culture. Whatever cultural identity that did exist would be ironic rather than authentic, playful rather than seri-ous, dedicated to form rather than substance, freely chosen rather than as-signed by historical tradition or linguistic, religious or ethnic identity, and

---

26 Quoted by Lenard J. Cohen, "The Destruction of Yugoslavia," in *The National Idea in Eastern Europe,* ed. Gerasimos Augustinos (Lexington, MA: D.C. Heath, 1996), 151.
27 J. Hillis Miller, *The Ethics of Reading* (New York: Columbia University Press, 1987), 58.

the accident of birth. Rorty, who appreciates the ephemeral character of multiculturalism, argues for a pragmatic approach in which there are "no high altars, and instead just …lots of picture galleries, book displays, movies, concerts, ethnographic museums, museums of science and technology, and so on…lots of cultural options but no privileged central discipline."[28]

Cultural identity of this sort would have the same value as a Japanese tea ceremony. Behind the mock diversity would be a fundamental agreement on first principles, one that would have the effect of producing a universal homogenous condition of humankind, not dissimilar to the epoch imagined by Hegel. But in that universal homogeneous era, true multiculturalism and diversity will cease to exist. In order to fully examine the issue, we must turn to the playful pragmatist Richard Rorty.

Rorty and Pragmatism

In a remarkably candid statement in *Philosophy and Social Hope*, Rorty lays out his personal beliefs. The precocious Rorty entered the University of Chicago at age fifteen in search of a unified theory of philosophy and ethics that would explain and complete the disparate elements of his life. Like any good philosopher, he entered the field for the most personal reasons; he wanted to know how to live well. Following some initial flirtations with various schools of philosophy, he discovered that unity and wholeness continued to elude him. There were too many philosophic positions – all somewhat plausible – but inevitably having no points of agreement in large or small matters. After much reflection, he concluded that the *problem* with both philosophy and social theory is that both seek a unified theory, a foundation from which to make judgments about policies and issues that is both true and good. In the end, Rorty came to see the root of the problem is Plato, who was the first to claim that perfect knowledge about the good is possible.[29]

Rorty concludes that virtue does not exist. Virtue, along with any proposition about morality, is nothing more than a linguistic construction that we have come to believe are true because speech constructs our

28 Rorty, *Essays on Heidegger*, 132.
29 Richard Rorty, *Philosophy and Social Hope* (New York: Penguin Books, 1999), 20; Paul Stern, "Antifoundationalism and Plato's *Phaedo*," *The Review of Politics* 51 no. 2 (Spring, 1989), 190–217.

understanding of reality. Postmodern and deconstruction schools assail claims that "the truth" exists and that there is such a thing as "the good." Leading contemporary philosophers such as Paul de Man, Jacques Derrida, Michel Foucault, and Rorty himself have labored mightily to undermine the claim that there is a foundation to knowledge or morality.[30] And Rorty explains:

> [T]here is no way to think about either the world or our purposes except by using our language. One can use language to criticize.... But...the attempt to say "how language relates to the world" by saying what *makes* certain sentences true, or certain actions or attitudes good or rational, is... impossible.... [T]rue sentences are not true because they correspond to reality...there is no need to worry "makes" [something] true.[31]

For Rorty, there can never be such a thing as objective standards of good and bad because there are no objective standards of truth. Indeed, there are no "objects." As he puts it, sentences do not explain the world; they merely explain other sentences:

> The basic anti-intuitionist and antifoundationalist point common to Derrida and these others is that knowledge is a matter of asserting sentences, that you cannot validate an assertion by confronting an object (e.g., a table the concept "tablehood," or the Platonic Idea of Table), but only by asserting other sentences. This point is linked to lots of other holist and antiessent doctrines that make it possible to set aside the subject-object, representationalist notions of knowledge we inherited from the Greeks.[32]

---

30 See for example, Jacques Derrida, *Of Grammatology*, trans. Gayatri Chakravorty Spivak (Baltimore: Johns Hopkins University Press, 1976); Michel Foucault, *Power*, ed. James D. Faubion, trans. Robert Hurley, et. al. (New York: New Press, 2000); Paul de Man, *Blindness and Insight*, 2nd ed. (Minneapolis: University of Minnesota Press, 1983); Richard Rorty, *Objectivity, Relativism, and Truth* (Cambridge: Cambridge University Press, 1991).

31 Richard Rorty, *Consequences of Pragmatism* (Minneapolis: University of Minnesota Press, 1982), xvi.

32 Rorty, *Essays on Heidegger*, 110.

Rorty ridicules the naiveté of those deluded souls who still believe that there is such a thing as truth, explaining, "Lovably old-fashioned prigs of this sort may provide the only excuses which...I have for staying in business."[33]

Rorty traces his anti-foundational ideas to Heidegger, who maintains that we cannot know what virtue is because we can never understand the purpose of Being. Being is the precondition of all that exists, but its being is forever shrouded in mystery. Postmodern or deconstruction thinkers employ something like Derrida's *sous rapture*, translated as "under erasure," a word that is necessary but inadequate for explanation. Heidegger conceived of the notion to explain the elusive character of Being (~~Being~~), which is always present but inexorably hidden. Being is concealed because we live within the world of phenomena and events. These things take up our time and pervade our consciousness but owe their existence to Being, the meaning of which we cannot penetrate.

According to Rorty, it is impossible for us to get outside a linguistic understanding of reality. We interpret experience, and language is the medium of interpretation. We can never understand the essence of things, merely how things appear to us because all reality is mediated by the mechanisms of the cultural milieu in which our awareness has grown. Rorty gives the example of essentialists who bang their head on a table in an effort to show that there is an intrinsic, nonverbal arena of experience. Rorty notes that such a thought experiment gets us no closer to understanding the essence of the table. Whatever we know, we know because language has taught us.[34]

Yet, is not Rorty being too easy on himself? If language constructs reality, Rorty should have jumped out of a fourth-floor window in Cabell Hall while he was writing his book on the campus of the University of Virginia. He could then have proven that language *constructs* reality, because he could have called the experience *flying* and landed safely on Mr. Jefferson's lawn. That Rorty never undertook this experiment is testament to his common sense, prudence, as well as to the inaccuracy of his theory.

It is one thing to say that language is the medium by which we "see" the world, but it is quite another to maintain that language makes things happen in the world. And if language does not make things happen, then phenomena have an independence from language that must be taken into account. According to Glenn Tinder, my defenestration example is the inevitable result of Rorty's principles. Tinder writes:

33 Rorty, *Essays on Heidegger*, 66, 86.
34 Richard Rorty, *Philosophy and Social Hope* (New York: Penguin Books, 1999), 56.

If there are no foundations, then language becomes like a ship without an anchor. It cannot be secured by attaching it to external realities. To elaborate on the simile, it also lacks portholes, for there is nothing outside to be seen, as well as navigational instruments, for there is nowhere to go. It is a prison ship, a craft built of words without meaning and destined to be everlastingly adrift. And that is not the worst of it. Lacking external referents, language becomes vulnerable to "deconstruction." Our prison ship of words is far from being a secure habitation. It is continually having holes torn in its sides, allowing the cold winds and seas of nothingness to sweep in.[35]

Rorty claims that there is no such thing as a giraffe. Of course, there are animals that look like giraffes, but only because we learned the word giraffe and apply it to the beast with a long neck. From the perspective of space or the microbes crawling around in their bellies, there are no giraffes. We have an interest in naming them only because it is "useful" to us.[36]

In the same book, however, Rorty also claims that words can hurt: critics who called him "weird" and "frivolous" hurt him.[37] Of what use was being hurt to Rorty? What was his interest in the sentences calling him weird and frivolous? Words are not objects, like giraffes, but we all know they can hurt. How can an incorporeal thing hurt? What accounts for the feelings about which Rorty felt compelled to write sentences? The answer is that human beings have an inner life. We experience pain, anguish, sorrow, and loss. These are human sensations that cannot be dismissed as just words. If suffering is real for us, so too is the experience of a fellow human being acting honorably, courageously, or justly. We cannot prove that giraffes exist, except we have all seen them. We cannot prove that metaphysical phenomena exist, except we have all experienced them.

Rorty's position is similar to Al-Ghazali's in *The Incoherence of the Philosophers*. The two of them argue that because philosophers cannot give sure and certain answers to the questions they pose, philosophy is useless. Yet both Al-Ghazali and Rorty employ philosophic reasoning in order to undermine philosophy. In doing so, have they really gone beyond Socrates' knowing, yet not knowing?

35   Glenn Tinder, "At the End of Pragmatism"*First Things*, (September 2008): 43–46, http://www.firstthings.com/article/2008/09/004-at-the-end-of-pragmatism
36   Rorty, *Philosophy and Social Hope*, xxvi.
37   Rorty, *Philosophy and Social Hope*, 5.

Plato's teaching is more complicated than Rorty is willing to concede. Plato creates much of what we know about Socrates. Plato does not assert that there are full and complete answers to life's questions. It is Plato's dialogues, in which Socrates is a character, that leave us with unanswered questions about the nature of truth, courage, friendship, and knowledge. If there were clear answers, it would mean the end of philosophy as well as of human freedom and dignity.

Not only does Rorty misread Plato, he also seems to willfully misread Nietzsche. He claims that Nietzsche and John Dewey agree on almost everything except the worth of democratic politics. However, in the *Use and Abuse of History,* Nietzsche warns against the deadening effects of historicism of the kind Dewey and Rorty admire. Nietzsche understands that once people's horizons are destroyed, once they lose faith in the goodness and truth of the principles they strive to implement, they will cease striving. Historicism is true, but deadly.

Rorty seems to have a project, although one that is never "beyond the reach of play."[38] His goal is pragmatism. He writes of his playful devotion to the cause:

> Pragmatists...do not believe that there is a way things really are.... they want to replace the appearance-reality distinction [with] ...less useful and...more useful. When the question "useful for what?" is pressed, they have nothing to say except "useful to create a better future." When they are asked, "Better by what criterion?" they have no detailed answer....Pragmatists can only say something as vague as: Better in the sense of containing more of what we consider good and less of what we consider bad. When asked, 'And what exactly do you consider good?' pragmatists can only say...with Dewey, "growth." "Growth itself," Dewey said, 'is the only moral end." They are limited to such fuzzy and unhelpful answers because what they hope is not that the future will conform to a plan...but rather that the future will astonish and exhilarate.[39]

According to Rorty, pragmatists should do the things that work and avoid the things that do not. For Rorty, America works – or, at least the *idea* of a progressive America works.[40] He argues that there is no ground for favoring

38 Rorty, *Philosophy and Social Hope,* 20.
39 Rorty, *Philosophy and Social Hope,* 27–28.

democracy over any other form of social arrangement. For him, human beings are "centerless networks of beliefs," humans understand nothing but "discourses," and none of them authoritative. No idea, no practice, no way of life is superior to any other. Rorty holds that relativism, multiculturalism, and eclecticism are most compatible with the liberty and tolerance guaranteed by democracy. Why does he favor liberty or tolerance? He falls back on convention to defend democracy. When "historical circumstance allows," it is possible to have "agreement about political topics." In other words, for people who by chance are born and raised in a democratic culture, democracy is beneficial and a worthy choice because other people of the same culture will have similar proclivities. As for those with "unusual views" who disagree with his democratic sentiments, Rorty admits, "Extensive attempts at an exchange of political views have made us realize we are not going to get anywhere."[41]

Rorty claims to be "sentimentally patriotic about America."[42] It is fair to ask, therefore, if America could have come into being had its Founders been guided by Rorty's principles. To make the point, one need only imagine a Postmodern General George Washington addressing his ill-clad, poorly equipped, hungry troops at Valley Forge as they struggled to secure America independence. "Now men," the Rorty-like Washington might say, "we have suffered defeat after defeat at the hands of the British. Notwithstanding our dire situation, I'm here to ask you to sacrifice your lives, fortunes and honor for a playfully contingent cause. Your descendants may or may not enjoy the blessings of liberty, and by the way, who can be sure whether liberty is good anyway? We will have to wait and see if it's something worth having. The British disagree with us, and who's to say they're wrong? There is no ground for saying anyone is right or wrong. Our revolution is the first to have no foundation and to be based fully on the pragmatic hope that things might work out."

Neither the revolution that gave birth to America nor the government formed to manage its affairs would have been successful without Washington, and he was not particularly pragmatic or playful. Rather, he was renowned for his integrity and virtue, qualities to which his countrymen responded with devotion. Perhaps virtue is not as verifiable as the laws of nature uncovered by scientific experiments, but human beings know it exists. Without Washington's virtue, the American Revolution would not have succeeded, and Rorty's pragmatism would not have found a home.

40 Rorty, *Philosophy and Social Hope*, 17.
41 Rorty, *Objectivity, Relativism, and Truth*, 191.
42 Rorty, *Philosophy and Social Hope*, 17.

Rorty does admit to having a number of heroes, and Václav Havel is among them.[43] Would Rorty admire Havel had he been a pragmatist? Havel was one of the worst practitioners of that doctrine in history. Had Havel been a pragmatist, he would never have written *Protest*, a play that shows how pragmatism can devolve into cowardly self-interest. If Havel had been a pragmatist, he would have adapted to his environment and become a communist in 1957. As a communist, like many of his contemporaries, he could have attended Charles University rather than being excluded from higher education because of lack of compliance. If Havel had been a pragmatist, he would never have become a dissident. If Havel had been converted to pragmatism while serving a jail sentence as a dissident, he would have left the awful conditions of his incarceration and come to the United States, where he would have been greeted warmly. The list goes on.

The qualities that Rorty admires in Havel and Americans admired in Washington are not pragmatic: they are what people once called virtue – courage, prudence, determination, skill in leadership, and forbearance of the shortcoming of others. Rorty claims to be a kind of realist. He does not want theory to influence events. What of the phenomenon of virtue? Is his realistic theory not leading him to deny what is everywhere apparent in social life: his fellow men and women striving to live by codes of behavior?

Rorty mistakes the *forms* of virtue for their *practical expression*. "The idea of a universally shared source of truth called 'reason' or 'human nature,'" Rorty explains, "is for us pragmatists….misleading." These concepts are misleading because they cannot become "the *destiny* of humanity."[44] A Platonist would respond that the idea/form of the chair is not a particular chair. The idea informs what all the chairs are in order to be chairs. The idea/form of virtue acts as an ideal, explaining to people what proper conduct should be. The idea does not have to be practical in every case to be real. In fact, it would no longer be an ideal if it were always practical. Virtue does not have to become the destiny of humanity for it to be able to influence the way human beings think about their lives.

Rorty too has an ideal. "It is…a fully democratic, fully secular…community in which everybody thinks that it is human solidarity, rather than knowledge…that really matters."[45] Does not this pragmatic ideal posit a

---

43   Richard Rorty, "The Seer of Prague: Review of *Jan Patočka: Philosophy and Se-lected Writings*," *The New Republic* 205 no.1 (1 July 1991), 35.

44   Rorty, *Philosophy and Social Hope*, xxxii.

45   Rorty, *Philosophy and Social Hope*, 20.

belief in happiness? What conditions lead to happiness? Are certain harmonious arrangements more likely to bring about happiness than others?[46] If so, why? What is there in the human condition that makes one set of social conditions lead to happiness and another lead away from happiness? Is not Rorty sneaking in some sort of human nature, one that takes account of our freedom to choose good or bad social outcomes?

If democracy and solidarity are not Archimedean first principles, what are they? Do not they need some sort of defense or justification? Must not reason, if perhaps not philosophic certainty, be put to the task of explaining why such a democratic future is good for us? Or is Rorty just playing when he says he cares for humanity?

Rorty might counter that he can convince only people who already accept the democratic, rights-oriented way of life of the validity of his statements However, if no truth and no principle of nature or reason exists to enable Rorty to persuade people that he is correct, could we not conclude that he is trying to manipulate people to accept his view? To put the point in Nietzsche's terms, Rorty may be merely asserting his will to power. Tinder maintains that the consequences of pragmatism are not solidarity and democracy, but power. He explains:

> If language cannot tell us of the truth, or be used to search for the truth, then philosophy, the love of wisdom, dies. It is replaced by rhetoric. It becomes an effort to convince-which is to say exercise power over-other people. All relationships become power relationships of one kind or another. In that situation, authority is inconceivable. If all speech is rhetorical, there can be no authoritative speech. There can be no relationships based on mutual recognition of the truth.[47]

Rorty's playful pragmatism has a darker side. We should wonder what will curb a person who can "speak persuasively if any of his misdeeds come to light, and use force when needed."[48] Plato raises the same issue in *The Republic*. His answer, of course, is that people need to be restrained by virtue.

---

46 Rorty, *Philosophy and Social Hope*, 277.
47 Tinder, "At the End of Pragmatism."
48 Plato, *Republic* 361b.

Chapter Three
Nietzsche's *Genealogy of Morals*

The practice of judging and condemning morally is the favorite revenge of the intellectually shallow on those who are less so, it is also a kind of indemnity for their being badly endowed by nature, and finally, it is an opportunity for acquiring spirit and BECOMING subtle – malice spiritualizes. Nietzsche[1]

Truth

No work presents a more devastating assault on the idea that moral considerations are natural to human beings than does Friedrich Nietzsche's *The Genealogy of Morals*. The *Genealogy* was written at the apogee of Nietzsche's powers. In it, he uses his substantial gifts of analysis and rhetorical flourish to challenge the humanitarian goals of social justice and equality. Put simply, Nietzsche condemns the idea that the morally good person is good for the human race. He states:

> Nobody, up to now, has doubted that the "good" man represents a higher value than the "evil," in terms of promoting and benefiting mankind.... But suppose the exact opposite were true. What if the "good" man represents not merely a retrogression but even a danger, a temptation, a narcotic drug enabling the present to live at the expense of the future? More comfortable, less hazardous, perhaps, but also baser, more petty – so that morality itself would be responsible for man, as a species, failing

---

1   Friedrich Nietzsche, *Beyond Good and Evil*, trans. Helen Zimmern (Project Gutenberg Literary Archive etext) http://www.gutenberg.org/dirs/etext03/bygdv10.txt, 2002): aphorism 219.

to reach the peak of magnificence of which he is capable? What if morality should turn out to be the danger of dangers?[2]

The Genealogy of Morals has fascinated scholars and philosophers, prompting myriad diverse, often conflicting interpretations.[3] Nietzsche's

2   Nietzsche, *Genealogy of Morals*, 155.
3   There are two collections of essays dedicated solely to analyses of *The Genealogy of Morals*: *Nietzsche's On the Genealogy of Morals: Critical Essays*, ed. Christa Davis Acampora, (Lanham, MD: Rowman & Littlefield, 2006); *Nietzsche, Genealogy, Morality: Essays on Nietzsche's Genealogy of Morals*, ed. Richard Schacht, (Berkley, CA: University of California Press, 1994). See also the following full-length studies: David B. Allison, R*eading the New Nietzsche* (Lanham, MD: Rowman & Littlefield, 2000); Daniel Conway, *Nietzsche's 'On the Genealogy of Morals': A Reader's Guide* (New York: Continuum International Publishing Group, 2008); and the following articles: Kristen Brown, "Possible and Questionable: Opening Nietzsche's Genealogy to Feminine Body," *Hypatia* 14 (Summer 1999): 39–58; David Campbell, "Nietzsche, Heidegger, and Meaning," *The Journal of Nietzsche Studies* 26 (2003) 25–54; Andrew Jason Cohen, "In Defense of Nietzschean Genealogy," *The Philosophic Forum* 30 no. 4 (December 1999): 269–288; Philip J. Kain, "Nietzschean Genealogy and Hegelian History in '*The Genealogy of Morals*,'" *Canadian Journal of Philosophy* 26 no. 1 (March 1996): 123–48; Brian Leiter, "Nietzsche and the Morality Critics," *Ethics* 107 no. 2 (January 1997): 250–85; David Lindstedt, "The Progression and Regression of Slave Morality in Nietzsche's *Genealogy*: The Moralization of Bad Conscience and Indebtedness," *Man and World* 23 (January 1997): 83–105; Karl Löwith, "Nietzsche's Doctrine of the Eternal Return," *Journal of the History of Ideas* 6 no. 3 (June 1945): 273–84; David Owen, "Nietzsche's Event: Genealogy and the Death of God," *Theory & Event* 6:3 (2002): 1–56; David Owen, "The Contest of Enlightenment An Essay on Critique and Genealogy," *The Journal of Nietzsche Studies* 25 (2003): 35–57; Bernard Reginster, "Nietzsche on Ressentiment and Valuation," *Philosophy and Phenomenology Research* 57:2 (June 1977): 281–305; R.R. Reno, "Nietzsche's Deeper Truth," *First Things: A Monthly Journal of Religion and Public Life* 179 (January 2008): 33–40; Aaron Ridley, "Guilt Before God, or God Before Guilt? The Second Essay of Nietzsche's *Genealogy*," *The Journal of Nietzsche Studies* 29 (Spring 2005): 35–45; Robert C. Solomon, "Nietzsche on Fatalism and 'Free Will,'" *The Journal of Nietzsche Studies* 23 (2002) 63–87; Charles D. Tarlton," Idealism and the Higher Morality versus Democracy: Using Nietzsche's *Genealogy of Morals* to Revisit Bradley's Ethical Studies," *Theory & Event* 8 no. 4 (2005): 1–64; Rudi Visker, "Can Genealogy Be Critical? A Somewhat Unromantic Look at Nietzsche and Foucault," *Man and World* 23 (October 1990): 441–452; Jerry Weinberger, "But Which God Will Save Us? The Political Legacy of Nietzsche and Heidegger," *The Political Science Reviewer* 16 (Fall 1986): 353–412; Kathleen J. Wininger, "On Nietzsche, *The Genealogy of Morals*," *The Journal of Value Inquiry* 30 (September

analysis of morals is not only an effort to undermine morality, but is an account of the final and inevitable historical collapse of Western metaphysics. And if there is no metaphysics – the things beyond the physical – there can be no virtue. Morality and virtue exist in the realm of judgment and choice, attributes that are never merely physical.

Nietzsche begins the *Genealogy* with what seems an odd admission: the thing closest to us – the self – is the most difficult to comprehend. When we consider our own being, the conscious part of the mind is not the same as the objective part we are examining. The thinker can never quite be captured by the thought. This unknowability of the self to itself is a psychological truth, an inherent condition of human existence that became plainly evident only in the modern world as the final historical fact of Western metaphysic.[4]

Nietzsche argues that even if common sense tells us that our experiences are accurate, we can never quite be sure. Truth is elusive because our comprehension of sense perception is organized by a whole array of learned cultural and historical presuppositions. Truth is mediated by what we are taught. For example, is an unusually bright light in the sky an indication that the Messiah has arrived, as people in religious eras might have thought, or it is a supernova exploding, as we in a culture dominated by scientific thinking might conclude?

Nietzsche argues that his work runs counter to the age-old goal of philosophy, knowing the truth. There is no simple way to ascertain the truth as such. All philosophic "thoughts should grow out of our values with the same necessity as fruit grows out of a tree." Values derive from authenticity, not commonly shared objective standards. In the most profound sense, then, it does not matter whether we "find these fruits unpalatable," for whatever "truths" we adopt will be a personal choice.[5]

Nietzsche makes fun of Kant's effort to overcome what has been called the clash of civilizations and to universalize moral dictates by locating them in the processes of human reason. Nietzsche recounts a personal story, one that indicates just how particular and individualistic morality can be:

> Already as a thirteen-year-old lad, I was exercised by the problem of the origin of evil. At an age when one's interests are

1996): 453–470; Robert J. Antonio, "Nietzsche's Antisociology: Subjectified Culture and the End of History," *The American Journal of Sociology* 101 (July 1995): 1–43.

4 Ken Gemes, "We Remain of Necessity Strangers to Ourselves," in Acampora, *Critical Essays*, 191–208.

5 Nietzsche, *Genealogy of Morals*, 150.

"divided between childish games and devotion to God," I wrote my first essay on ethics. My solution of the problem was to give honor to God, as is only just, and make him the father of evil. Was this what my *a priori* demanded of me – that new immoral, at the very least unmoral *a priori* – and that mysterious anti-Kantian "categorical imperative" to which I have hearkened more and more ever since, and not just hearkened?[6]

From these considerations, two questions arise. First, if all thought is mediated by culture, how can Nietzsche's own ideas run counter to his age? Should not his principles, like all others, be products of his time rather than "thoughts out of season"? Second, if there is no ground for metaphysical "truth," then is not truth itself – and not only values – a matter of personal choice?

Nietzsche's response to these two questions is revealing and indicates why Martin Heidegger believes that Nietzsche, despite his dismissal of metaphysical ideas, is himself a part and continuation of the Western tradition of metaphysics. In the Third Essay of *Genealogy*, Nietzsche argues that some people – philosophers – move beyond the ideas of their societies. In fact, Nietzsche is an idealist, for he contends that the ideas of philosophers establish the cultural horizons in which the rest of us live.

Nietzsche's view of "truth" is an odd one. To state the obvious, if truth is a matter of personal perspective, then the words on the page can be interpreted any way any reader decides. Nietzsche's work can be read as an endorsement of weakness, servility, and a strict adherence to "slave" morality – hardly the result that Nietzsche intends.[7] It is clear that Nietzsche has a specific "authorial intent." He claims that "reading is an art," and that, to be understood correctly, his work requires "careful reading," one that employs "a whole science of hermeneutics."[8] Yet, as Heidegger argues, if truth grows out of values, then what a person values will establish the truth.[9]

---

6 Nietzsche, *Genealogy of Morals*, 151.
7 For an analysis on "perspectivism" see Brain Leiter's analysis of the "received view," of Nietzsche's perspectivism. Brain Leiter, "Perspectivism in Nietzsche's *Genealogy of Morals*," in Schacht, *Nietzsche, Genealogy, Morality*, 334–57. For the origin of "perspectivism" see Arthur Danto, *Nietzsche as Philosopher* (New York: MacMillan, 1965).
8 Nietzsche, *Genealogy of Morals*, 157.
9 Martin Heidegger, *Nietzsche*, vol. 3, trans. by David Ferrell Krell (San Francisco: HarperSanFrancisco, 1991), 191–200.

How can there be truth and no truth? Heidegger argues that the dilemma is resolved only if we understand Nietzsche's fundamental truth: the will-to-power. Heidegger states:

> All objectivity is "subjective." This does not mean that being comes to be a mere point of view and opinion set down by some casual and arbitrary "I." That all objectivity is "subjective" means that what encounters us comes to be established as an object standing in itself. "Beingness is subjectivity" and "Beingness is objectivity" say the selfsame thing.[10]

Nietzsche's strange "truth" proclaims that the will-to-power demands that truth exist. The role of will-to-power is to bring health and vitality to all living things. The will-to-power *is* the truth of existence. Humans cannot thrive unless they believe that their lives make sense, and life does not make sense unless we think that validity, significance, consistency, or accuracy are real. Therefore, the will-to-power requires that humans believe that some things are true. But Nietzsche reveals that truth is merely an assertion of the will-to-power, not the eternal, immutable form Plato imagined. In a way, there is "truth," but only because the will-to-power decrees it into existence.

Nietzsche's goal in the *Genealogy* is to attack metaphysics in such a way as to undermine the most strongly held "truth" of his age, the "preference for and overestimation of pity."[11] He objects to egalitarianism, universal human rights, social justice, and economic equity. He argues that societies that pursue such goals inevitably take their bearing from the most basic needs of the neediest people. Those dedicated to humanitarian principles – often the best and brightest – constantly worry about the weak, downtrodden, sick, maladroit, and lazy. Humanitarians deny their own accomplishments in order to fulfill the wants of others; their ambitions become a kind of self-denial in service to inept underachievers. According to Nietzsche, egalitarian societies sink to the lowest level of humanity. Any mark of beauty, merit, or accomplishment is lost in a sea of mediocrity and sameness. The masses, taken literally to mean an indistinguishable throng, come to dominate life. Life among the masses is boring, tedious, and mundane – even, it turns out, for the masses. Individuals who make up the

10 Heidegger *Nietzsche*, vol. 3, 221.
11 Nietzsche, *Genealogy of Morals*, 154.

masses need exciting deeds and virtuous heroes to bring meaning and purpose to their lives. Humanity requires inspiration, and great human beings provide it.

Slaves and Masters

Nietzsche begins his assault on the truth of modern morality in the *Genealogy's* First Essay "'Good and Evil' and 'Good and Bad.'" He discounts theories that explain the origin of morality. These schemes speculate that a fortuitous act of kindness in the distant past must have been praised, which led to further acts of generosity. Concern for others became habitual as the community's respect for altruism grew. Over time, the first acts of kindness, generosity or compassion were forgotten, but the habit of kindness and regard for others became the norm.

Nietzsche argues that this theory must be incorrect for there is no reason why the original good deed would have been overlooked. Instead, Nietzsche uses his training as a philologist to investigate the origin of the word *good*. Good at first meant strong, powerful, distinctive, and excellent. Its opposite was weak, common, plebian, and ordinary. The original meaning of *good* provides a clue to the beginning of morality. The aristocracies of the ancient world, especially Greece and Rome, celebrated their achievements and skills, with little thought for the unwashed many – except by way of contemptuous comparison:

> It was the "good" themselves, that is to say the noble, mighty, highly placed, and high-minded who decreed themselves and their actions to be good, i.e., belonging to the highest rank, in contradistinction to all that was base, low-minded and plebeian. It was only this *pathos of distance* that authorized them to create values and name them.[12]

The strong were good because they were strong. The weak could not match the physical prowess or determination of the strong, and so they were bad. The strong used their vitality to establish political societies in which the weak had to do the strong's bidding. The strong did not attempt to rule by force alone, but they solidified their superiority by creating laws, cus-

12   Nietzsche, *Genealogy of Morals*, 160.

toms, and beliefs that made obedience to their commands a matter of legal, social, and religious obligation. Success at defending the community with extraordinary deeds and valor was named virtue. The strong embraced the mores and practices they established. They considered their superiority spiritual as well as physical, believing the gods had ordained their elevated place in society. They assumed their primacy was proper, just, natural, and sanctioned by religious principles. The justification of the social hierarchy became metaphysical as well as physical (for example, the Pharaohs of Egypt were believed to be gods, not tyrants).

The metaphysical defense of social hierarchy led to the first setback for the rule of the strong. A priestly class arose whose task was to interpret and justify the social order. These people came to have an interest and outlook different from the warrior-rulers. Nietzsche claims that there was "from the very start, something unwholesome about the priestly aristocracies." They experienced swings between "brooding and emotional outburst" because they eschewed action, instead practicing abstinence, fasting, sexual continence and other forms of "anti-sensual metaphysics."[13] The virtue of grand achievement was transformed by priests into moral inhibitions.

In time, the priests came to have a perspective opposed to the warrior rulers; their metaphysical kingdom competed with the political-military for dominance. The contest was one-sided: brawny, aggressive, dull-witted nobles were no match for the "cerebral and poisonous" priests. The nobles had "the innocence of wild animals" returning from "an orgy of murder, arson, rape and torture, jubilant and at peace...as though they had committed a fraternity prank." The priests calculated, planned, and succeeded. They gained people's loyalty by ruling their minds, and in doing so they altered the human race forever. Humans became "interesting creatures," capable of more than merely following their animal instincts. "Human history," Nietzsche explains, would have been "a dull and stupid thing without the intelligence furnished by its impotence."[14]

Once the idea of a transcendent realm took hold among people, it was inevitable that one group would lay claim to a special relationship with the deity. With an extraordinarily powerful – and we know now, dangerous – rhetorical flourish, Nietzsche blames the most "priestly people," the Jews, for inverting a moral code that reduced and inhibited the vitality of the

13 Nietzsche, *Genealogy of Morals*, 166.
14 Nietzsche, *Genealogy of Morals*, 166–67, 174.

human species.[15] The Jews took revenge on their militarily stronger, politically more powerful, and culturally more successful enemies by attacking their claim to dominance:

> It was the Jews who with frightening consistency, dared to invert the aristocratic value equations: good/noble/powerful/beautiful/happy/favored-of-the-gods and maintain, with the furious hatred of the underprivileged and impotent, that "only the poor, the powerless, are good; only the suffering, sick, and ugly, truly blessed. But you noble and mighty ones of the earth will be damned to all eternity. . . ."[16]

The Jewish religion was the foundation of the trans-valuation of values, according to Nietzsche, a moral revolution in which what the aristocrats condemned as bad (weakness and humility) was taken to be right, and what was thought to be good (spirited assertiveness) was damned as sin. The bad became good, and the good became sin. In the metaphysical world of morals, the strong are constrained from using their superiority; their assertive virtue is evil. Weak people, who in reality have no physical capacity for superiority, transform their lack of ability into the virtues of piety, humility, and humanity – for which they are rewarded with eternal salvation.[17]

Nietzsche maintains that the moral restraint of the weak is not truly a virtue. The weak have no choice but to exhibit moderation because they are incapable of asserting themselves physically. They rage against their natural limits and social inferiority, turning their rancor against the mighty. Nietzsche's *Genealogy* argues, then, that morality is not admirable, noble, or desirable, but rather is merely a manifestation of the seething resentment of the weak, a psychological sleight of hand that has had the effect of making lack of ability a virtue.

According to Nietzsche, the slaves have won. Everything noble, beautiful, grand, and dangerous is disparaged, not just by the many, but also by the leading minds of the age. The era of "the last man" – who does little but

---

15 As Yirmiyahu Yovel argues Nietzsche disliked and criticized anti-Semites, even his sister. Yet few can doubt that his powerful rhetoric and brilliance gave credence to virulent forms of 20th century anti-Semitism. Yirmiyahu Yovel, "Nietzsche and the Jews: The Structure of an Ambivalence," in Acampora, *Critical Essays*, 277–290.

16 Nietzsche, *Genealogy of Morals*, 167.

17 Nietzsche, *Genealogy of Morals*, 181.

shop, eat, pursue mindless entertainment (and complain bitterly about high prices and the lack of good shows on television) – has arrived.[18]

Conscience and Guilt

Yet, do not people have a natural moral sense? Do we not feel the pangs of conscience when we commit a thoughtless, cruel, or evil act? No. The sense of guilt and regret we feel after having done something wrong is certainly not, Nietzsche declares, a sentiment imprinted by nature on our souls instead it is the result of successfully taming our animal instincts.

Nietzsche elaborates by asking how it is possible for animals to keep promises. Of course, animals cannot keep promises, because they never make any. Human beings need to make promises because their actions are not motivated by pure instinct. They can defer eating when they are hungry or drinking when they are thirsty. They can say one thing and do another. Humans need not behave in a straight-forward manner, making it possible for them to mislead. Because humans can deceive, they need to make promises to each other not to mislead. They must swear to keep their word. In order to keep their promises, they must bind their future actions with their present words. Then, to honor those words, humans must project themselves into the future and purport to control their actions in a time that does not yet exist. But how did this peculiar trait of forethought arise in humans?

At the starting point of social life, Nietzsche claims, people felt no guilt: they did as they pleased – stealing, killing, lying, cheating – without a second thought. They made promises and reneged on them with no regret. So from where arose the concept of a guilty conscience, of remorse or shame? Nietzsche dismisses the Biblical account, that guilt was a consequence of the disobedience of Adam and Eve. Rather, he maintains, when people started living together, they found they needed rules. Punishment for violating them was simple and fierce. We know that thieves lost limbs, and murderers lost their lives, and adulterers suffered equally harsh treatment.

These penalties were not meant to reform the guilty or even to prevent future crimes; they were the ways primitive societies compensated an individual who had been wronged. How was the aggrieved person comforted? According to Nietzsche's account, the victim's compensation was the great good of seeing another person suffer.

18   Robert O. Solomon, "One Hundred Years of *Ressentiment*," in Schacht, *Nietzsche, Genealogy, Morality*, 95–138.

"My money is gone," or "My wife has dishonored my name," or "My brother is dead," but "I will feel better watching the thief, adulterer, or murderer writhe in agony," Nietzsche's archaic people might have thought. Those punished felt little guilt for their misdeeds; they accepted their penalty, he says, as "if some terrible unforeseen disaster had occurred, if a rock had fallen and crushed" them.[19] At some point, however, people began to engage in cost-benefit analysis. They decided to try to avoid the pain associated with violating the rules.

What happened to their natural animal instincts, to the desire to take what they pleased, to rape, plunder, and murder? No longer able to express these urges outwardly against neighbors or foes, civilized humans turned their passions against themselves:

> Hostility, cruelty, the delight in persecution, raids, excitement, destruction all turned against their begetter. Lacking external enemies and resistances, and confined within an oppressive narrowness and regularity, man began rending, persecuting, terrifying himself, like a wild beast hurling itself against the bars of its cage. This languisher…who had to turn *himself* into an adventure, a torture chamber, an insecure and dangerous wilderness…became the inventor of "bad conscience"…. His sickness of himself, brought on by the violent severance from his animal past…. Let me hasten to add that the phenomenon of an animal soul turning in upon itself, taking up arms against itself, was so novel, profound, mysterious, contradictory, and pregnant with possibility, that the whole complexion of the universe was changed thereby. This spectacle…required a divine audience to do it justice. It was a spectacle too sublime and paradoxical to pass unnoticed on some trivial planet.[20]

Nietzsche's analysis reverses the traditional order of the moral universe. For him, it was not God who dictated commandments to limit and control the base aspects of human nature. It was the inner compulsion of humans to justify the taming of their instincts that created both God and the concept of moral codes. Moreover, although Sigmund Freud is said to have avoided reading Nietzsche before he wrote his psychoanalytic theory, there is a clear

19   Nietzsche, *Genealogy of Morals*, 215.
20   Nietzsche, *Genealogy of Morals*, 215.

path from the *Genealogy* to the concept of the sublimation of the id for the sake of the ego and superego.[21]

If Nietzsche's theory about archaic societies is accurate, it is evident why ancestor worship became so widespread in almost every ancient society. Those who established the first conventions created human consciousness. How do we repay our forbearers for the ability to think in temporal ways? How do we repay the debt of being human? Nietzsche claims that rituals idolizing ancestors become more elaborate, complex, and awe-inspiring until the venerated ones become gods. Yet the very capacity of people to stage increasingly sophisticated ceremonies only shows how extraordinary humans being are, making the debt to past generations who established the moral foundations of civilization even greater. People feel guilt because they can never pay back what is owed to the godlike founders. Civilization's advances established a mandate of eternal guilt.

Here Christianity developed its most important and powerful belief: Christ the redeemer absolved humans of their sins:

> Then suddenly we come face to face with that paradoxical and ghastly expedient which brought temporary relief to tortured humanity, that most brilliant stroke of Christianity: God's sacrifice of himself for man. God makes himself the ransom for what could not otherwise be ransomed; God alone has power to absolve us of a debt we can no longer discharge; the creditor offers himself as a sacrifice for his debtor out of sheer love (can you believe it?), out of love for his debtor. . . .[22]

Who but the almighty can make such a sacrifice to absolve humans of their sins? Christianity drives human beings ever further into guilt and despair. They can never live up to the example of a crucified Christ even when they attempt to follow God's laws; his sacrifice is too enormous. They can never rid themselves of the debt and must always humbly submit to divine commands that require inhibiting their strongest passions and desires.

Christian morality is the final victory of the Jewish religion. According to Nietzsche, Jews had to kill Christ to fully achieve the trans-valuation of

---

21 See Eric Blondel, "Nietzsche' Style of Affirmation" and Alan D. Schrift, "Nietzsche, Deleuze, and the Genealogical Critique of Psychoanalysis," in Acampora, *Critical Essays*, 67–76, 245–255.

22 Nietzsche, *Genealogy of Morals*, 225.

values. Jews transformed the moral world by making a martyr of its central figure, although paradoxically the Jewish people became social outcasts to achieve this metaphysical victory.

Rule of Philosophers

The Third Essay of the *Genealogy*, entitled "What Do Ascetic Ideals Mean?" is accompanied by a misogynist aphorism: "Wisdom likes men who are reckless, scornful and violent; being a woman, her heart goes out to a soldier."[23] The relationship between ascetics, wisdom, and reckless soldiers becomes clear only at the end of the essay.

Nietzsche begins by raising the question of the phenomenon of asceticism. This cooping up of physical desires is associated with many human activities: religion, sports, art, and philosophy. Creative people instinctively understand that living abstemiously will benefit their work (or at least exercising self-control will allow their energies to be channeled into their creation). Despite this inclination toward asceticism, artists cannot explain the impulse, and so priests explain it as a commandment from God.

To help us accurately understand the ascetic ideal, Nietzsche turns to philosophers, who, of course, attempt to explain everything. Philosophers practice the ascetic ideal because it is their way. The driving passion of their lives is to understand, an obsession aided by inhibiting physical impulses. They forswear "shiny, loud things – fame, princes, and women," in order to pursue solitary contemplation.[24] Few philosophers marry, and still fewer have children. They follow these "anti-biological" practices not because of a commitment to virtue, nor to inhibit or restrain the will, but rather to fulfill the "natural conditions of their optimal existence."[25] Philosophers best pursue their drive to know in quiet, responsibility-free, meditative surroundings.

Notwithstanding their reclusive practices, political and religious leaders in almost every society have distrusted – even persecuted – philosophers. Until the Enlightenment, philosophers were frequently in danger of attack because their views were at odds with prevailing conventions. Moreover, philosophers were suspect because they cast a skeptical eye on gods, whose existence can be proven only by myth, tradition, and faith.

---

23 Nietzsche, *Genealogy of Morals*, 231.
24 "that malicious Socrates got married in a spirit of irony," Nietzsche, *Genealogy of Morals*, 242.
25 Nietzsche, *Genealogy of Morals*, 243–45, 253.

According to Nietzsche, philosophers command a powerful tool of self-defense, a weapon more formidable than the physical strength of the ruling elites: they understand the power of ideas. They employ a potent rhetoric to convince people of a realm beyond the physical – a sphere more real and truer than experience can grasp. One need think only of Plato's theory of the forms in which the phenomena of daily life are but a poor second-hand copy of the real world of ideas. What we cannot see becomes "truer" than what we can.

Nietzsche contends that philosophers invented the metaphysical world – with its emphasis on self-discipline, moderation, and morality – in order to legitimize their own way of life. They made a virtue of not acting, of inhibiting and restraining the vigorous elements of human nature as practiced by the warrior elite. Asceticism, the denial of the physical, became an ideal, indeed, *the* ideal. The many accepted the metaphysics of the philosophers even if they could not adopt the actual discipline of philosophy. The many tried to live a moral life, suppressing their desires and living according to a moral doctrine that promoted helping the poor, weak, and humble. Slave morality triumphed, and Christian charity became the dominant moral prescription of Western civilization. Nietzsche calls its metaphysical principles, "Platonism for the people."[26]

While the ascetic life may be good for philosophers, it is not necessarily good for everyone else. Although Platonic metaphysics has not quite vanquished the savage beast in the human species, it has succeeded all too well for Nietzsche's taste. Morality turns people's striving away from achievement and toward caring for the poor, weak and, underprivileged. It compels the best to be in the service of the worst. It reduces the human species to mediocrity, because it turns attention away from achievement and towards pity. Nietzsche, by contrast, would have the best seek greatness:

> if there are any such in the realm beyond good and evil grant me...the sight of something perfect, wholly achieved, happy, magnificently triumphant, something still capable of inspiring fear! Of a man who will justify the existence of mankind. . . . The leveling and diminution of European man is our greatest danger; because the sight of him makes us despond. . . .[27]

---

26 *Beyond Good and Evil*, Preface.
27 Nietzsche, *Genealogy of Morals*, 177.

Philosophers have given meaning to human existence. They have pretended to discover the truth, but, in fact, they have invented it. The philosophic way of life has provided the human race with a purpose, although that purpose results in a life that hems in and restricts our physical nature:

> Until the advent of the ascetic ideal...the animal man, had no meaning....His existence was aimless; the question, "Why is there such a thing as man?" could not have been answered.... [T]here rang...a refrain..."In vain!".... [S]omething was lacking....[Man] did not know how to justify...himself. His...meaning was an unsolved problem and made him suffer....yet what bothered him was not his suffering but his inability to answer the question "What is the meaning of my trouble?" Man...does not deny suffering per se: he wants it... provided that it can be given a meaning.... [T]he ascetic ideal arose to give it meaning.... Suffering had been interpreted.... No doubt that interpretation brought new...suffering: it placed all suffering under the perspective of guilt.... All the same, man had saved himself... he was no longer a leaf in the wind.... We can no longer conceal from ourselves what...the ascetic ideal, signifies – this hatred of...animality, of inert matter; this loathing of the senses, of reason even; this fear of beauty and happiness.... It signifies...a will to nothingness, a revulsion from life, a rebellion against the principal conditions of living. And yet, despite everything, it is and remains a will. Let me repeat, now that I have reached the end, what I said at the beginning: man would sooner have the void for his purpose than be void of purpose....[28]

The aphorism is now explained. Philosophers create our horizons with a bold assertion of their will. We live in a world of constructed meaning made possible because of the daring rhetoric of superior minds. For Nietzsche, there is nothing noble, natural, or holy about morality. Morals are the consequence of human desires and emotions – fear, anxiety, envy, or resentment against the high and mighty. Philosophers made those low passions into a metaphysical teaching that we have mistakenly come to accept as the natural or spiritual order of existence.

28   Nietzsche, *Genealogy of Morals*, 298–99.

Assessment

Nietzsche presents a number of criticisms of morality. As we have seen, he argues that the strong created morality as an act of will; morals are little more than resentment against the strong – the revenge of the weak against their own inadequacies; the will-to-power is the one true principle of existence; and that the metaphysical realm of morals was created, not discovered, by philosophers and therefore does not truly exist.

Did the strong establish morality with no thought to the weak, "the other"? As Mark Migotti points out, there may be some truth to Nietzsche's claim that "All truly noble morality grows out of triumphant self-affirmation. Slave ethics, on the other hand, begins by saying *no* to an 'outside,' to an 'other,' a non-self, and that *no* is its creative act."[29] Yet, human consciousness seems to be more multifaceted than Nietzsche's polemic admits. After all, strength is a comparison between one's own capacity and that of others, an evaluation that must take account of "the other."[30] Aristocrats constantly compared themselves to others. It was exactly because they did not want to be needy and weak that they behaved as if they had no weakness. It was the fear of appearing fragile, not mere haughty indifference, that motivated the strong to act as they did. They wanted to exhibit their mastery over fortune, chance, and vulnerability because they knew a reverse could alter their status in an instant. Chinua Achebe's leading character, Okonkwo, in *Things Fall Apart* (whose life falls apart) beautifully exhibits both the awareness of failure and fear of disgrace that motivate the strong.[31]

The involvement of human beings with other people is so ubiquitous and necessary that it can never be dismissed. We are, as Alasdair MacIntyre puts it, "dependent rational animals."[32] We need our parents when we are young, we need our children when we are old, we need love, companionship, and admiration throughout life. Even the archetypal fictional hero of Western civilization, Achilles, unburdened his frustration, fear, and anxiety on his mother. The strong require "the other" as associates to carry out their commands. Shakespeare's *Coriolanus* is the most eloquent literary example of a person trying to be utterly independent of his confederates, but tragically failing.

29 Nietzsche, *Genealogy of Morals*, 170.
30 Mark Migotti, "Slave Morality, Socrates, and the Bushman," in Acampora, *Critical Essays*, 109–29.
31 Chinua Achebe, *Things Fall Apart* (London: Heinemann, 1958).
32 Alasdair C. MacIntyre, *Dependent Rational Animals: Why Human Beings Need the Virtues* (Chicago: Open Court, 1999).

There can be no consciousness of existence without others. People are taught to speak and reason. The awareness of life beyond the moment is partly a social construct. It was not only the self assertion of the strong that taught humans to keep promises, but also the appreciation of human vulnerability. Social interaction entails giving thought to the needs, demands, and desires of others. To get and do what we want, we must be alert to how our desires and demands might affect others. We must be able to put ourselves in their place in order to understand their motivations, even if we wish to control them. We are never really free of others. For the strong who seek the accolades of their fellow human beings, like Okonkwo and Coriolanus, the judgment of others is the driving force of their lives.

Others are not merely some distant anonymous "they," as Heidegger characterizes them. Others can be quite specifically associated with us. Others are our families, friends, teachers, and neighbors. They are the people who taught us how to discern one object from another, to name what we experience, and use what we understand. They taught us right from wrong.

The demands of social life require that there be rules of social interaction; there must be ways to curb people's selfish motivations. Morals and manners are the natural outgrowth of our neediness and our sociability. If we must live with others in order to survive and thrive, there must be rules for how we can coexist in harmony.

Although it may be true that powerful leaders delineated the limits and made the rules in ancient times, it does not follow that all morality is a result of that original compact. Rather, virtue and morality have a phenomenological basis. Rules of conduct arise because humans have the capacity to put themselves in the place of others. Even if, as Nietzsche maintains, the strong created the principles of order to privilege themselves, they did so by comparing themselves to others. As we have seen, in striving not to be weak, they tried to master their own neediness and vulnerability.

The morals of the weak, too, were grounded on a comparison. Those who were abused and tyrannized by the strong came to understand not only that their safety and interests were in jeopardy, but also that they were being treated unjustly, even by the standards of the strong. Nietzsche's *Genealogy* extols the virtues of the aristocratic Greeks and therefore focuses on heroic and tragic poetry. But he ignores comedy. The comic poet Aristophanes satirized the pretensions of the aristocrats. Aristophanes' plays often illustrate what the common people thought, since, in order to be popular, comedy must take account of the perspective of the many. Aristophanes showed that there was a view of reality not dependent on the will of the masters. Perhaps the point of view of the common person – sometimes called common sense – is a better way to approach living. As Hegel argued, having to produce food, build roads, care for livestock, and trade with neighbors gives people an understanding and appreciation of life superior to that in the upper classes whose needs are met by servants. Because most ordinary people in the ancient world were either illiterate or semiliterate, this common viewpoint gained voice only in the work of comic poets like Aristophanes. However, it did exist. We might conclude, therefore, that the masters did not create or establish truth with their assertion of the will-to-power. The phenomena of social life established that reality, including an awareness of its benefits, responsibilities, and duties.

Heidegger identifies will-to-power as the key doctrine of Nietzsche's philosophy. The will-to-power defines Being since all things exist by making themselves present. If the will-to-power is the core of existence, then those who most vigorously assert that will live closest to what Being directs. Although the will-to-power does not tell us what to do, it does mandate that whatever we do must be done with great verve. Nietzsche's *ubermensch* (overman) is the culmination of this line of reasoning. The overman does as he pleases with no regard for the morals or manners of society and without consideration of the consequences of his actions. The overman acts on the proposition that if God is dead, all things are possible; with no metaphysical realm or rules to guide him, he takes his bearings from his own choices.[33]

Although the doctrine of the will-to-power is taken to be novel, Plato had actually considered it in Book I of the *Republic*. Thrasymachus proclaims that justice *is* the interest of the stronger, implying that whoever has the power both creates and institutes the rules according to his will. Socrates asks Thrasymachus what he means by stronger. Does he assert that Polydamas is the source of Athens' principles of justice? Polydamas is a professional wrestler – huge, formidable, and skilled. Of course, Socrates is making one of his ironic jokes at Thrasymachus' expense. Nevertheless, if Thrasymachus really were to test his strength against Polydamas, the result would probably not be humorous, at least for Thrasymachus.[34]

If "the strongest," then, does not mean physical prowess, there must be another, non-physical measure, of might. Thrasymachus next suggests that

33 Martin Heidegger *Nietzsche*, vol. 3 and 4, trans. by David Ferrell Krell (San Francisco: HarperSanFrancisco, 1991), 243–45.
34 Plato, *Republic*, 338c.

whoever has power makes the rules. But he changes his formulation slightly: justice is the advantage of the stronger. Hence, justice is politically and existentially a creation of the strong, a theory almost exactly in line with Nietzsche's overman asserting the will-to-power.

Again Socrates raises a question: do powerful rulers ever make mistakes about their advantage? Thrasymachus does not reply; he is smart enough to understand where it might lead. But Cleitophon addresses the question, claiming that "the advantage of the stronger is what the stronger believes to be his advantage." If justice is whatever the stronger say it is, then whoever is in charge defines justice. In such a contest, if the "weak" take over, they get to decide the nature of virtue – they have become the stronger. Might makes right; there is no standard beyond the rules posited by whoever happens to be in power.[35]

Nietzsche's polemic against the weak in the *Genealogy* contradicts his vision of the overman expressing the will-to-power. The weak have triumphed. They have actualized their will-to-power and revolutionized our understanding of morals; the ethos of equality has defeated its adversaries. According to Nietzsche's theory, the weak ought to have won, since their will has proved stronger than that of the aristocrats. If the will-to-power *defines* what we take to be the order of Being, on what grounds can anyone object? Nietzsche is free to assert his will and endeavor to change what we believe. If no one listens, he is in much the same position as Thrasymachus in the *Republic*, who loses the argument to that first voyager into the metaphysical realm, Socrates.

We can see remnants of Nietzsche's principles in Libertarianism, especially in the work of Ayn Rand. Rand wanted talented people to declare their superiority. She argued that inventors and entrepreneurs should demand a larger share of society's resources because they make prosperity and progress possible. However, the Randian will-to-power is checked by consumer sovereignty, fleeting tastes, and public sentiment. Here too, the many decide the fate of the few.

Even as he demonizes morality, Nietzsche does not attack virtue as excellence. In fact, he celebrates self-discipline, dedication, and achievement. For him, the will-to-power supplants virtue. Nietzsche promotes excellence while he discards morality.

Feminists are particularly sensitive to the misogynistic implications of Nietzsche's ideas. They maintain that traditional notions of virtue privilege

35   Plato, *Republic*, 340b.

male attributes such as "independence, autonomy, intellect, will, wariness, hierarchy, domination, culture, transcendence, product, asceticism, war, and death," as they undervalue culturally determined feminine qualities like "interdependence, community, connection, sharing, emotion, body, trust, absence of hierarchy, nature, immanence, process, joy, peace, and life."[36]

One the other hand, some feminists appreciate that Nietzsche's will-to-power is not connected to a foundation. It paves the way for postmodern principles. Postmodernists have transformed the will-to-power into an assertion of personal values with no hierarchy. Anything can become both personal and a value. Thus, Nietzsche's ideas can herald liberation by undermining culturally established roles for males and females.[37]

Virtue, however, encompasses both strength *and* care for others. As David Campbell explains, "Virtues such as courage, generosity, and courtesy are analogous to one another and form a class in that each is in its own way an expression of 'strength,' that is, heightened vitality in exercising coping skills."[38]

Nietzsche's analysis brings us no closer to comprehending the enduring appeal of virtue. To understand that vibrancy, we must first turn to Heidegger, the most important critic of Nietzsche, Western metaphysics, and every principle of proscriptive actions.

36 Alison M. Jaggar, "Feminist ethics," *Encyclopedia of Ethics*, eds. L. Becker and C. Becker, (New York: Garland Press, 1992), 364.

37 Barbara Helm, "Combating Misogyny? Responses to Nietzsche by Turn-of-the-Century German Feminists," *The Journal of Nietzsche Studies* 27 (Spring 2004) 64–84.

38 David Campbell, "Nietzsche, Heidegger, and Meaning," *The Journal of Nietzsche Studies* 26 (Autumn 2003), 32–33.

Chapter Four
Heidegger's World

Only when the strangeness of beings oppresses us does it arouse and evoke wonder. Only on the ground of wonder – the revelation of the nothing – does the "why?" loom before us. Only because the "why" is possible as such can we in a definite way inquire into grounds, and ground them. Heidegger[1]

The Wonder of Being

Wonder. Why are sunsets beautiful? Why do people cry at both weddings and funerals? Why are there so many creatures? Why do they all die? Why is the universe so big and we so small? Why is music enchanting? Where do we come from and where are we going? Why does anything even exist? Why do we wonder about such things?

Why do so few interpreters of Martin Heidegger mention wonder? He is enthralled by the notion, although he rarely uses the exact world. Yet much about Heidegger's work makes us wonder.[2] His writing is strange, almost impenetrable. Although he uses the language of philosophy, his style is more poetic than systematic. Sometimes it is as if he has adopted the vocabulary of Kant to express and aphorisms of Nietzsche. He repeats himself, making the same point in a variety of ways, as if holding an object up to the light and turning it round to apprehend its shape and composition.[3] He makes ironic statements meant to become iconic: "Language is the house of Being." "Man is not the lord of beings, but the shepherd of Being." "Only a god can save us now."[4]

---

1   Martin Heidegger, "What Is Metaphysics," in *Martin Heidegger: Basic Writings*, ed. and trans. David Farrell Krell (New York: Harper & Row, 1977), 111.

2   Heidegger, "Letter on Humanism," in *Basic Writings*, 111.

3   George Steiner, *Martin Heidegger* (Chicago: University of Chicago Press, 1987).

4   Heidegger, "Letter on Humanism,'" in *Basic Writings*, 193, 221; Martin Heidegger, "Interview in *Der Spiegel*,"with Rudolf Augstein and Georg Wolff, 23 September

Heidegger's wonder leads him on a grand mission. He hopes to find again or perhaps discover for the first time the origin of everything. He does not seek a scientific account of the beginning, such as the Big Bang, or a religious narrative as given in Genesis. He strives to understand how the universe, God, and human awareness came to be. He asks, "What is Being?" and this simple yet profound question drove his life's work. Heidegger believes that the pace and trajectory of modern existence have made us lose sight of this most important inquiry.

Being is not an easy thing to grasp. In fact, it is not a thing at all. Being is the precondition that brings things into existence. In his lectures, Heidegger, standing at the lectern, not moving or speaking, gave a sort of philosophy lab on Being. The audience would shift uneasily, bored, with nothing to do, nothing to hear. Ultimately, he would tell them that they had experienced Being. Being is no-thing.

While it may be possible – rarely – to touch Being itself (in a "moment of *vision*" which "discloses the authentic 'there,'" he says), for the most part, Being is an unfathomable mystery.[5] As George Steiner points out, we get some sense of Being in the strange command music has over us. Music can move, calm, inspirit, encourage, console, cheer, and arouse. Music is ineffable. It accomplishes all these various effects without engaging our rational sense.[6] Plato maintains that musical "rhythm and harmony…insinuate themselves into the inmost part of the soul."[7]

According to Heidegger, Being is so ineffable that we can best make sense of it by explaining what it is not:

> Have we not confined ourselves to negative assertions in all our attempts to determine the nature of this state of Being? Though… Being…is…fundamental, we always keep hearing about what it is *not*….[T]here is nothing accidental about our characterizing it predominantly in so negative a manner. In doing so we have rather made known what is peculiar to this

1966; published 31 May 1976, http://web.ics.purdue.edu/~other1/Heidegger%20Der%20Spiegel.pdf.

5   Heidegger, *Being and Time*, I have followed MacQuarrie and Robinson in capitalizing Being in order to distinguish it from the beings – things that can be experienced.

6   George Steiner, *Martin Heidegger* (Chicago: University of Chicago Press, 1987).

7   Plato, *Republic*, 401d.

phenomenon, and our characterization is therefore…appropriate to the phenomenon itself.[8]

Being There

Actually, Heidegger is not as interested in Being as he is in human beings' relationship to Being. The entire known universe acts according to some law or principle of nature. Physics, chemistry, and biology determine every-thing's fate, but not people's destiny. It is true that some animals have com-plex cognition, but they are so busy with daily survival that they have almost no recollection of the past and little awareness of the future.[9] We might con-vey Heidegger's point by making some observations. A deer climbs to the summit of a hill and sees the far-off horizon, the rolling emerald woods, and the red-yellow sun dipping over a remote peak. But it does not stop to reflect on the meaning or beauty of the scene. We know this because there is no deer poetry.

If animals had foresight, our nearest primate relative long ago would have armed themselves against exploitation of their rainforest habitat.

Somehow, human beings have been liberated from the causal chain since they possess both forethought and wonder. Their future actions are difficult to calculate. Heidegger writes:

> The fact that physiology and physiological chemistry can scien-tifically investigate the human being as an organism is no proof that in this 'organic' thing, that is, in the body scientifically ex-plained, the essence of the human being consists.[10]

Heidegger names the human way of experiencing the world Dasein – literally *there being,* but better in English as *being there.* Dasein is unique.

8   Heidegger, *Being and Time*, 85.
9   Martin Heidegger, *The Fundamental Problems of Metaphysics: World, Finitude, Solitude*, trans.William McNeill and Nicholas Walker (Blommington, IN: Indiana University Press, 1995), 228–39. See also William McNeill, "Life Beyond the Or-ganism: Animal Being in Heidegger's Freiburg Lectures," in *Animal Others: On Ethics, Ontology, and Animal Life*, ed. Peter H. Steeves (Albany: State University of New York Press, 1999), 197–248.
10 Heidegger, "The Age of World Picture," in *Question Concerning Technology*, 148–50.

Everything else just *is*, but Dasein wonders *why* it is. It worries about a time when it will not be there. "Dasein is an entity which does not just occur among other entities," Heidegger explains. "Rather it is ... distinguished by the fact that, in its very Being, that Being is an *issue* for it."[11] To be or not to be? is a question only a being with Dasein could ask.

Heidegger argues that Dasein is our contact with Being. It comes before all the beings in the world. Dasein makes possible an awareness of all that exists. Things might have existed before Dasein, but nothing took notice of them. Heidegger answers the question of whether a tree falling in the woods makes a noise. Of course it does, he says, but no one knows or cares. If Dasein comes into being to make Being present, then nothing in the world can influence Dasein; certainly no-thing can guide it.

Heidegger argues that mood can influence our behavior. When we are in a bad mood, we can be short, testy, even cruel. We often do not know why our mood changes. Does that imply that reason is dependent on something we cannot control? When we are in a bad mood, we say we are "out of sorts," and when we are feeling better, we claim to be "back to normal." An element of consciousness is prior to reason. Heidegger calls that pre-rational element Dasein.

Heidegger contends that humans have anthropomorphized Being. For example, the Israelites made Yahweh – which might be translated as all the tenses of the verb "to be" (I was, I am, I will be) – into the notion that there is a knowing, caring God. However, if Being just is and has no Dasein, it does not care what happens to people. Unlike God, it provides no guidance for our thoughts or actions.[12]

The unique relationship between Dasein and Being is almost the same as the mysterious no-thingness of Being. This does not mean that we are unaffected by our surroundings. Quite the contrary, according to Heidegger's formulation: we are "thrown" into a world full of myriad objects not of our making and out of our control.[13] There we also find people and cultures that explain and make sense of the phenomena. We learn from both experience and culture the way to interpret beings. Anti-foundationalists follow Heidegger in arguing that language shapes our understanding of life.

11 Heidegger, *Being and Time*, 32.
12 Mark Blitz, *Heidegger's Being and Time and the Possibility of Political Philosophy* (Ithaca, NY: Cornell University Press, 1981), 35.
13 Heidegger, *Being and Time*, 175.

Being and Belief

If Heidegger claims that his way of thinking has "no result" and "no effect," what does all this have to do with virtue?[14]

Heidegger's philosophy presents a great challenge to virtue. It is not that Heidegger opposes virtue. Along with Nietzsche, he laments the loss of belief accompanying the nihilistic trajectory of Western civilization. Heidegger's flirtation with Nazism was likely an effort to restore the sort of spirited devotion that is the basis of virtuous action. He hoped that "in the questioning confrontation with National Socialism, a new path, the only one still possible, to a renewal might possibly open up."[15]

Heidegger's political hopes turned, as Jacques Derrida phrases it, into little more than "flame and ashes."[16] Even more, his philosophy *undermines* virtue because it calls into question all metaphysical principles, of which virtue is one. According to Heidegger, most people at most times have not asked the right questions. We approach the activities of daily life by asking what is it? how does it work? how can I use it? Heidegger gives a name to this commonly felt familiarity with our surroundings – everydayness.

We are creatures caught up in the times when we live. It as if we were asleep and suddenly woke up in a place where nothing makes sense. But we learn from our surroundings and the people in them to adapt. In fact, we become so familiar with our world that we lose sight of wonder. Everyday life becomes routine, the objects around us readily identified and employed. We forget that everything we know is thrust upon us by the civilization, place, and time in which we live.

Everydayness is the ordinary, commonplace, and routine way human beings encounter, understand, and deal with the world. We hardly ever wonder about daily occurrences; not much reflection goes into brushing our teeth, tying our shoes, or drinking coffee. We rarely ponder why the sky is blue or the sun comes up in the east. We take for granted that we drive on the right-hand side of the road, unless we drive in Britain. We take the things ready-at-hand to be natural, reasonable, and the way they should be. "Because this average everydayness makes up what is…proximal," Heidegger explains, "it has again and again *passed over*…. That which is…closest and well known…is…farthest, and constantly overlooked."[17]

14   Heidegger, "Letter on Humanism,'" in *Basic Writings*, 236.
15   Heidegger, Interview in *Der Spiegel*.
16   Jacques Derrida, *Of Spirit: Heidegger and the Question,* trans. Geoffry Bennington and Rachel Bowlby (Chicago: University of Chicago Press, 1989), 1.
17   Heidegger, *Being and Time*, 69.

Everyday life "enframes" us.[18] We almost never comprehend how much of what we assume to be natural actually is culturally determined. It is as if some distant anonymous "they" have established a set of rules and definitions that we all are compelled to follow. Heidegger explains that:

> In ...making use of information services such as the newspaper, every Other is like the next. This Being-with-one-another dissolves one's own Dasein completely into a kind of Being of 'the Others,' in such a way, indeed, that the Others, as distinguishable and explicit, vanish more and more....We take pleasure and enjoy ourselves as *they* take pleasure; we read, see, and judge about literature and art as *they* see and judge; likewise we shrink back from the 'great mass' as *they* shrink back; we find 'shocking' what *they* find shocking. The 'they', which is nothing definite, and which all are, though not as the sum, prescribes the kind of Being of everydayness.[19]

Heidegger calls such a life fully submerged in everydayness "inauthentic," because it does not stalwartly face non-Being – death.[20] That is not to say that people are passive and uninvolved in everyday life. Quite the contrary: they might be fully engaged in activities that satisfy or delight them. "Care" is Heidegger's name for our attitude toward life. Put simply, we care what happens next because it matters to us.

Care is what people do even while living inauthentic lives within the horizon of everydayness. They care because they are always ahead of themselves – thinking what to donext. Care does not necessarily seek to gratify a particular passion or interest. Care is not, as Thomas Hobbes maintains, always an effort to satisfy bodily needs. People can care about anything. Heidegger's care is similar to Ludwig von Mises' notion of interest. People pursue goals, but there is no way to tell which goals they will set for themselves.

Science Leads to No-thing

One way in which humans express their care is to lessen their anxiety about death and suffering. To accomplish this, they attempt to put nature to the

18 Heidegger, "The Turning" in *Question Concerning Technology*, 36–49.
19 Heidegger, *Being and Time*, 164.
20 Heidegger, *Being and Time*, 279–311.

service of human needs. The most important development in the quest to harness nature has been the application of scientific discoveries to engineering and technology. Technology has been successful in manipulating, organizing, and mastering the material world. Heidegger maintains that technology has turned the planet into "standing reserve," objects and processes ready to be bent to our will whenever a need or yearning arises. The extraordinary success of scientific-technological progress has created the impression that humans are capable of conquering chance and of becoming the lords of Being, or existence. "Everything functions, and the functioning drives us further and further to more functioning, and technology tears people away and uproots them from the earth more and more,"[21] he says.

Heidegger gives the example of the Rhine River, about which Germans created myths that define them as a people. The river has been enframed:

> The hydroelectric plant is set into the current of the Rhine... to dispatch electricity....even the Rhine itself appears to be something at our command. What the river is now, namely, a water-power supplier, derives from the essence of the power station. In order that we may even remotely consider the monstrousness that reigns here, let us ponder for a moment the contrast that is spoken by the two titles: "The Rhine," as dammed up into the *power* works, and "The Rhine," as uttered out of the *art* work, in Hölderlin's hymn by that name. But, it will be replied, the Rhine is still a river in the landscape, is it not? Perhaps. But how? In no other way than as an object on call for inspection by a tour group ordered there by the vacation industry.[22]

No matter how much we try to conquer chance and contingency, Heidegger warns, we cannot fully solve the mystery of existence. There will always be part of life beyond our control. Bad luck, old age, loss of loved ones, and, of course, our own ultimate death, are the most obvious examples of our tragic fate. For Heidegger, "Man is not the lord of Being, but the shepherd of Being."[23]

Even the fullest depiction of what the world is and does cannot explain

21 Heidegger, Interview in *Der Spiegel*.
22 Heidegger, *Question Concerning Technology*, 16.
23 Heidegger, "Letter on Humanism,'" in *Basic Writings*, 231.

how we should live. Comprehension of things, whether through science, philosophy, or just common sense, does not help us understand what to *do* with the knowledge or mastery we obtain. For Heidegger, the modern scientific explanation of existence is similar to owning a sophisticated GPS but knowing neither the starting point of our trip nor our destination. Since we cannot know Being, which is both the beginning and end of existence, all assertions about the meaning of life are groundless. He explains:

> *Basically, all ontology, no matter how rich and firmly compacted a system of categories it has at its disposal, remains blind and perverted from its ownmost aim, if it has not first adequately clarified the meaning of Being, and conceived this clarification as its fundamental task.*[24]

Although people in every age seek to reduce the contingency in their lives by using inventions that increase productivity, there is a difference between the founder of the modern scientific method, Rene Descartes, and the pre-Socratics natural philosophers. Descartes' science hopes to render Being comprehensible so that people can extract the greatest benefit from it. Heraclites takes nature as it is and merely expresses the view that humans comprehend the phenomena before them.[25]

For Heidegger, Descartes' modern scientific project could not have led to anything but nihilism. Nihilism does not naively deny that truth exists; its basic tenet is that there is no final truth to explain the purpose of life. Descartes attempts to ground the truth not in speculation about transcendent ideas, as did Plato, but in the certainty of repeatable scientific experiments and mathematical formulas. For Descartes, all beliefs must be assessed according to the certainty that science provides. But this method of establishing the truth necessarily undermines belief in God, metaphysics, and transcendence, because none of them can pass the test of science.

Metaphysics is a Dead End

Immanuel Kant attempts to overcome the problem that Descartes' method causes for morals by suggesting that metaphysical principles exist in the

24 Heidegger, *Being and Time*, 31. Italics original.
25 Heidegger, "The Age of World Picture," in *Question Concerning Technology*, 148–50.

structure of human reason. But Heidegger says that Kant merely worsens the predicament by making metaphysics into a being, a thing that can be known with certainty. Kant's project falls short, Heidegger insists, because Being is not one of the beings.[26]

Heidegger encapsulates the spiritual crises of Western civilization with a phrase taken from Nietzsche: God is dead.[27] When God was alive, people had a transcendent rationale for existence. But now, he says, there is no evidence that God exists, especially if Descartes' method is the sole way to establish proof. When science killed God, the West lost its conviction.

Heidegger blames Plato for launching the West on what turned out to be a dead end. Plato created the theory of the forms/ideas to articulate how human beings describe and categorize the phenomena and experiences of life. Plato's philosophy made comprehending truth easier, but it reduced the wonder of Being to the mundane. Clarity was gained, but understanding was lost. Being was classified and enframed as if it were a table or chair. Aristotle calls the study and indexing of the non-visible phenomena "metaphysics." But Heidegger objects to classifying and ossifying our understanding of existence. He explains:

> Metaphysics does not ask about the truth of being itself. Nor does it therefore ask in what way the essence of the human being belongs to the truth of being. Metaphysics has not only failed up to now to ask this question, the question is inaccessible to metaphysics as such. Being is still waiting for the time when It itself will become thought-provoking to the human being.[28]

Heidegger maintains that Dasein always projects itself into the future. It exists both in the now and in a time that does not yet exist. We propel ourselves into the future. Common sense tells us to base our future behavior on what we have learned from the past, either from experience or from studying and contemplating the results of an action. But the future is never fully determined. It can always be different from the past. Hence, nothing in the past need be relevant to our decision about what to do in a time that

---

26 Martin Heidegger, *Kant and the Problem of Metaphysics*, trans. Richard Taft (Bloomington, IN: Indiana University Press, 1997).

27 Heidegger, "The Word of Nietzsche: 'God is Dead,'" in *Question Concerning Technology*, 53–112.

28 Heidegger, "Letter on 'Humanism,'" in *Basic Writings*, 203.

has not come. Nothing in the past binds the future. More generally, our destiny cannot be based on experience or historical precedents. There can thus be no "foundational" principles. Nothing that is particularly human – that is, based on Dasein – can help us know how to live well. The nature of humans is constructed on the mysterious and unknowable future, not on a comprehensible past. Our Being is connected with time.

Since there is no foundation on which to rest metaphysical principles, according to Heidegger, all morality, virtue, and thought are temporal. Because people can believe their future may be different from the lives and beliefs of their predecessors, they have changed what is "true." All thought is "true" only for its time and place. Hegel is wrong. There is no absolute moment when the relative truth of different historical epochs or cultures can be comprehended – making them all part of a whole that reveals itself as a dialectic. The disparate "truths" of different eras are really true, for truth reveals itself differently at different times.

Awareness of the meaninglessness of existence causes our age to be plagued with confusion, doubt, and anxiety. People feel alienated and alone because they have no purpose. In a rare compliment to the founder of Communism, whose doctrine he loathed, Heidegger claims "the Marxist view of history is superior to…other…accounts… [b]ecause…estrangement attains an essential dimension of history."[29]

People in the past were rooted in their cultural beliefs, committed to family, community, nation, and religion. Their beliefs gave significance to their activities exactly because they accepted them as truths. We live in a more skeptical time. The same principle on which modern science is based – believe only what you can prove – has undermined attachment to God, country, and, indeed, any non-physical concept of virtue, morality or truth. For us, the ultimate meaning of life is an impenetrable mystery, a mystery that becomes more apparent as we live longer, more prosperous lives. Today, even religiously oriented people understand that faith is a choice and that an alternative truth exists – the scientific view of the world that is indifferent to human fate. Our awareness of the possibility that our lives may be pointless is the source of our anxiety. As Heidegger puts it, "Homelessness is coming to be of the destiny of the world."[30]

Even philosophy that aspires to reach beyond the constraints of convention is submerged in a set of given ideas and concepts. One set of ideas

29   Heidegger, "Letter on 'Humanism,'" in *Basic Writings*, 219.
30   Heidegger, "Letter on 'Humanism,'" in *Basic Writings*, 219.

follows, criticizes, and changes another. Nihilism developed as a consequence of the criticism of Hegel's effort to make sense of the historical process.[31] Heidegger agrees with Nietzsche that philosophy reveals not the "truth," but merely the principles of its historical epoch. It was inevitable that philosophy eventually would uncover the no-thingness of Being and come to the conclusion that nothing is true.

Values

In an age when science is the highest authority in establishing truth, it is impossible to prove that God exists, or that courage is better than cowardice. Yet people still value things. In projecting themselves into the future, they inevitably try to find out what they should do. They believe that some actions and beliefs are better than others, and therefore they value them more. Hence, in the post-metaphysical era, values become the standard of good and bad, noble and base, virtue and vice. People choose values based on what is important to them.

We may state the problems raised by values as follows. We look in the mirror and we see ourselves. We are not sure 0 what we are. Are we good-looking, funny, attractive, witty, or talented? We are a mystery to ourselves. We form our identity from what others say about us. Teachers, coaches, friends, sibling, parents, and lovers create our impression of self. However, there is a sense in which the self is empty unless it identifies with something beyond itself. As Derek L. Phillips argues, when the self is disconnected from principles outside itself, such as religion or patriotism, there is a loss of self. Self-help books are an effort to "find oneself" or be true to oneself.[32] The self, however, is hard to find or even to know, so "being true to oneself" is meaningless if people are unsure about their self-worth in the first place. Self-help books that teach people to be good to themselves sometimes have the effect of making people self-absorbed. Since we do not understand ourselves, we are preoccupied with a self that is uncertain. The result is that the self becomes subject to the whims of momentary moods. It is little wonder that people who buy self-help books almost never find what they are

---

31 Martin Heidegger, *Hegel's Concept of Experience*, trans. Kenley Royce Dove (New York: Harper & Row, 1970).

32 Derek L. Phillips, "Authenticity or Morality?" *The Virtues: Contemporary Essays on Moral Character*, eds. Robert B. Kruschwitz and Robert Campbell (Belmont, CA: Wadsworth Publishing Co. 1987), 23–35.

looking for. Peter Lawler blames the elusive nature of the self for our feelings of being "alien" even in our home country. We are alienated from ourselves because our self is such a mystery.[33]

We want to identify with permanent things. We do not want everything we know and care about to disappear when our consciousness ceases. We want a knowing and caring God to watch over us and reunite us with loved ones after death. On the other hand, we want to have our own values and refuse to let God order us around. So in place of this controlling God comes "spirituality." Spirituality is unlike traditional religious principles. "Spiritual" people can pretty much do whatever they please, and God neither judges nor scolds. In fact, the spirituality God has no rules whatever, so that the self is just as lost as it was on its own.

People with values as their guiding principles are likely to be peaceful. Values rarely inspire great devotion. We may take them seriously, but we realize they are just our individual choices. "No one dies for mere values," Heidegger comments.[34] He also worries that people in values-oriented societies will be fully immersed in and enframed by everydayness. No decisive events or epoch-altering cataclysms will occur in the future. Life will be boring. Heidegger asks whether life will be fulfilling when brilliant deeds, so prized in the past, are no longer needed. What will happen to the human spirit if heroic effort becomes antiquated and pathetic? "Thinking in terms of values," Heidegger claims, "precludes in advance that Being itself will attain to a coming to presence in truth."[35]

What is true?

Heidegger claims that there cannot be trans-historical truth because truth comes into Being only when Dasein recognizes it. "That there are 'eternal truths' will not be adequately proved," he claims, "until someone has succeeded in demonstrating that Dasein has been and will be for all eternity."[36]

Heidegger's point may be true, but it also could be that the truth coexists with Dasein. As long as there is Dasein, the truth will exist eternally. This objection makes us wonder about Dasein. Where does it come from? Is it

---

33 Peter Augustine Lawler, *Aliens in America: The Strange Truth about Our Souls* (Wilmington, DE: Intercollegiate Studies Institute, 2002).

34 Heidegger, "The Age of World Picture," in *Question Concerning Technology*, 142.

35 Heidegger, "The Word of Nietzsche: God is Dead," in *Question Concerning Technology*, 108.

36 Heidegger, *Being and Time*, 269–70.

present in all human beings? The answer is no. Dasein is not present in humans who cannot reason or have not been brought up in human society. Dasein is partly natural, since all but severely handicapped people can acquire it. Perhaps this is why Aristotle considers temperance one of the foremost virtues. Without it, people would be at the mercy of mindless passions and be less likely to exercise foresight, an intrinsic element of Dasein.[37]

We are taught Dasein – an awareness of our surroundings. What do we learn? We learn to grasp the relationship between the experience of the outside world – the beings – and a comprehension of their meaning. We categorize them in groups by dimension, texture, colors and the like.[38] These are chairs. Some are red. Some bigger than others. Those are farther away. The more comfortable chairs are the bigger chairs in the back. All of the attributes are things we had to be taught – in one way or another, the specifics had to be conveyed through language. Therefore, Heidegger maintains that language mediates reality.

"Language is the clearing-concealing advent of Being itself," according to Heidegger.[39] Yet there could be no language without society. Language is a social mechanism. With whom would solitary beings converse? There might be society without language, but in order to act together, all the individuals who make up the society would have to be drones, blindly following instinct. And people are not fully determined by instinct – they would not have Dasein if they were.

Heidegger does not stop there. As we have seen, he argues that the "they" provides ready-made explanations of all that we see and experience. While it is true that we are thrown into a world of ready-made accounts of life and the things in it, it is also true that Dasein need not be content with the ready at hand. Some people are not satisfied with usual or conventional explanations. They wonder whether conventions are natural. From where did the "they" get their ideas?

If Dasein is a social construct, perhaps in its nature Dasein has an awareness of the importance of others. We learn from others, and we learn to think about others. A sort of empathy coexists with Dasein. Since we can categorize phenomena, perhaps there are natural categories for the things that make society possible and livable. Empathy is a way of putting ourselves in the place of others. Along with the skill of categorization, we learn to consider

---

37   Aristotle *Ethics*, 1117b–1119b.
38   Aristotle, *Metaphysics*, 1017a-b.
39   Heidegger, "Letter on 'Humanism,'" in *Basic Writings*, 206.

what others do and what they say. We have relationships with others so that we come to understand their pain, moods, and joys. We also learn the categories of human attributes – friendship, honor, anxiety, justice, and the like. The development of Dasein would then be synonymous with awareness of human categories. It is possible to understand metaphysical attributes, and among them would be the virtues. Heidegger seems to admit that human beings need metaphysics to explain existence, so long as they have reason:

> As long as man remains the *animal rationale* he is also the *animal metaphysicum*. As long as man understands himself as the rational animal, metaphysics belongs, as Kant said, to the nature of man.[40]

Although Heidegger claims to have no agenda other than giving an account of Being, it is likely he, like Nietzsche, thinks that nihilism will destroy humanity. People will believe in nothing; life will become so meaningless that people might not want to go on living. The alternative is that people will become mindless drones, so utterly enframed by everydayness that their true majesty – angst before Being and non-Being – will be lost. He worries that everydayness will "dissolves one's own Da-sein completely into the kind of being of 'the others.'" In a sense, identification with "others" will become total as it becomes "inconspicuousness" and "unascertainability." It is at the point when the authority of others is not perceived that "they unfolds its true dictatorship." Heidegger protests against the "leveling down of all possibilities of Being."[41]

For Heidegger, nihilism and the loss of devotion and achievement have precipitated the crisis of the West. He hopes to restore humanity by abandoning reason and the metaphysical morass into which it has fallen. At least before "The Turning," he hoped that a new revelation of Being would bring about a new human condition. He says, "If our thinking should succeed in its efforts to go back into the ground of metaphysics, it might well help to bring about a change in human nature, accompanied by a transformation of metaphysics.[42]

40 Martin Heidegger, "The Way Back into the Ground of Metaphysics," in *Existentialism from Dostoevsky to Sartre*, ed. and trans. Walter Kaufman (New York: New American Library, 1975), 267.

41 Heidegger, *Being and Time*, 1962, 164–65.

42 Heidegger, "The Way Back into the Ground of Metaphysics," in *Existentialism from Dostoevsky to Sartre*, 267.

After "The Turning," he rethought his position and called for thinking and waiting instead of action:

> Philosophy will not be able to bring about a direct change of the present state of the world. This is true not only of philosophy but of all merely human meditations and endeavors. Only a god can still save us. I think the only possibility of salvation left to us is to prepare readiness, through thinking and poetry, for the appearance of the god or for the absence of the god during the decline; so that we do not, simply put, die meaningless deaths, but that when we decline, we decline in the face of the absent god.[43]

In "The Turning," Heidegger comes very close to maintaining that Being shows itself in whatever way is proper for its time and place. Although the experiences of people living in Medieval Europe, the Han Dynasty, or the contemporary world are quite different from each other, Being, "in keeping with its own coming to presence in the midst of whatever is," is present in all of them.[44] Heidegger realizes that his new position must make peace with the nihilistic effect of technology, which empties the world of all higher meaning. Since it is today's reality, it therefore should exist. What is – whatever might be – ought to be.

Heidegger's supine acceptance of fate is more profound than that of the Stoic philosophers. At least the Stoics attempted to shield themselves from the winds of ill-fortune by practicing traditional virtues. Heidegger's acceptance of the vagaries of the chance movements of Being prevents him from objecting to even the worst situations. However, Heidegger's own furious activity in trying to understand Being belies this acquiescence. Surely Heidegger must have thought there was something true in his presentation of Being. He tried to reveal and therefore control Being by letting his readers act upon that reality. Heidegger's life, if not his later philosophic positions, shows that most people are not passive as they look toward the future. In fact, as noted above, Dasein is always thrusting itself into the future. People project their actions, asking, "What should I do next?"

The Greek philosophers were as aware of the tenuous nature of the truth as was Heidegger. After all, Socrates claimed his wisdom amounted to

---

43   Heidegger, Interview in *Der Spiegel*.
44   Heidegger, "The Turning" in *Question Concerning Technology*, 38.

knowing that he did not know. In almost every Platonic dialogue, Socrates undercuts his interlocutors' certainty. Socrates' questions make the virtues disappear; we are left wondering just what we know. Nevertheless, Socrates would have had nothing to talk about if the forms were really absent. He surely would not have continued to discuss the nature of the virtues with his friends if the virtues did not exist.

Plato's dialogues attempt to make the forms visible not only in speech, but in the actions of his characters. For example, we read the speeches about love in *Symposium*, but the attributes of love – longing, shame, anticipation, and the urge to dominate – are visible in the relationship between Socrates and Alcibiades. The scene is more instructive than the words; the phenomena more revealing than the language.[45]

Does language really create love, friendship, courage, honor, and justice? Or does speech attempt to categorize and explain the phenomena? There seems to be a relationship between our recognition of time and the metaphysical principles of virtue. When we project ourselves into the future, we always think of what we should do. The practice of thinking about the "should" places expectations on ourselves. Our present actions and state of mind try to measure up to a project that we conceived in the past. Is not this practice of placing expectations on ourselves the mental process we use when we apply ethical principles? The moral "should" of our past thinking becomes the "ought" of the present and future. Of course, there is no guarantee that what we decide to do will be moral. Someone could say, "I need money; I should rob a bank." While Heidegger argues that metaphysics and therefore virtue are unknowable, perhaps it is more accurate to say that we can comprehend virtues, but we choose to ignore them.

Poetry, Music, and Civil Society

Heidegger suggests that the world of Friedrich Hölderin's poetry is more authentic than the metaphysical explanation of existence. If that is true, then there must be better and worse accounts of Being. If there is no eternal truth, how do we know which truth or truths are more accurate? Perhaps an experience of Being could solve the dilemma.

Is there any way to have a direct encounter with Being? Mystics report

---

45   Plato, *Symposium*, 212d–222b; William A. Johnson, "Dramatic Frame and Philosophic Idea in Plato," *The American Journal of Philology* 119:4 (Winter, 1998): 577–598.

a sense of becoming one with everything. Just before his epileptic seizures, Fyodor Dostoyevsky claimed to experience an ecstatic aura. But most of us remain mired in everydayness. We come closest to Being when we hear music. As Arthur Schopenhauer explains:

> Music…stands quite apart from all the others [arts]. In it, we do not recognize the copy, the repetition, of any Idea of the inner nature of the world. Yet it is such a great and exceedingly fine art, its effect on man's innermost nature is so powerful, and it is so completely and profoundly understood by him in his innermost being as an entirely universal language.[46]

Music makes us feel a part of something beyond ourselves without making the experience into a form. Music can change our mood or create a sensation or attitude about experience. Music can make us happy, sad, invigorated, and contemplative. It can evoke a marshal spirit or a romantic impulse. It connects directly with some part of consciousness that need not be explained. Plato frets about music in *The Republic*, fearing that music can have unintended consequences. Nietzsche was so enthralled by Richard Wagner's music that he believed it could bring about a "return to Nature, health, good spirits, youth, *virtue!*"[47]

Can we construct anything practical on the basis of music? Music, like Being, is ineffable. Its mysterious effect on us provides a glimpse of Being. But music's elusive power is hardly helpful in organizing and dealing with a world of beings. Music's inability to tell us about how we should behave is perhaps evidence that Being has little to do with understanding our lives or constructing virtue. Heidegger argues that Being is somehow connected both to the way we *actually* live and the way we *should* live. Being is important.

Yet no society has ever been based on music alone. Music can elicit patriotic feeling, but it cannot build a nation. Although music is almost as old as civilization, it has never been important in constructing social life. For music to have a practical effect, it must be accompanied by words, which, in order to be understood, must be comprehended as forms.

Would poetry be successful in establishing a decent society? Heidegger recommends that Hölderin's poetry become the basis of a renewed German

---

46 Arthur Schopenhauer, *The World as Will and Representation*, trans. E.F.J. Payne (New York: Dover Publications, Inc., 1969), 256.

47 Friedrich Nietzsche, *The Case Of Wagner*, trans. Anthony M. Ludovici (Edinburgh, UK: T. N. Foulis, 1911), 5.

culture. He complains that Plato's art "stands far below truth in...meta-physics....it... is placed under the guidance of philosophy as knowledge of the essence of beings."[48] Plato destroyed the fleeting glimpse of Being that poetry gives Dasein by launching metaphysics. Plato established the philosophic tradition of the West in which Being becomes one of the beings.[49]

Heidegger apparently did not study Book 10 of the *Republic*. It ends with a poetic myth about the nature of existence in which virtue is extolled, but it is far from a philosophic defense of virtue. Instead of attempting to make life knowable through the forms or scientific proofs, Plato does exactly what Heidegger suggests. Art, not philosophy, explains existence. Perhaps Plato's intent is to show how Socrates "makes present" virtue in the lives of the young people, in this case Plato's brothers.

Since we make the virtues present as a construction, works of art are able to exhibit a purer form of the thing than is perceived in real life. Homer's Achilles has greater courage than any real life man does. The power of art to complete or perfect what we perceive through experience is one of the many lessons of Plato's *Republic*. Plato banishes the poets twice. Once he bans them from his perfect city, and, more importantly, he warns against the perfection that we can construct with the mind's eye – a perfection impossible in everyday life.

Plato's goal is to establish ideals on which people can base their lives. The virtues stand as distant goals, never quite reached, and just beyond our grasp. Despite his claim to have no interest in political life, Heidegger hopes that a poetic account of Being can rescue Western civilization from nihilism and bring about a new order in civil society.[50] However, he provides no practical roadmap for how we can bring his concepts into being. Quite the opposite: his philosophy undermines ideals, including virtue, by questioning the capacity of reason to understand anything. His solution to the crises of the West seems only to make the illness more acute.

Heidegger and the Ends of Philosophy

Heidegger's goal, as he states many times, is to make us wonder about Being. But what is the point of discovering Being? How will people live

48   Martin Heidegger, *Nietzsche*, trans. David Ferrell Krell, vol. 1 (San Francisco, CA: HarperSanFrancisco, 1991), 187.
49   Heidegger, "The Origin of a Work of Art in *Basic Writings*, 149–87.
50   Heidegger, "The Origin of a Work of Art," in *Basic Writings*, 373–92.

differently after discovering a better account of Being? At times, Heidegger suggests that his philosophy has no political implications, and the answer to the question is that nothing will change. But if Heidegger does anticipate some political, social, or even individual alteration in the way people live, shouldn't he have been more concerned with the moral codes required in decent societies? Should he have been attuned to the deconstructive power of all philosophic inquiry, especially his?

If Heidegger's philosophy was not intended to have an effect, why then did he teach and write? Was he not attempting to create something better, something good? This raises a broader question about the aim of philosophy. All philosophers attempt to explain what is true and to have an influence over what others think and how they behave. Philosophy imitates the forms. It attempts to uncover the truth, yet – since the forms defy a fully satisfying explanation – philosophy endeavors to influence how the forms can be best understood.

Philosophers cannot fully construct what is true. They cannot rule like tyrants, as Nietzsche claims, because certain human longings, issues, and questions are constant in life and therefore beyond even the greatest minds' power to alter. Philosophers can transcend the way people in particular cultures at particular times address the concerns of life; they can even influence how people comprehend the eternal questions. Philosophers write so that people will understand existence. Philosophy attempts to illuminate and thereby instruct in order to make things better. If philosophers did not think their writing was true or good, it is questionable whether they would bother to write.

Plato's idea of the good is not as far-fetched or metaphorical as many interpretations of the *Republic* claim. Philosophers seem to care about bringing what is good into being. Their Dasein cares about the good. Should we not infer that some form of the good seems to have guided even Heidegger's mission to discover Being? If the search for the good is responsible for the philosophers' quest, Being is not no-thing, for the philosophic activity is at the service of a trans-historical yearning for the good.

Heidegger objects to the characterization of *Being and Time* as a "blind alley." [51] He claims that we can learn something even when a book points out the absence of meaning. He writes:

Understood from out of metaphysics (i.e., out of the question of Being, in the form What is it to be?), the concealment essence

---

51   Heidegger, "Letter on 'Humanism,'" in *Basic Writings*, 222.

of Being, denial, unveils itself first of all as absolutely not-having-being, as Nothing. But Nothing as that Nothing which pertains to the having-of-being is the keenest opponent of mere negating, Nothing is never nothing; it is just as little a something, in the sense of an object....it is Being itself, whose truth will be given over to man when he has overcome himself as subject.[52]

What practical expectations does this idea of confrontation with nothing give us? How will this new revelation of Being influence us? Heidegger's poetic allusion to something created out of nothing entails forgetting the history of Western metaphysics. We would have to discard much of what we know. We would again have to live in the enchanted world of myths – the world Hölderin longed to recapture.

Unless civilization somehow is destroyed and only uneducated stragglers remain, the human race cannot disregard metaphysics any more than individuals can forget all the events of their past. The pre-Socratic Greeks lived in a cultural horizon founded on poetic myths. Even the best of our writers could not return us to such a condition.

Perhaps Heidegger imagined the destruction of civilization. He quotes Nietzsche's statement, "We are conducting an experiment with truth. Perhaps, mankind will perish as a result! Splendid!" and comments only that the statement is a riddle, one that must be solved by pondering other riddles.[53]

Here I would like to make a personal observation. I have lived and taught in Iraq, a place where all too many people perish, and civilization teeters on the brink of destruction. It is a country where decent people seek not a riddle, but answers to human questions about how best to live.

After World War II, Heidegger was discredited because of his association with Nazism. In the "Letter on 'Humanism,'" he was asked to explain his attitude toward his fellow human beings. He hardly gives a direct answer. He argues that true humanism entails pondering Being. Thinking about Being is the most humane of all activities, because through people, Being discloses itself. Thus, a person who philosophizes about Being can come to no harm. He explains:

Thus to 'philosophize' about being shattered is separated by a chasm from a thinking that is shattered. If such thinking were

---

52 Heidegger, "The Age of World Picture," in *Question Concerning Technology*, 154.
53 Heidegger, *Nietzsche*, vol. 2, 38.

to go fortunately for someone, no misfortune would befall him. He would receive the only gift that can come to thinking from being.[54]

Heidegger almost says that it is good to philosophize. He assumes that there is a good. He describes a positive relationship between humans and thinking. He suggest that it is good for humans to think. How is this different from the idea of the good expressed in the *Republic*?

Heidegger maintains that "With this utterance, 'Life is will to power,' Western metaphysics completes itself; at its beginning stands the obscure statement 'being as a whole is *physis*.'"[55] This assertion contradicts his view that Plato's theory of the forms set Western civilization on a false and nihilistic path, for Plato did not believe that Being was reduced to the formulas of physics. Plato made a point of showing that as a young man Socrates hoped to understand the meaning of life through the study of natural science. The quest was a failure. An older, chastened Socrates was compelled to undertake a second sailing, a journey of the mind that led him to ponder the recurring human qualities most apparent and important in our lives. He investigated experiences such as love, justice, friendship, courage, and honor, phenomena that could not be comprehended in the same way as the laws of physics.

Heidegger's comes closest of any interpreter to understanding the character of Plato's forms, yet his claim that Plato thought the forms were material objects is mistaken. Plato believed that the forms were the way humans understood the world because making sense of sensations cannot be achieved merely by having senses. When we look at an object, we are not certain what it is until we can place it into a category – its form. As Heidegger says, a bed frame becomes a bed frame only when we locate the object in the abstract conception "bed frame"; the impression of the bed frame itself has no meaning. It is our minds, not our eyes, that make out the bed frame.[56]

Despite his analysis of Plato's ontology, Heidegger argues that Plato tried to make the forms into entities. Heidegger then misunderstands the forms, especially those concerned with human things such as love, justice, courage, and friendship. If the forms of human things were entities, they

54 Heidegger, "Letter on 'Humanism,'" in *Basic Writings*, 223.
55 Heidegger, *Nietzsche*, vol. 3, 18.
56 Heidegger, *Nietzsche*, vol. 1, 172–73.

would not disappear during Plato's Socratic dialogues. The fact that a full account of the forms always seems to elude Socrates indicates their odd character for human understanding.

When Socrates investigates an attribute such as friendship, his companions begin with a notion of what it is. But after some discussion, they get lost. What they assumed turns out not to be true. They are no longer certain what they know. Yet, they could not know that the forms had eluded them unless they already knew something about what they should know – that is, unless they were aware of the form. To put the concept in Heidegger's terms, their hiddenness discloses their uncoveredness. We know that we do not know because we have an idea of what a full understanding should be.

Are there truly forms of the virtues? Do the virtues have a natural foundation? Can human beings know what is good? Plato understood the ephemeral nature of uncovering the truth, especially the character of the virtues. But he was aware that decent societies can rest on secure foundations only if people believe that morals and virtues are proper and fitting goals for human beings. If Plato erred, it was in presenting his moral teachings in ways that attracted people to a decent and moderate way of life. One need only consider the education of Plato's brothers in the *Republic* to understand Plato's humanistic purposes.

It was not Plato, but Niccolò Machiavelli, who demanded that certainty be brought into human affairs. Machiavelli thought speculation about "imagined principalities" was in vain. He wanted to fully conquer chance, a feat that could not be accomplished so long as the metaphysical world took precedence over the physical. In a quote quite similar to Nietzsche's aphorism, Machiavelli counsels that we take our destinies into our own hands and work to conquer nature:

> For my part I consider that it is better to be adventurous than cautious, because fortune is a woman, and if you wish to keep her under it is necessary to beat and ill-use her; and it is seen that she allows herself to be mastered by the adventurous rather than by those who go to work more coldly. She is, therefore, always, woman-like, a lover of young men, because they are less cautious, more violent, and with more audacity command her.[57]

57 Nicolò Machiavelli, *The Prince*, Ch. 25, trans. W. K. Marriott, http://www.constitution.org/mac/prince00.htm.

It was not the "metaphysics" of the West that turned the world into what Heidegger calls "standing reserve," a condition in which people almost fully control and use material things, but in which they have no guiding principles about what to do with their more bountiful, calm, and longer lives. It was not Plato who made the world into standing reserve, but the "anti-metaphysical" doctrines of Machiavelli, Thomas Hobbes, and Descartes, men who endeavored to master fate by reducing Being to the beings.[58]

Plato's metaphysics originates in the undeniable fact that human beings experience friendship and love, and sacrifice their physical interests to pursue acclaim and honor. They prize courage and evaluate actions (more often, perhaps, the actions of others) on the basis of whether they are fair or just. By their very nature, these phenomena are not present in our lives like physical experiences, yet they live in our consciousness; they exist. In order to exist, they must have a form that makes them comprehensible. We know, for example, that courage and friendship are different, although we may hope that our friends are courageous. If the non-physical phenomena that are so important in our lives have forms, Plato's philosophy makes us aware that those forms can instruct or guide us in discovering the nature of the virtues.

Heidegger's phenomenological method is meant to displace Plato's forms/ideas as the source of truth. Heidegger argues that the theory of the forms, in which the truth is discovered by distrusting common-sense observations, was the origin of the scientific approach. And that in turn led to a world empty of meaning and purpose – to nihilism.[59] Phenomenology is better than the Platonic method at finding the "unhiddenness" of beings and can get beyond or under the ready-at-hand explanations of the world that both explain yet obscure the truth.

Yet Plato's dialectic method also attempts to disentangle the true from the merely conventional. The *Republic's* myth of the cave explicates how entwined human beings are in the cultural mores of their time and place. What is true, he taught, is the pure form of a thing uninfluenced by the

---

58 For an exhaustive analysis of the difference between ancient and modern politics and metaphysics, see the three volumes of Paul A. Rahe, *Republics Ancient and Modern: New Modes and Orders in Early Modern Political Thought*, (Chapel Hill, NC: University of North Carolina Press, 1994). Heidegger seems to acknowledge a difference between the ancient philosophers and the Enlightenment philosophers who created modern natural science. Martin Heidegger, *The Essence of Truth*, trans. Ted Sadler (New York: Continuum, 2002), 45.

59 Heidegger, *The Essence of Truth*, 44–45.

explanations of particular cultures. Although we can never know the form of a thing fully – complete knowledge of the form eludes us – dialectic inquiry can help us know more about the nature of the subject of an inquiry. If there were no forms, there would be no inquiry, for questions about a better account of the thing would not arise. It is the lack of a clear account that compels us to wonder. On the other hand, if there were a full account of the forms – if everything in life were clear – there would be no Dasein. We, like the rest of nature, would exist without consciousness, without reflection, in utter certainty.

Heidegger maintains that Plato's method ultimately reduced Being to the beings. In trying to overcome this problem, Heidegger applied the rigorous discipline of phenomenology. But Heidegger could not ground his ideas in nothing. He still had to trust that his observations were accurate. As Plato makes clear in his presentation of the divided line, knowledge is impossible without trusting that sensation, experience, and judgment make sense.

Insofar as Heidegger details his ideas – Being, Dasein, thrownness, everydayness – he makes them into forms. Forms or ideas are the way human beings differentiate one thing from another. We explain what we mean by giving a definition of it and fitting it into its particular category. Heidegger's long account of Being makes its character clearer to his readers. We understand it because Heidegger has explained its nature or form. Human beings cannot escape this kind of reasoning so long as they wish to comprehend anything in the world. Our awareness of the phenomena is in fact an awareness of the forms. Dasein makes the world comprehensible by placing objects and ideas into their proper forms. If forms are the way we understand the world, then it is possible that the forms of the human things, including the virtues, are real.

Heidegger discounts everyday common-sense perceptions almost in the same way as Plato's *Republic* dismisses the images in the cave.[60] Although Heidegger interprets the myth of the cave quite closely, he seems to miss (or, more likely, consciously ignore) the most important point. The *Republic* is a dialogue about justice. Heidegger rarely discusses the virtues, for he assumes the obvious, although unstated, view that we must know what the truth is before we can know the truth about human attributes. Heidegger's phenomenology leads him to disregard the most obvious phenomena. By dismissing the political elements of the myth of the cave, Heidegger fails to appreciate Plato's effort to nurture what is noble and decent in actual cities

---

60   Compare Plato, *Republic*, 503b–511e and Heidegger, *The Essence of Truth*, 17–68.

and real people like Glaucon and Adeimantus. Heidegger sees no disjunction between the salutary (but debatable) beliefs that support political societies and the ruthless quest to uncover the truth through philosophic inquiry. His lack of moderation on this point makes his philosophic analysis strikingly similar to the ideologies of the 20th century that attempted to bring a perfect form or idea into being.[61]

Thinking about Being can be destructive of order and tradition if it shows that all human activities are groundless and futile. After all, as Heidegger argues in many places with great command, Being is a mystery, and we cannot grasp it. What good does it do to ponder Being if the effort leads us to ignore the questions, phenomena, and controversies right before us? Heidegger ignored the obvious and recommended that great minds stay aloof from everyday life:

> The thinker and sayer of this utterance is "a destiny." This means that the Being of this thinker and of every essential Western thinker consists in an almost inhuman fidelity to the most covert history of the West. This history is the poet's and thinker's struggle for a word for beings as a whole. All world-historical publicity essentially lacks the eyes and the ears, the measure and the heart, for the poet's and thinker's struggle for the word of Being. The struggle is in play beyond war and peace, outside success and defeat, is never touched by clamor and acclaim, and remains unconcerned about the destiny of individuals.[62]

It is because the ground of morality and virtue is not clear-cut that decent societies can easily be engulfed in war, disharmony, and unrest. The classical philosophers were more prudent in their political approach than either Nietzsche or Heidegger, perhaps because they had learned the lessons of the Persian invasions of Greece and the catastrophic Peloponnesian War. Societies are easily destroyed, and entire civilizations can perish.[63] The

---

61　Mark Blitz, *Heidegger's Being and Time and the Possibility of Philosophy* (Ithaca, NY, Cornell University Press, 1981); Mark Blitz, "Reading Heidegger: A review of *The Essence of Human Freedom* and *The Essence of Truth* by Martin Heidegger," *Claremont Review of Books*, Summer 2005, http://www.claremont.org/publications/crb/id.1086/article_detail.asp.

62　Heidegger, *Nietzsche*, vol. 3, 19.

63　Victor Davis Hansen, *A War Like No Other* (New York: Random House, 2005), 1–23.

classical philosophers did not attempt to master Being; they strove to high-light those ever-present human longings for the good and noble. If they erred on the side of caution, describing human nature in more optimistic terms than is warranted, it was because they were aware that people need encour-agement to be good, and that noble and beautiful things are often difficult to achieve and fragile to maintain.

We are not faced with a nihilistic end of history despite all the global-izing and homogenizing signs to the contrary. We still wonder about what is good for us. Our longings for a good life both direct us to that inquiry and make us unsatisfied with the answer. So long as we are perplexed, we will not be fully content. So long as we are not content, we will seek better alternatives. So long as we seek better alternatives, the quest for virtue will continue.

Chapter Five
What Is Virtue?

Notwithstanding the corruption of Manners so justly complain'd of every where, this moral sense has greater influence on Mankind than is generally imagin'd, although it is often directed by…imperfect Views of the publick Good, and overcome by Self-love. Francis Hutcheson[1]

No book on virtue, especially one that supports classical notions of the concept, can escape the Socratic question. What is virtue? The answer is especially difficult today because people hardly use the term *virtue* at all. Virtue is associated with repression of our natural urges. In our post-neo-Freudian age it is not considered healthy to keep our yearnings at bay. Virtue looks like a relic of a quaint, narrow-minded, uptight age. We now believe that virtue is probably unhealthy and surely not good for our self-esteem because it is taxing to keep our passions under control. Virtue is also undemocratic, since some people exhibit it to a greater extent than others. Of course, defining virtue has never been an easy task. Socrates does not give a satisfying description and professes to think virtue unteachable.[2] Plato's view, which shall be discussed, maintains that virtue rests on knowledge of the forms.

Virtue may be a Greek concept, but it is a Roman word. Virtue originally meant manliness, connoting mastery, self-control, pride, courage, and loyalty. Classical virtue was not primarily concerned with the good of others, but rather with one's claims to merit. Real men sought honor because it showed they excelled in virtue. One can attain honor only in service to others. Love of honor roused men to do great deeds for their country.[3] Others benefitted from a man's virtue because he would keep his word, deal honestly with them, provide for his family, and protect his community.

1   Francis Hutcheson, *An Inquiry into the Original of Our Ideas of Beauty and Virtue*, ed. Wolfgang Leidhold (Indianapolis, IN: Liberty Fund, 2004 [1726]), 162.
2   Plato, *Meno* 70a–100b.
3   James Bowman, *Honor: A History* (New York: Encounter Books, 2006).

The term virtue had a different meaning when applied to women. Chastity, temperance and fidelity were the chief feminine qualities honored by the Romans. In all cases, virtue implied choice and the discipline required to resist the easy road in order to follow the proper one.[4]

Charles Dickens captures the original sense of a virtuous man in *Bleak House*:

> He would on the whole admit Nature to be a good idea (a little low, perhaps, when not enclosed with a park-fence), but an idea dependent for its execution on your great country families. He is a gentleman of strict conscience, disdainful of all littleness and meanness, and ready, on the shortest notice, to die any death you may please to mention rather than give occasion for the least impeachment of his integrity. He is an honorable, obstinate, truthful, high-spirited, intensely prejudiced, perfectly unreasonable man.[5]

The most natural of the virtues is temperance because overindulgence, although it can be fun, hurts. Even in our permissive age, people who are intemperate feel as if their lives are out of control, as a visit to an Alcoholic Anonymous meeting would show. They seek counseling, and, if substance abuse is their problem, they go to clinics to get help. They achieve a measure of gratification when they become temperate because intemperance means that their desires control them. Most people are not happy and do not feel good about themselves when they cannot manage their lives. Temperance seems to lead to happiness.

Human beings aspire to control their bodily functions. When we are ill, we sometimes feel so bad that we forego daily activities like brushing our teeth and combing our hair. To help ourselves recover, we make an effort to resume these everyday routines, sometimes at the prompting of a good nurse. Often, resuming these small daily routines makes us feel better. There seems to be a social role involved in tidying up. We also want to look better for those around us, although it is unclear whether we return to grooming

---

4   Andreas A.M. Kinneging, *Aristocracy, Antiquity & History* (New Brunswick, NJ: Transaction Publishers, 1997), 147–150. See also Harvey C. Mansfield, *Manliness* (New Haven, CT: Yale University Press, 2006).

5   Charles Dickens, *Bleak House,* An Electronic Classics Series Publication Classic, ed. Jim Manis (Hazelton, PA: The Pennsylvania State University, 1999–2013).

for others or ourselves. Our self-mastery, regaining control of our lives, is related to how others perceive us and how we believe others will perceive us.

Stephen L. Carter reflects on the relationship between manners and the moral sense. Every culture has rules of etiquette that act as ideals for the way people should act. Manners are the mechanism by which people interact with others in a peaceful and polite way. They are the application of moral principles to daily life.[6]

Rules of decorum also show how humans attempt to rise above and control their physical nature. Every society expects that certain acts be cloaked. We do not eat like beasts. We hardly ever put our faces in a bowl of food even though it may be a more efficient way of getting nourishment into our bodies. Instead, we use cutlery and wipe our chin. Even in those cultures where people eat with their hands, table manners apply. We are pleasure seekers, but usually we want to experience gratification in a human way.

Bathrooms usually have doors; we acknowledge that some bodily functions require privacy. We do some things in private because doing them in public is beneath us. We compartmentalize certain aspects of our lives. Most people do not make a public spectacle of sexual relations, choosing instead to keep intimacy private (although the Internet seems to be helping some to overcome this taboo).

In our easy-going times such as ours, people choose to live more "naturally," and the idea of manners is considered quaint. We are much less proper than in times when manners were strictly enforced by social conventions. We dress in leisurely ways that are more comfortable than formal. Yet, despite all the informality, fashion and stylish attire are quite important and publically displayed. Exotic and alluring images are regularly flaunted in magazines and on the internet. Although most people prefer comfortable attire, fashion shows that we seek to go beyond the merely natural and that we have an ideal of how we look at our best.

The simple activities of manners, grooming, and style reveal much about the human psyche. In every society, as Carter points out, customs prescribe how people should master and channel the physical desires. Humans seem to want control over desires, interests, passions and bodily functions. We want to be more than our animal element. Virtue is also a way of showing our mastery over the beast within us. It is an ideal about how people should carry themselves and interact with others. We might surmise that

6   Carter, *Civility*.

virtue is at odds with nature, since it seeks to control and even deny nature's commands. However, such a conclusion fails to account for the difference between nature and human nature.[7]

Theories of Virtue

There are a variety of theories about virtue. This chapter takes up those ideas. However, it is not an exhaustive study. If it were, the book would be encyclopedic rather than insightful. In presenting theories I have considered relevant, I have taken the opportunity to offer both their strengths and weakness in an effort to distinguish my own stance on virtue.

Aristotle

Aristotle's *Ethics* makes an effort to categorize the virtues.[8] Aristotle stresses the practical nature of virtue. He takes his bearing from the actions of a decent person, not the musings of philosophers.[9] For Aristotle, virtue is good both for people who exercise it and for those who benefit from it. Virtue is not like morality, which demands that people deny their desires, passions, and interests. In spite of the discipline needed to attain it, virtue can lead to happiness. Those who exercise it are aware that they, not their passions, are in command. Virtue is pleasurable because people are pleased when they do the right thing. Virtue makes people proud because it is more difficult to do the right thing than to succumb to self-interest. Aristotle explains that "It is harder to fight with pleasure than with anger...virtue [is]... always concerned with what is harder; for even the good is better when it is harder."[10] Since it is demanding, virtue is an achievement. Virtue is a kind of excellence; it is nobler than what common people commonly do. Aristotle is aware that many people do not live up to the ideals of virtue. He maintains that nature not only explains the way people act, but also the way they should act.

Aristotle contemplates alternatives to virtue. What if people had so much wealth that they did not have to worry about self-restraint? What if

7   Carter, *Civility*.
8   Aristotle, *Nicomachean Ethics*.
9   Aristide Tessitore, *Reading Aristotle's Ethics: Virtue, Rhetoric, and Political Philosophy* (Albany, NY: State University of New York Press, 1996).
10   Aristotle, *Nicomachean Ethics* 1105a.

machines multiplied nature's bounty such that they overcame the persistent and sometimes catastrophic shortages common in pre-industrial societies? If there were more commodities to go around, perhaps people would not have to worry about virtuously limiting their desires so as not to deny subsistence to others. Instead, as Libertarians suggest, they could seek to fulfill their interests and benefit others. Would virtue then be unnecessary?

Aristotle seems to have considered the scientific-technological project that would increase the amount of goods available. He wonders what would happen, "If shuttles could weave and picks played lyres themselves, master-craftsmen would have no need of assistants and masters no need of slaves"?[11] In other words, what if machines took the place of human labor? Would technology alter the human condition?

Aristotle rejects technology in favor of virtue. He is fearful that technology might be turned into weapons of war or employed by ruthless tyrants seeking to strengthen their grip on power. He is uncertain whether producing more material goods improves the human condition if it results in neglect of self discipline. Unlike Machiavelli, Aristotle does not seek to master fortune by beating it into submission. Rather he tries to encourage attributes that build character. Virtue is a discipline people practice because they recognize the limits of human will. Nature cannot be fully conquered. People grow old and die. Strong character may be needed to face such a prospect.

Virtue must have some authority over people if they are to follow it. For Aristotle, virtue is natural. Nature means more than the origin of a thing, such as its biology or cellular structure. Nature is a guide; it directs things to their end or completion.[12] For example, it is the nature of acorns to become oak trees. Most acorns never become trees, but all would with luck and the proper conditions. It is in the nature of people to develop their uniquely human characteristics. Speech and reason imply, but do not dictate, that decisions be made not merely based on desires, but upon reflection and judgment.

Aristotle also emphasizes the beauty of virtue. For example, when an athlete does something extraordinary, we call it "a beautiful play." The excellence of the athlete's skill is attractive, and that ability, while sometimes innate, is primarily the result of discipline and training. To be a superior athlete, to prepare for high-level competition, one has to deny, or at least restrain, everyday longings for rest and comfort. This form of virtue is similar

11 Aristotle, *Politics* 1253b.
12 Aristotle, *Politics* 1252b.

to morality in that people have to say no to certain kinds of desires. They deny themselves, however, not merely to be good, but rather to be good at their sport. In that they are like the virtuous who restrain themselves because it is noble and because it makes them good people.

Aristotle's *Ethics*, as many have noted, is partly an effort to understand ethical behavior and partly a polemic intended to make virtue appealing to those who long to distinguish themselves.[13] He makes virtue noble, something beautiful to act as a guide for those who long to show their superiority over animal nature and the common behavior of common people. Virtue becomes an ideal that decent people seek to attain. An ideal is something to which we aspire – something possible but just out of reach. For example, tying our shoes is not an ideal. But if we were in an accident and seriously injured, we might think, "If only I could tie my shoes, I'd know that I will be all right." Tying our shoes would then be an ideal. Aristotle's prescriptions are ideals meant to motivate upright people to become virtuous.

A person who holds high political office obviously has many opportunities to use the position for personal gain, and for some politicians, the temptation is too great. People who refuse to be corrupted by power show their self-mastery by not giving in to self-interest. Politicians who use an office for the common good demonstrate virtue. They make decisions based on judgment and discernment, not passion or the potential to enrich themselves. The best leaders endeavor to convince their fellow citizens of the rightness of their policies, using force only when required. They have much responsibility thrust upon them and rise to the occasion by making the best possible choices. Especially in times of crisis or change, political life demands that people develop the peculiar skills of speech and reason. They must employ good judgment to solve their country's problems. They receive inner satisfaction from succeeding at a difficult task. They enjoy honors for their public service. Sometimes their fellow citizens even call them great. For those like Alexander Hamilton who believe that "fame" is "the ruling passion of the noblest minds," virtue leads to a particularly grand kind of happiness.[14]

Whenever I present Aristotle's ideal political leader to students, they object that no such politician exists. But, their discontent proves that they are Aristotelians. They crave leaders who are virtuous (talented and decent).

13 Tessitore, *Reading Aristotle's Ethics*; Bowman, *Honor*; Thomas L. Pangle, *Aristotle's Teaching in the Politics* (Chicago: University of Chicago Press, 2013).
14 *Federalist Papers* #72.

Perhaps, just as Aristotle hoped, their longing will inspire them to behave virtuously if they are ever in a position to do so.

Aristotle's teleological doctrine of virtue has resonated through Western Culture. Thomas Aquinas made it the governing principle of the Catholic Church in his synthesis of Christian theology and Classical philosophy.[15] The fusion fell apart during the Reformation and Enlightenment. Thomas's synthesis was condemned by religious theorists for being too worldly and by secular thinkers for being impractical. "Don't attach yourself to Aristotle, or to other teachers of a deceitful philosophy," Luther enjoined his followers, because it had covered the church "in a Greek mask."[16] Thomas Hobbes labeled "Aristotelity" the "tenets of vain Philosophy."[17] It misled people into believing in teleology, personal conscience, republican government, and aristocratic virtue.[18] Both sides agreed that virtue was not natural, Luther because goodness came from God, not reason, and Hobbes because the teleological ideals were speculation, not science.

In our age of egalitarian ideals, Aristotle is out of place. He lived in a time when small homogeneous countries were still viable, and when aristocracy, not democracy was the most widely practiced form of government. He takes his bearings from the decent person, not the average guy. He tries to point people in a particular (noble) direction, rather than allowing them to do as they please. He suggests that pride, not moral scruples be the source of good behavior. He elevates those who seek fame and achievement over everyday heroes. Most importantly, he condemns technological discoveries instead of slavery. Aristotle has much to teach us about virtue, but he seems out of step with the temper of our time.

Natural Law

Present-day thinkers have tried to revive natural law, too many to analyze here.[19] But some contemporary ideas about natural law deserve

---

15 Servais Pinckaers, *Morality: the Catholic View* (South Bend, IN : St. Augustine Press, 2003).

16 Quoted in J. H. Merle D'Aubigné, *History of the Great Reformation*, trans. Henry Beveridge, vol. 1 (London: R. Groombridge and Sons, 1845), 154, 165, The Project Gutenberg EBook, http://www.gutenberg.org/files/40858/40858-h/40858-h.htm.

17 Thomas Hobbes, *Leviathan*, ed. C. B. Macpherson (New York, Penguin Books, (1651) 1982), Ch. 26.

18 Hobbes, *Leviathan*, Ch.1, 4, 12, 15, 17, 21, 24, 44, 46, 47.

19 Brian B. Tierney, "Natural Law and Natural Rights: Old Problems and Recent Approaches," *The Review of Politics* 64:3 (Summer 2002): 389–406.

consideration. Robert P. George presents a "defense" and J. Budziszewskia "vindication" of natural law.[20] Their theories, like Aristotle's, attempt not only to explain how people act, but also how they *should* act. Both scholars attempt to apply general moral principles to particular social, political and personal choices.

They argue against abortion and homosexual marriage. Their practical recommendations are controversial because people are free to believe that their preferences are rational. Since people display a wide range of behavior and follow quite different systems of belief, it is impractical to decide which of them is rational or natural.[21] If natural law is really natural, why do so few people follow it, or even know what it is? Why did Enlightenment principles and then nihilistic doctrines of relativism so readily undermine natural law theories?

It is unclear whether Aristotle subscribes to natural law. His theory is aimed at persuading decent gentlemen that they should behave nobly. He argues that virtue depends on habits, not on law.[22] But as Thomas L. Pangle's analysis points out, Aristotle's political counsel varies greatly depending on the situation.[23] There is a difference between natural law and natural right. Natural law is teleological; it prescribes behavior in advance, as positive law proscribes it. Natural right maintains that there is one best way to behave in any particular set of circumstances. The naturally right choice is a combination of what is best and what is possible. In extreme conditions, natural right might resemble Machiavellian behavior. While natural law attempts to regularize behavior, natural right takes complexity and diversity into account.

An example of one of the virtues, justice, will demonstrate the difficulty. Is it more just for an unhappy couple to stay together for the sake of their children, or to get a divorce leaving a love-less and conflict-ridden marriage? The choice is difficult and cannot be made without knowledge

---

20   J. Budziszewski, "A Vindication of the Politics of Virtues," American Political Science Association, New Orleans, 1985; Robert P. George, *In Defense of Natural Law* (Oxford, UK: Oxford University Press, 2001).

21   Nicholas White, "Harmonizing Plato," *Philosophy and Phenomenological Research* 59:2 (June 1999): 497–512.

22   James Bernard Murphy, "Nature, Custom, and Reason and the Explanation and Practical Principles of Aristotelian Political Science," *The Review of Politics*, 64:3 (Summer 2002): 468–495.

23   Thomas L. Pangle, *Aristotle's Teaching in the Politics* (Chicago: University of Chicago Press, 2013).

of the particular circumstances. Even then, there is no perfect solution or painless option. The naturally right decision may not have a happy ending, even though there may be some reward for doing the right thing.

The statue that usually represents justice is a goddess wearing a blindfold and balancing scales. In this image justice is blind because she takes no notice of wealth, social status, personal or familial connections. The goddess is holding scales because justice is not merely a formula readily applied. There are always facts to be uncovered, details to be weighed, extenuating factors to be evaluated, and alternatives to be considered before judgment is rendered. Justice is a fluid doctrine, which may lead to a variety of choices depending on the what, when, where, who, and how of each particular situation.[24]

The problem with natural law (even more with the metaphysics of Kant and the skepticism of Rorty) is that it wants justice to be simple, universal, and readily visible. Since we must apply justice after taking particulars into account, it can never live up to such a standard.

Still our ability to make Being present, to make sense out of our experiences, to order the phenomena into comprehensible forms or categories, makes the concept of justice possible. If people could not conceive of justice, then the message of the goddess symbol would not be so clear.

Natural law is a friend of virtue. However, natural law fails to take into account the tenuousness of virtue. Because natural law tries to make virtue into decrees, it is attacked by Libertarians for stifling creativity and by anti-foundationalists for making conjectures about the nature of humans. Natural law fails to perceive how much of life is socially constructed.[25] Natural law mistakes the conventional for the natural. The Catholic Church's natural law teaching on physics and astronomy has been abandoned, and its natural law defense of monarchy and patriarchy are relics of the past. One wonders if its position on celibacy, homosexuality, and female clergy will alter under Pope Francis I. In Heidegger's language, natural law has shown itself to be temporal, not natural.

Virtue Ethics

Virtue Ethics is a school of thought that tries to restate the case for virtue in the contemporary world. Michael Slote maintains that morality is an

---

24   Carl J. Friedrich, "Justice: The Just Political Act," *Justice, Nomos VI*, eds. Friedrich, Carl J. and John William Chapman, (New York: Atherton Press, 1963), 24–43.

25   J. L. Mackie, *Ethics: Inventing Right and Wrong* (New York: Penguin, 1977).

insufficient way to understand good behavior. Morality ignores the motives or moral character of the person doing a good deed. Virtue Ethics attempts to avoid Kantian morality, which requires that people take no account of their well being or self-interest when acting. Morality demands that they give no thought to themselves. Virtue Ethics tries to explain the complicated intentions of people. They do things for others and themselves. Virtue Ethics also disagrees with the Libertarian claim that people judge things only by what is good for them. What benefit do we get from ethical actions, according to Slote? We receive honor and acclaim from others. We experience a sense of self-satisfaction, accomplishment, and self-worth.[26] Self-regarding virtues are not necessarily bad, because one has to do things for the community to receive approval. As has been stated earlier, Hamilton maintains, "The love of fame is the ruling passion of the noblest minds and…prompt a man to plan and undertake extensive and arduous enterprises for the public benefit."[27]

Phillipa Foot, a leading proponent of Virtue Ethics, argues that because moral behavior is ubiquitous, there must be a reason for it. While moral theories have failed to provide adequate grounds or a theoretical basis for moral action, it persists in everyday life. This prevalence of natural goodness indicates for Foot that "acting morally is part of practical rationality."[28] We see innumerable examples of parents raising children, children looking after aging parents, people giving money to charities, a young person giving up his seat on the bus to an elderly person. Instances of goodness are ubiquitous.

Foot asks a simple but important question. Why are people good to each other? For philosophers, the question is controversial, perhaps, insoluble.[29] For Foot, and for most in the Virtue Ethics School, the answer lies in the phenomena of life. Something propels people to be good. There is a "should" associated with most practical judgments. We should brush our teeth, we should watch our weight, and we should be truthful.[30] This "should" carries over to moral reasoning, although Foot does not confront the theoretical issue of why this is so.

26 Michael A. Slote, *From Morality to Virtue* (New York: Oxford University Press, 1992), 3–58.
27 Alexander Hamilton, *Federalist Papers* (New York: J. and A. McLean, 1788), No. 72.
28 Philippa Foot, *Natural Goodness* (Oxford, UK: Oxford Univerity Press, 2001), 9.
29 Foot, *Natural Goodness*, 43.
30 Foot, *Natural Goodness*, 67.

The theoretical response to her question is the subject of this book. Libertarians are indifferent to the problem, because they argue that actions, not ideas, matter. People always act to promote their self-interest. Kantian humanists are not opposed to virtue, but they claim its scope is too narrow. Virtue might be attached to a particular country, religion, or national identity. It need not encompass all human beings. Anti-foundationalists find all virtue suspicious because it requires people to act in traditionally restrictive ways. It might be true that people do seek honor, but is not that desire a mere appetite to attain rewards prized by the conventions of society? Anti-foundationalists doubt whether a ground exists that can justify virtue, honor, or any other form of human behavior. Feminists oppose Virtue Ethics because it sets the bar for personal behavior so high that women might feel guilty if they cannot measure up. They could find the experience "alienating." Feminism maintains that the "focus" of "lives" should be "on the personal and the particular rather than on the universal and abstract."[31]

Despite these criticisms, Aristide Tessitore maintains that Aristotle's influence has experienced a Renaissance in both the general public and academia.[32] The most important proponent is Alasdair MacIntyre.

MacIntyre laments the confusion about moral principles so common today. In *After Virtue*, he points out that leading thinkers come to radically different conclusions about what is good. Their arguments are logically consistent and rationally sound, but they begin with different premises. The divergence of opinions – all intelligently supported – causes people to believe that all judgments are based on "emotivism." MacIntyre explains emotivism:

> In moral argument the apparent assertion of principles functions as a mask for expressions of personal preference.... There is and can be *no* valid rational justification for any claim that objective and impersonal moral standards exist.[33]

To counter the quagmire into which emotivism has thrown moral decision-making, MacIntyre restates the case for Aristotle's approach, but in an

---

31 Sarah Conly, "Why Feminists Should Oppose Feminist Virtue Ethics," *Philosophy Now* (March/April 2014), http://philosophynow.org /issues/33/Why_Feminists_Should_Oppose_Feminist_Virtue_Ethics.

32 Aristide Tessitore, ed. *Aristotle and Modern Politics: The Persistence of Political Philosophy* (Notre Dame, IN: Notre Dame Univesity Press, 2002), 2–6.

33 Alasdair C. MacIntyre, *After Virtue: A Study in Moral Theory*, 2nd ed. (Notre Dame, IN: University of Notre Dame Press, 1984) 19.

odd way. A variety of traditions foster virtue, he claims, while some under-mine it, and so people must choose among them. It is impossible to stand outside tradition and skeptically deny validity to all of them. One of the tra-ditions has already made that claim.[34] MacIntyre claims that "the Aris-totelian...tradition" gives "its adherents...a high measure of confidence in its epistemological and moral resources."[35]

After Virtue attempts to recapture the Aristotelian notion that virtue is personal achievement. Aristotle claims that virtue is aimed at "some good." MacIntyre argues that prowess is connected with what we usually think of as moral self-possession. Truly virtuous people will not use their superiority for narrowly selfish ends, and if they do, they will not fully achieve the "good" they seek. Thus, vicious chess players will never be fully content despite winning all their competitive matches. They are skilled, but their victories are tainted by the absence of a sense of true goodness – something they might have achieved with less skill but more restraint.[36]

After Virtue supports virtue by showing that alternatives to the concept of virtue have failed to provide an adequate basis for sustaining morality. MacIntyre rests his view on the historical record of failed efforts to discover an adequate foundation for belief.[37] His method, although far more elaborate and well documented, is similar to that of Alan Dershowitz.[38] In essence, what has worked has survived the test of time, what has failed has been dis-carded for a new and better theory. For MacIntyre, what has lasted longest is Aristotle's concept of virtue.

One might ask, however, whether MacIntyre's historicist approach is needed to justify Aristotle's views. Aristotle's presentation of virtue is so long-lasting because it comes close to capturing the essence of virtue. We see the continuing power of virtue in the phenomena of everyday life. The-ories after Aristotle, especially those that sought a kind of scientific cer-tainty, were less able to explain the characteristics of virtue – perhaps because of all its caveats and intricacies.

MacIntyre argues that virtue is expressed differently in different cul-tures; it is mediated by culture. What if these cultures clash? Whose set of virtues is correct? Which tradition is right? MacIntyre answers this

---

34 Alasdair C. MacIntyre, *Whose Justice? Which Rationality?* (Notre Dame, IN: Uni-versity of Notre Dame Press, 1988).

35 MacIntyre, *After Virtue*, 277.

36 MacIntyre, *After Virtue*, 274–75.

37 MacIntyre, *After Virtue*, 264–73.

38 Alan Dershowitz, *Rights from Wrongs* (New York: Basic Books, 2004).

challenge by contending that even quarrelling cultures may see common threads in their mutual appreciation of particular virtues.

We are left to wonder if Macintyre's support of Aristotle is little more than an argument from authority – Aristotle created a long-standing ethical tradition in the West. But it is unclear whether Aristotle would agree with Macintyre's tradition-based conclusion. Aristotle, as opposed to the tradition he established, makes an effort to judge the practices of various cultures according to their ability to produce both sound political practices and decent human beings. For instance, Aristotle claims that Carthage – a non-Greek city – has a superior political system when compared to Sparta and Crete.[39] Therefore, Aristotle does not judge cities simply on the basis of Greek, or any other, tradition. In defending virtue, MacIntyre does not recognize the kind of philosophic detachment necessary to judge between traditions. He does not distinguish between philosophy, which has no home, and politics, which always must be grounded in a particular society. Philosophers endeavor to have no prejudice or cultural bias, although they may choose, as Socrates did, to live in a certain community and devote their energies to it.

MacIntyre rethought his views, perhaps in response to criticisms of *After Virtue*.[40] Critics wondered how tradition could be a rational source of virtue and why someone from another tradition would respect Aristotle's theories. Moreover, why is reason the final arbiter of the superiority of a tradition? As anti-foundationalists point out, reason itself is suspect. Perhaps the kind of reason that supports Aristotelian epistemology is little more than a linguistic construction defending the privileged position of that tradition.

Because of these difficulties, MacIntyre abandoned the Aristotelian position he had so forcefully defended in *After Virtue*. In *Dependent Rational Animals,* he attempts to ground virtue in human weakness and fallibility. *Dependent Rational Animals* begins by comparing humans to animals, showing the Darwinian origins of sociability and trust. MacIntyre argues that we gain our longing for virtue, not by an assertion of prowess, as he had claimed in *After Virtue*, but from a sense of communal necessity and personal vulnerability. Virtue is acquired not from strength but from contingency.

Nature genetically guides us to be social animals, MacIntyre states, and social animals take care of the members of their society. The members of the society most in need of care, the most helpless – children, the sick and infirm – teach us most about our responsibilities to the community.

---

39   Aristotle, *Politics* 1269a–1273b.
40   MacIntyre, *After Virtue*, Postscript to Second Edition, 264–278.

MacIntyre then applies this argument to society. If we learn virtue from weakness and contingency, then we owe a social debt to the most vulnerable who provide our moral compass. Indeed, social responsibility to the downtrodden should be our most pressing duty.

MacIntyre's political argument in favor helping the poor and infirm is certainly humane, but his philosophic position combining Aristotelian teleology with care for the least fortunate is untenable. It is as if Aristotle delivered the Sermon on the Mount. Aristotle and the MacIntyre of *After Virtue* are more interested in the person exercising virtue than in the beneficiary of the virtuous person's largesse. *Dependent Rational Animals* is focused on helping those in need. In contrast to MacIntyre, Aristotle believes that the sense of pride and accomplishment attracts people to virtue. Although he cares about equity, Aristotle is more interested in accomplishment, hence the principle of teleology which directs people away from what is most base in human nature.

The effort to restate Aristotelian rationality also is undermined because MacIntyre neglects the source of emotivism. Emotivism is not merely concerned with the inability to choose rationally among alternative traditions. Emotivism arose because people came to doubt the authority of reason. No one expresses that distrust with more insight than Heidegger, and yet MacIntyre fails to mention Heidegger in *After Virtue*. Elsewhere he refers to Heidegger, but merely as one party to a dispute.[41] He does not examine the challenge that Heidegger's ideas present to Western metaphysics, of which virtue is an element.

Darwin and Virtue

MacIntyre abandons Aristotelian teleology in all but name in *Dependent Rational Animals*. He dismisses as an illusion Aristotle's ideal of the great-souled man.[42] Where Aristotle argues that pride leads men to virtue (vice is

---

41 Alasdair C. MacIntyre, *Three Rival Versions of Moral Enquiry: Encyclopaedia, Genealogy, and Tradition* (Notre Dame, IN: University of Notre Dame Press, 1990), 12–13, 46, 71, 166, 209.

42 Alasdair C. MacIntyre, *Dependent Rational Animals: Why Human Beings Need the Virtues* (Chicago: Open Court, 1999), 127. Tessitore's careful analysis makes a strong case that Aristotle has doubts about making *megalopsycho* (great-souled men) the teleological ideal of life. MacIntyre accepts that *megalopsycho* is Aristotle's ideal and dismisses it without analysis. Tessitore, *Reading Aristotle's Ethics*, 31–35, 42, 106, 108.

beneath their dignity), MacIntyre adopts biological determinism as the mechanism of human virtue.[43] He compares humans with other social animals, such as dolphins, to explain why humans develop virtue, an argument Aristotle specifically rejects.[44] Since we are dependent on parents, elders, and fellow citizens, MacIntyre reasons, we develop a sense of responsibility toward others. We realize that we needed others when we were weak and vulnerable, from which we draw the general conclusion that we should aid others who are in a similar position.

The confusion in finding the illusive philosophic or metaphysical ground of virtue demonstrated by MacIntyre's contradictory analyses, has spawned the field of evolutionary ethics.[45] Proponents of evolutionary ethics begin with Charles Darwin's *Origin of the Species*. Darwinians maintain that we need not rack our brains in metaphysical disputations in order to discover the basis of good behavior; we need only look to our genes. We can know human nature with as much certainty as a chemistry experiment. Larry Arnhart proclaims that, "Political science could become a true science by becoming a biopolitical science of political animals."[46]

According to Darwinians, species disseminate traits that allow them to survive and flourish. Individual members of a species that thrive are more likely to live long enough to breed and to pass on these genes to their progeny. Even though individuals seek only to spread their own genes, natural selection chooses those attributes that best suit the continuation of the species. Humans with cooperative genes are more successful because people need group action to survive. Steven Pinker explains, "A gene's metaphorical goal of selfishly replicating itself can be implemented by wiring up the brain of the organism to do unselfish things, like being nice to relatives or

43 MacIntyre, *Dependent Rational Animals*, x.
44 Compare Aristotle, *Politics* 1253a and MacIntyre, *Dependent Rational Animals*, 13, 21–27, 41, 57–59, 63–68, 82–83, 96.
45 Matt Ridley, *The Origins of Virtue: Human Instincts and the Evolution of Cooperation* (New York: Viking, 1997); Robert Richards, "A Defense of Evolutionary Ethics," *Biology and Philosophy* 1 (1986): 293–297; Steven Pinker, "The Moral Instinct," *New York Times Magazine*, January 13, 2008: 32–36, 52, 55–56; Pinker, *Better Angels*; Nigel Barber, *Kindness in a Cruel World: The Evolution of Altruism* (Amherst, NY: Prometheus Books, 2004); Larry Arnhart, "Biopolitical Science," *Politics and Life Sciences* 29:1 (March 2010): 24–47; Larry Arnhart, *Darwinian Conservatism* (Exeter, UK: Imprint Academic, 2005); Larry Arnhart, *Darwinian Natural Right: The Biological Ethics of Human Nature* (Albany, NY: State University of New York Press, 1998).
46 Arnhart, "Biopolitical Science," 24.

doing good deeds for needy strangers."[47] Since natural selection responds to the environment in which members of the species live, the success of humans depends on how well they adapt to the social environment they create. These social traits not only produce virtue, but also insure that progress will take place. Those civilizations that allow more people to survive out-compete those with slower population growth. In fact, some Darwinians, such as Matt Ridley, advise that people stop fretting our social, environmental, and existential woes. He asserts that our genes will produce an adaptation that will resolve our problems.[48] Ridley might rephrase Heidegger's pronouncement as follows: we do not need a god to save us; our genes will do the job.

Darwinians do not stop at using natural selection to explain human behavior. They argue that genetic coding can be prescriptive as well. For example, Arnhart maintains that evolution can show us that virtuous actions, private property, family values, and small local government are the proper way for people to live.[49]

Since people have the ability to choose, however, biology is not destiny. People could decide to live in large cities, avoid family responsibilities, depend on social welfare, not act virtuously, and still have many children. Are not their genes successfully passed on to posterity?

Moreover, Darwinian theory can account for human behavior only until people are old enough to breed. Once individuals successfully pass on their genes, the dictates of evolution are less apparent. Could this be the reason that for most of human history patriarchy was the preferred social arrangement? Men could compel young, healthy women to carry their genes onto the next generation. Even today, patriarchal societies produce more children than people who accept Darwinian principles.[50]

Darwinians would have us believe that erotic desires lead to virtue. Mating and procreation are the instruments that establish successful ethical codes. Those rules ensure stable societies where people can live long enough to procreate. However, the experience of virtue seems to contradict this claim. Whatever genetic heritage has programmed into us, it did not make virtue simple, easy, or natural in the same way that eating,

---

47   Pinker, "the Moral Instinct," 55.
48   Ridley, *The Origins of Virtue.*
49   Arnhart, *Darwinian Conservatism.*
50   Peter Augustine Lawler, "American Nominalism and Our Need for the Science of Theology," *First Principles*, March 28, 2008, http://www.firstprinciplesjournal.com/print.aspx?article=523&

sleeping, and procreating are easy. If nature really were directing us toward virtue, it might have chosen a less challenging vehicle to pass on our genes.

If Darwinian teleology is natural, why do the advocates of Darwinian teleology differ so much about the goals that people should pursue? MacIntyre argues that Darwinism leads to social democracy in which the most successful have a moral duty to care for the weak. Ridley maintains that limited government, protection of property rights, and voluntary cooperation are the evolutionary goals of the human species. As Robert Richards points out, Darwin's ideas have been used to justify the free market, Marxism, the social welfare state, and even the Third Reich.[51] Attempting to explain why genes lead to certain social behaviors may fall into the category of *post hoc ergo propter hoc* – speculating on the cause from the effect.

Oddly, teleological Darwinism is similar to Rorty's pragmatism and Dershowitz's progressive historicism. All argue that history, whether genetic or cultural, eliminates attributes that are harmful to people and selects traits that are good. Darwinians end up agreeing with post-modernists that human nature is constructed by history, a series of events in our past that over millennia created our current characteristics. Human nature has adapted to its environment. There is no guarantee, however, that what we observe presently will remain indicative of people because the species may adapt in the future to altered circumstances. Therefore, we cannot conclude that any particular action is natural, for nature depends on evolution to exist. Darwinian principles seem to agree with Heraclitus – being is becoming. If being changes over time, then the anti-foundationalist are correct. Virtue has no ground; its definition changes according to the time and place in which it reveals itself. Darwinian virtue turns out to be speculation about the good, not science.[52]

Human choice seems to be at odds with Darwinian teleology. Nature gives impulses to people, and we, unlike beasts, must decide which to follow. Some people may even decide that life is too much of a burden. What is the survival value in suicide?

These issues seem to have caused the leading Darwinian to rethink his position. In *The Better Angels of Our Nature,* Steven Pinker argues that genes cannot account for everything. There are multiple reasons for human

51   Richards, "A Defense of Evolutionary Ethics," 293–297.
52   Peter Augustine Lawler, *Stuck with Virtue* (Wilmington, DE: ISI Books, 2005).

behavior that interact and overlap in complex and unexpected ways. Among other developments, they have caused people to establish humane societies.[53]

Religion and Virtue

Religion has been associated with virtue since the dawn of recorded history. Prescriptive principles gain authority when required by the gods and reinforced by divine sanction. As Machiavelli puts it:

> The observance of divine institutions is the cause of the greatness of republics, so the disregard of them produces their ruin; for where the fear of God is wanting, there the country will come to ruin, unless it be sustained by the fear of the prince, which may temporarily supply the want of religion.[54]

Gods of ancient worlds were deities of the political community or the family. Religions were polytheistic and civil. They promoted civic virtue as a cornerstone of domestic harmony and the willingness to sacrifice for the security of the community in desperate situations. But the Greek philosophers cast a skeptical eye on the irrational myths that supported religion. Plato explains that "to seem to speak well of the gods...is far easier than to speak well of men to men: for the inexperience and utter ignorance of his hearers about any subject is a great assistance to him who has to speak of it, and we know how ignorant we are concerning the gods."[55]

Biblical religions were not interested in virtue as much as in righteousness. Obedience to an all-powerful God was more important than human judgment, as the story of Abraham's divine command to kill Isaac demonstrates.[56]

Unlike Aristotle's view of virtue as excellence, monotheism originated with prohibitions on action – "thou shalt not" – in the Ten Commandments. Since Judaism was the religion of one people, however, it diverged, but did not fundamentally alter, the idea of civic duty. Virtue was expressed as

---

53 Pinker, *The Better Angels*.
54 Niccolò Machiavelli, *The Prince and the Discourses*, Modern Library Edition (New York: Random House, 1950), 147–48.
55 Plato, *Critias* 107b.
56 *Genesis*, 18, 22.

responsibility to the Hebraic law and the Jewish people, through which the word of God spread.[57]

Christianity changed the way people thought about their lives. It turned them inward, making them aware of their inner thoughts, not merely their outer actions. In the New Testament, St. Paul denigrates the physical self and celebrates the inner spirit which is closer to God:

> For we know that the law is spiritual: but I am carnal, sold under sin. For that which I do I allow not: for what I would, that do I not; but what I hate, that do I. If then I do that which I would not, I consent unto the law that it is good. Now then it is no more I that do it, but sin that dwelleth in me. For I know that in me (that is, in my flesh,) dwelleth no good thing: for to will is present with me; but how to perform that which is good I find not. For the good that I would I do not: but the evil which I would not, that I do. [58]

The psychological and metaphysical effects of Christianity both deepened and weakened the human soul. The Christian God is universal and perfect. Such a doctrine undermines civil religion like the pagan worship of the ancient world. The laws and traditions of a nation no longer define what is right or wrong. Instead, individuals are personally responsible for observing the moral codes commanded by the deity. Biblical religion intensifies anxiety, for people are continually left to wonder whether their actions and even thoughts live up to requirements of religion. What was once consciousness become self-consciousness. Humans owe a duty, not just to their family, friends, and country, but – following Christ's example – to all people.

Machiavelli writes that Christianity "places the supreme happiness in humility, lowliness and a contempt for worldly objects, whilst [pagan religion]...places the supreme good in the grandeur of soul, strength of body, and all other such qualities as render men formidable."[59]

David Hume explains that:

> Where the deity is represented as infinitely superior to mankind, this belief...is apt, when joined with superstitious terrors, to sink

---

57 Meir Y. Soloveichik, "The Virtue of Hate," *First Things*, February 2003, http://www.firstthings.com/article/2003/02/the-virtue-of-hate.

58 *Romans* 7: 14–25.

59 Machiavelli, *Discourses*, 285.

the human mind into the lowest submission and abasement, and to represent the monkish virtues of mortification, penance, humility, and passive suffering, as the only qualities which are acceptable to him. But where the Gods are conceived to be only a little superior to mankind...we are more at our ease in our addresses to them, and may even...aspire sometimes to a rivalship and emulation of them. Hence activity, spirit, courage, magnanimity, love of liberty, and all the virtues which aggrandize a people.[60]

In a sense, Christian virtue led people to be concerned with moral issues, but at the same time made them intolerant of those who disagreed with that moral code. As Edward Gibbon makes clear, religion became a kind of ideology:

> The most sublime representations of...the Deity were sullied by an idle mixture of metaphysical subtleties, puerile rites, and fictitious miracles: and they expatiated, with the most fervent zeal, on the religious merit of hating the adversaries, and obeying the ministers, of the church. When the public peace was distracted by heresy and schism, the sacred orators sounded the trumpet, of discord and...sedition. The understandings of their congregations were perplexed by mystery, their passions were inflamed by invectives: and they rushed from the Christian temples . . . prepared either to suffer or to inflict martyrdom.[61]

It was partly because of the sectarian violence spawned by the Reformation that Enlightenment philosophers such as Descartes proposed a radical shift in the way human beings confronted existence. The Enlightenment sought to replace faith in divine authority with absolute trust in human judgment. The burden of proof for establishing the correctness of any proposition shifted from speculation about the ends (purpose) to experimentation to discover the means (how it works). The Enlightenment thinkers wanted this new emphasis to rid the human race of ignorance, superstition, narrow-mindedness, and prejudice.

---

60 David Hume, *The Natural History of Religion,* Online Library of Liberty (London: A. and H. Bradlaugh Bonner, 1889), section 10, http://oll.libertyfund.org/titles/hume-the-natural-history-of-religion.

61 Edward Gibbon, *The History of the Decline and Fall of the* , ed. David Wormersley (London: Penguin, 1995), 783.

Science would also increase the store of material goods available for human consumption. Life would be at once more bountiful, peaceful, and tolerant. Perhaps the greatest allure of the Enlightenment was its promise to use science to cure the maladies that afflict people's bodies, and to a lesser degree, their minds.

We live in an age when that promise seems to have been fulfilled. Our doctors know an astounding amount about how to keep us healthy. Our stores have enough goods to delight even the most rabid consumer. Our communication and transportation systems make possible a global economy. We can experience events from the farthest reaches of the globe almost instantaneously.

The success of the scientific revolution has affected virtue in a number of ways. People no longer believe that a doctrine urging self-restraint is as necessary as it was when nature was less bountiful. Most people count on scientific discoveries and technological innovation to solve the most pressing human problems. We expect the economy to grow, wages to increase, and life spans to lengthen. Over time, science has eroded the need for and belief in religion and virtue. In the words of Havel, ours is the "first atheistic civilization…we are going through a great departure from God which has no parallel in history."[62]

Of course, religion remains an important element in many people's lives. Religions still preach virtue to believers, as expressed by the elegantly simple and forceful statement of the Archdiocese of Saint Paul and Minneapolis:

> Human virtues form the soul with the habits of mind and will that support moral behavior, control passions, and avoid sin. Virtues guide our conduct according to the dictates of faith and reason, leading us toward freedom based on self-control and toward joy in living a good moral life. Compassion, responsibility, a sense of duty, self-discipline and restraint, honesty, loyalty, friendship, courage, and persistence are examples of desirable virtues for sustaining a moral life.[63]

62 Václav Havel, *Disturbing the Peace: A Conversation with Karel Hvíž ala*, trans. Paul R. Wilson (New York: Knopf, 1990), 10–11.

63 "What is Virtue? Why Is It Important in the Christian life?" *Rediscover: Newsletter of The Archdiocese of Saint Paul and Minneapolis*, http://rediscover.archspm.org/meaning/topic.php?id=7276.

Pope Benedict XVI argues that science and religion are not necessarily in conflict. Christianity teaches that "not to act in accordance with reason is contrary to God's nature."[64] God would not have given humans reason if He meant to make moral choices irrational. Benedict also maintained that Catholic Christianity is partly founded on Greek rationalism. Benedict's formulation means that rationalism existed before and independent of revelation. The virtues extolled by the Greek philosophers were discovered independently of revealed religion.

The most perceptive contemporary religious thinkers thematically face the loss of belief. Vigen Guroian proposes the novel idea that in the postmodern age, where form has replaced substance, complex ceremonies can fulfill the role once played by theology. At the very least, ecclesiastical Christianity gives people a sense of community and belonging.[65]

Tinder reminds us that Christianity never emphasized virtue. Rather, Christianity acknowledged the tragic nature of every human being's existence. Life is tragic, not only because our bodies die, but also because our plans rarely work out as we expect. Even when we want to do the right thing, it is difficult to know what the right thing is, and even more difficult to carry it out. For Christians, two fundamental limitations guide moral behavior. First, all people have a divine element. No matter people's virtues or vices, this spark of the eternal remains. It must be taken into account in all political and personal interactions. Second, humans are fallen. Tinder recommends a "hesitant radicalism," one that always seeks to improve the human condition, but is alert to the imperfections of all earthly institutions.[66]

Peter Augustine Lawler maintains that we are *Stuck with Virtue*. For him, virtue is necessary because nature places limits on human beings that can never be overcome, even by the cleverest scientific and medical discoveries. We cannot live forever, a fact that haunts our existence.

Ironically, as our power over nature has grown, our anxiety over death has increased. We tell ourselves that medicine can treat all illnesses and that science can foretell and therefore forestall natural calamities. Our worry and fear over the inevitably heart-rending trajectory of our existence has

---

64 Benedict XVI, "Three Stages in the Program of De-Hellenization," *Papal Address at University of Regensburg*, September 9, 2006.

65 Vigen Guroian, *Ethics after Christendom: Toward an Ecclesial Christian Ethic* (Grand Rapids, MI: Eerdmans Publishing Company, 1994).

66 Glenn Tinder, "Can We Be Good without God?" *The Atlantic Monthly*, December 1, 1989, 69, 72, 76–85.

created a therapeutic culture. Millions of mood-elevating drugs are daily prescribed to assuage our apprehension of aging and death.

According to Lawler, our misery over the ephemeral character of existence should not make us despondent. Rather, our restless discontent is a sign given by God to make us notice the perfection that could exist as opposed to the imperfection that does exist. Only belief in a personal God, one who cares about *our* soul, can soothe, even if it cannot cure, *our* anxiety.

Like Tinder, Lawler suggests that people should pursue morality and virtue, but like Tinder, he is more interested in salvation than virtue. Neither gives a full account of what virtue is.[67]

---

67 Peter Augustine Lawler, *Stuck with Virtue* (Wilmington, DE: ISI Books, 2005).

Chapter Six
The Good, the Bad, and the Unknown

It is not possible…that evil should be destroyed, for there will always be something opposed to the good….It must inevitably haunt human life and prowl about the earth.[1] Plato

This chapter is not about virtue. Instead, it attempts to enumerate the reasons why virtuous actions are so difficult. The account is admittedly brief, for a full explanation of evil would require a book dedicated to the topic. To understand virtue, it is necessary to cast a critical eye on the way people behave. To see good, we must imitate skeptics who focus on bad.

If virtue is natural, why is there so much wrongdoing and cruelty? How can the evil people do be explained? Should not something natural be effortless? The reasons why people are not good to each other are as complicated and varied as the reasons they are. Christianity answers the question with the doctrine of original sin. Somehow, even against our preference, we are fated to do evil. "In Adam's fall, we sinned all," said the New England Primer.[2] "According to that concept," Tinder maintains, the proclivity "toward evil is primarily an inclination to exalt ourselves rather than allowing ourselves to be exalted by God."[3]

Virtue is not simple because we are self-interested. We inhabit bodies that demand food, shelter, comfort and repose. We must satisfy those desires or cease to exist. Inevitably, we calculate our own good before considering broader principles of good or honor.

After all, life is cruel. Animals feed on one another and we on them. We regularly murder insects who prey on us. Even plants depend on the decay of other creatures for their nutrients. It is little wonder that the creature within humans thinks of survival, security, and comfort in such a heartless environment.

1 Plato, Theaetetus 174a5–6.
2 *The New England Primer*, ed. Paul Leicester Ford, (NY: Teachers College, Columbia U, 1962). http://www.jesus-is-lord.com/primer.htm.
3 Tinder, "Can We Be Good without God?" 69, 72, 76–85.

Moreover, our consciousness is singular. We have only our own thoughts. We can recognize the pain, suffering, and anxiety of others, but we *experience* those things only in ourselves. So strong is self-interest that Libertarians maintain it is the origin of all human action. When we think of our pressing needs, it is difficult to be virtuous because virtue demands that we rise above the immediate and consider the concerns of others. We all have seen selfish or thoughtless people, and we understand their behavior because we have all acted that way ourselves.

Virtue is also difficult because it is hard to define precisely what virtue is. As the anti-foundationalists argue, metaphysical principles such as duty, honor, courage, and others are difficult to know and harder to prove. It is even more challenging to apply general concepts of virtue to particular cases since circumstances alter the application.

James Bowman argues that the pursuit of honor is a widespread, if not always virtuous, human attribute. People want their lives to matter, so they seek to stand out from the crowd, to put a mark on their society. Men in particular like to make a show of their physical strength and mental adroitness. Even if they cannot exhibit their ability ethically, they pursue it nonetheless. Manly displays of violence, often against women, are required by long-standing cultural customs that place expectations on men to demonstrate dominance.[4]

Honor can be a strict mistress, but if the desire for honor is in the service of a cause, it can drive people to moderate their self-interest. Bowman uses the example of George Washington, who subdued his desires for power, riches, and even pretended not to hunger after honor in order to fulfill his longing to gain more honor.[5] But men and women can be honored for dedication to any cause, no matter how malevolent. Lust for honor thus can lead to both virtue and vice.

Bowman also argues that what look like acts of gratuitous violence are often done in response to slights or injustices. Acts of revenge to defend one's honor are efforts to balance and restore justice by punishing an evil-doer. Anxiety or feelings of mistreatment can compel people to strike out at others. The sense of injustice sparked two world wars – the first because of Serbian feelings of victimization, and the second because Germans felt betrayed at Versailles. The sense of injustice is so strong that it can often become the source of new injustice.

4   Bowman, *Honor*, 15–40.
5   Bowman, *Honor*, 275.

As long as human beings live in different countries, speak different languages, and follow different religions, there will be conflict. People are more attached to the familiar than the alien. People love their families more than their neighbors, but they are fonder of their neighbors than of their countrymen in general. They are attached more to their country than to other nations. They believe that their religion is the truest. But devotion wanes as objects of affection become more distant. As we have seen, civil society rests in part on dedication to the parochial. Conflict arises from the distrust people feel towards outsiders, who are dedicated to another community.

Martha Nussbaum argues that virtue depends on luck. Talented and decent people may never be in a situation to demonstrate their prowess, while individuals with less talent but more luck may be able to display their virtue because they happen to be in the right place at the right time. Talent itself is based on chance. Those endowed with extraordinary intellectual aptitude or physical strength have a greater ability to excel. They are also more capable of performing actions respected and honored by their fellow countrymen.

Nussbaum contends that some people do not have the wherewithal to be virtuous. If a child is raised by uncaring, arbitrary parents or in a social setting where thoughtless behavior is the norm, he or she is unlikely to exhibit virtue. Some social conditions are so dire that virtue is dangerous. When there is no civil society, people tend to think only of their safety. It is difficult for people to be virtuous if they are rendered amoral either by nature or nurture.

Even mood can influence people's ability to behave well. Someone who is sick, depressed, or just having a bad day, is less likely to be virtuous than someone for whom all is well.[6]

Generally, we do not feel pity or empathy for people who are not close to us. It is more difficult to sacrifice for people we do not know. It is not only the other that we find threatening and dangerous. We can also act against others when we think nothing of them. We give no thought to others as objects of sympathy. We do not see them as people with the same kinds of feelings as us.

However, it is this comparison with others that explains the dual nature of virtue. People have a desire to stand above the suffering or vulnerability of others. Empathy makes us realize that we could be in their shoes. But empathy is a double-edged sword: it can lead people to care for their fellow

---

6   Martha C. Nussbaum, *The Fragility of Goodness: Luck and the Ethics of Greek Tragedy and Philosophy* (Cambridge: Cambridge University Press, 1986).

human beings or to put distance between themselves and the suffering they want to avoid. As Charles Dickens makes clear in *Bleak House*, virtue is not always an appealing quality. It can be narrow, haughty, and disdainful. Dickens' character Sir Leicester Dedlock "is only a baronet, but there is no mightier baronet than he. His family is as old as the hills, and infinitely more respectable. He has a general opinion that the world might get on without hills, but would be done up without Dedlocks."[7]

Steven Pinker's *The Better Angels of Our Nature,* might aptly be named *The Sinister Character of Our Souls*. The book details ennumerable historical examples of the ways people torture, humilate, and murder one another.[8] Such practices have made skeptics doubt that virtue has a foundation. If such deeds are possible, how can virtue be part of the human make-up?

It is true that empathy can lead to kindness towards others, but, as we have seen, it can also lead us to compare ourselves to others. Since we understand people's suffering, we know how to inflict it. There is sense in which we rise above our fragility by cruelty toward and torture of others. Perhaps making them weaker and putting them under our will makes us less vulnerable.

The capacity to put ourselves in the place of others makes virtue possible. But it is one thing to understand what others feel but quite another to act on that knowledge. Virtue is not natural in the sense that it is common or easy. It is natural in that it provides an ideal of how people should behave. Christine McKinnon claims that, "Virtues and habits both manifest themselves in predictable regular behavior, but thoughts, actions, and speech of the virtuous agent are informed ….by conceptions of a good human life."[9] Even if the forms/ideas of virtue can be recognized, they are hardly self-executing. Perhaps this is why Aristotle is more interested in habituating virtue than explicating it.

It seems that humans have the ability to turn off their moral sense. For example, in ancient societies it was the practice to kill infants born with abnormalities. The children were not alive long enough for them to become part of the family; it was the custom to leave them exposed to the elements in remote locations. We feel little responsibility towards those things we cannot see or experience.

---

7   Charles Dickens, *Bleak House*, chap. 2, http://www.bibliomania.com/0/0/19/34/
     frameset.html.
8   Pinker, *Better Angels*.
9   Christine McKinnon, *Character, Virtue Theories, and the Vices* (Toronto: Broadview
     Press, 1999), 30.

There is part of human psychology that loves breaking conventional social restraints. As Nietzsche argues, some people revel in behaving outside society's rules. They flaunt their audaciousness, almost daring to be caught. It is as if they were prisoners released from an overbearing captivity.

All of us compartmentalize life. When we are alone, we do things that we would never do in the open in front of others. Plato makes a point of this in Glaucon's challenge to Socrates. If people had the Ring of Gyges to make them invisible, they would not be just. Justice may be necessary for social harmony, but it may not be natural. We do many things that are considered normal, even healthy, when we are alone. Our sex life is private. It is little wonder that it is difficult to draw the line between appropriate and inappropriate actions in public and private.

Adam Smith argues that our minds experience an impartial observer who guides our actions with disapprobation for vice. Of course, if there were a disinterested spectator, such a being would judge things with a view broader than our narrow self-interest. But it is sometimes difficult to behave honorably when one's interests are involved. The best way to establish what is good is not to have a stake in the matter at hand. Members of a jury or spectators at a play have no personal interest in the events and can have a dispassionate view of whatever the issue.

On the other hand, if people have no compelling interest to exhibit virtue, they may remain neutral and do nothing. There are two aspects of virtue: *knowing* what is good and *doing* what is good. People who are disinterested are more likely to know what is good, and people who are involved are more likely to do it. There is a tension between the ideal of virtue and its achievement. Aristotle tries to solve this problem by extolling the virtues of the magnanimous man whose disinterested pride spurs him to noble action. Plato depends on the independent philosophic judge, but such a person would have to be forced to take part in the life of the community.

It is sometimes said, occasionally by Heidegger, that his philosophic quest has no political agenda.[10] Yet Heidegger gives one of the most perceptive analyses of why there is so much suspicion, mistrust, and violence in daily life. Heidegger calls the concept "theyness." When something goes against our wishes, we blame "they." "They" is a distant anonymous force – perhaps even a conspiracy – that manipulates events to control our destiny. We hear "they" in everyday speech. "They" should make a law against that, or "they" should fix my street. "They" has no specific identity – although

---

10   Heidegger, Interview in *Der Spiegel*.

it might have a category. For example, the rich are greedy; the poor are lazy; the government is inept.

"They" was once outsiders – those from different countries who spoke unintelligible languages and followed odd customs. In our age of global communication and universalist perspective, "they" is more likely to be a corporation or government entity beyond our control. "They" is depersonalized in such a way as to make putting blame on a particular person or action unnecessary.

We can rationalization bad behavior against "they." When people file false insurance claims, they justify the action because, they argue, insurance companies are big, rich, anonymous entities that pay executives too much and charge exorbitant premiums for coverage. The concept of "they" allows people to do questionable things without thinking of the consequences of their actions because "they" is not a particular person but an abstraction.

Often people do evil in the name of doing good or remedying a wrong. The worst atrocities are often committed by people who believe they are doing the right thing. Even people living under totalitarian governments exhibited normal virtues such as patriotism, loyalty, and honesty, although for the sake of a depraved cause.[11]

The problem with ideas is that they can become too powerful in shaping our notions of what we should do. Ideas become ideology when we try to make reality conform to a pre-conceived notion of how the world should be constructed or people should behave. Heidegger is correct about the form of morals: moral ideas are easily transformed into ideology because they are not physical objects but things that we "make present" in our lives. Under the spell of ideology, people have instituted totalitarian governments and committed great atrocities in order to bring ideals into being.

For example, Marx's ideas promised to liberate people from social fetters, to make all people equal, and to resolve political conflicts. These ideals were so compelling that their devotees did almost anything to make society progress toward them. Millions were killed, tens of millions imprisoned, long-standing cultural norms destroyed, and the traditions of cultures throughout the world torn apart to bring Marx's ideas to reality. The ideas – the ideology – made communists blind to their crimes. The ideology justified the creation and maintenance of some of the worst regimes in human history.

11   David Wiggins, *Ethics: Twelve Lectures on the Philosophy of Morality* (Cambridge: Harvard University Press, 2006), 61.

Of course, communism was not alone in using ideology to rationalize inhuman behavior. Nazism was equally guilty. Sadly, even religion has been used to promote the most extreme savagery.

The very attributes usually considered virtue can be practiced for immoral purposes. When people believe their actions are virtuous, they often become self-righteous or smug. Virtue is an ideal, not a roadmap. People can misunderstand or misapply the principle.

Chapter Seven
Kant's Influence

Hypocrisy is a form of homage that vice pays to virtue. Francois
de La Rochefoucauld[1]

Virtue and Morality

For decades, researchers have tracked a decline in the acceptance of traditional moral principles and the rise of secular values, even among those who
profess belief in a Deity. Despite the weakening of long-established religious
prescriptions and proscriptions, people continue to make moral judgments.[2]
In fact, the contemporary social and political discourse is full of righteous
– one might even say self-righteous – denunciations.

 While no single element can account for the new morality, it is possible
to provide a partial explanation by investigating contemporary public

1   Francois de La Rochefoucauld, *Collected Maxims and Other Reflections* (New
    York: Peter Eckler Publisher, 1890), v218.
2   Phil Zuckerman, "Atheism, Secularity, and Well-Being: How the Findings of Social
    Science Counter Negative Stereotypes and Assumptions," *Sociology Compass* 3:6
    (2009): 949–971; Robert Fuller, *Spiritual but not Religious: Understanding
    Unchurched America* (New York: Oxford University Press, 2001); Bernadette
    Hayes, "The Impact of Religious Identification on Political Attitudes: An Interna-
    tional Comparison," *Sociology of Religion* 56:2 (1995): 177–94; Michael Hout and
    Claude Fischer, "Why More Americans Have No Religious Preference: Politics and
    Generations," *American Sociological Review* 67:2 (April 2002): 165–90; Ariela
    Keysar, "Who Are America's Atheists and Agnostics?" *Secularism and Secularity:
    Contemporary International Perspectives*, ed. Barry Kosmin and Ariela Keysar
    (Hartford, CT: Institute for the Study of Secularism in Society and Culture, 2007),
    33–39; Barry Kosmin and Ariela Keysar, *Religion in a Free Market: Religion and
    Non-Religious Americans* (Ithaca, NY: Paramount Market Publishing, 2006); Mark
    Shibley, "Secular But Spiritual in the Pacific Northwest," *Pacific Northwest: The
    None Zone*, ed. Patricia O'Connell Killen and Mark Silk (Walnut Creek, CA: Al-
    tamira, 2004), 139–67.

philosophy. In the past, as Edmund Burke explains, the greater part of morality and ethics grew out of one's specific national and cultural history.[3] This is no longer the case. We live in an era of universal ideals. Principles associated with a particular culture, religion, nation, or group are suspect. Indeed, conventional standards are condemned as being narrow-minded and bigoted. While the abandonment of time-honored moral judgments looks like relativism, it is not. Those who practice the new morality insist that long-established beliefs are a form of parochial bias related to gender, class, ethnicity, or culture. On the other hand, the new morality claims to be inclusive, especially of those considered outsiders under old belief systems.

Conventional wisdom once held that religion is necessary to promote virtue, and that virtue is necessary to establish civil society.[4] However, as Pinker shows, personal security has increased as religious faith as decreased. Pinker, however, discounts the horrendous wars and totalitarian carnage of the Twentieth Century. While slaughter of that magnitude is an important caveat, Pinker raises an important issue. Why has life in Western societies become safer as faith has waned?[5]

The most obvious answer is the natural rights revolution. The founders of the natural rights doctrine cared little for classical virtue. In fact, Hobbes reasoned that virtue is too rare to act as the basis of civil society.[6] Instead of virtue, Hobbes suggests that people follow their more certain motivations – the desire to enjoy peace, security, and prosperity.

Natural rights are at once easier and more difficult to practice than virtue. They are harder because people must give up the prideful protection of what they hold dear. For example, men can no longer claim women as possessions.[7] As feminists argue, natural rights and patriarchy – hallmarks of pre-Enlightenment social life – are incompatible.[8] Natural rights direct people to be tolerant of others, even those who are different. Natural rights

---

3   Edmund Burke, *Reflections on the Revolution in France*, ed. Jon Roland (Austin, TX: Constitution Society, 1790), http://www.constitution.org/eb/rev_fran.htm
4   Adam Ferguson, *An Essay on Civil Society*, ed. Fania Oz-Salzberger (Cambridge, UK: Cambridge University Press, 1995), 48, 89, 192.
5   Pinker, *Better Angels.*
6   Hobbes, *Leviathan*, Ch.14.
7   Lee Ward, *John Locke and Modern Life* (Cambridge, UK: Cambridge University Press, 2010), 141.
8   Mary Wollstonecraft, *A Vindication of the Rights of Woman, with Strictures on Political and Moral Subjects*, ed. Charles W. Hagelman, Jr. (New York: Norton, 1967).

are difficult because they ask people not to indulge in the human tendencies to envy, suspicion, malice, and domination.

Natural rights are easier because they allow people to do as they please. They do not distinguish between right and wrong, since people have a right to be wrong. They ask only that people leave others alone. As Libertarians note, natural rights create prosperity since people pursue self-interest in ways that add to their personal well-being and that in turn increases the general wealth of society.

The natural rights revolution helped establish bourgeois-middle class virtues. Although not as grand as the principles valued in antiquity, the middle class way of life is tranquil because it channels rivalry from personal conflict toward economic competition. Tocqueville calls the guiding ethos of the bourgeoisie "self-interest rightly understood." It stresses materialism, hard work, self-reliance, honesty, and diligence.[9]

There are difficulties within the natural rights doctrine. Natural rights can make people selfish, even solipsistic. Charles Dickens' *A Christmas Carol* perceptively demonstrates what happens to a man devoured by self-interest. People like Ebenezer Scrooge have few friends, hardly any pleasures, and no repose. They are wary that others may take advantage over them. They strive day and night to increase their wealth. Since they think only of themselves, they cannot participate in creating or supporting a civil society. Such people do not voluntarily obey the rule of law; they are restrained only by fear of punishment from a powerful government.

Kant understands this problem and attempts to show that natural rights are universal principles, not merely an assertion of individual autonomy. He also wants everyone to appreciate the natural rights and dignity of others.

How are these goals possible? First it is necessary to undermine traditional moral and religious codes, for they have been the source of conflict and division. He argues that long-established customs are merely a form of self-interest and that the pursuit of self-interest itself is immoral. Kant's ideas have had a hand in discrediting customs. He insists that even God must submit to the rules of morality or be dismissed as an immoral being. He explains:

> the Divine will…is a conception made up of the attributes of desire
> of glory and dominion, combined with the awful conceptions of

9   Tocqueville, *Democracy in America*, 190–91, 201 211–12, 218, 233, 359, 500–6, 538, 571, 575, 594–95.

might and vengeance, and any system of morals erected on this foundation would be directly opposed to morality.[10]

As this statement indicates, not only is Kant one of the most important founders of modern secularism, he is also a primary originator of spirituality. Although it is often reported in the media that believers are zealots, the vast majority of today's faithful have abandoned the fire and brimstone tenets of their ancestors and adopted the more Kantian view of a good-hearted deity that rewards his faithful but does not punish.

For Kant, it is not God's commandments but the categorical imperative that is the only source of morality. The categorical imperative holds that an action is moral only if it is free from calculation of reward or gain. To be truly moral, people must abandon all practical considerations based on their needs or desires; they must be directed entirely by good will. "Nothing can possibly be conceived in the world," Kant explains, "which can be called good, without qualification, except a good will."[11]

Since good will is the fundamental determinant of the worth of any action, neither bourgeois nor ancient virtues can rightly be called moral. Kant writes:

Moderation in the affections and passions, self-control, and calm deliberation are...far from deserving to be called good without qualification, although they have been so unconditionally praised by the ancients. For without the principles of a good will, they may become extremely bad, and the coolness of a villain... makes him far more dangerous.[12]

In order to insure that an action is unconditionally good, Kant breaks apart the elements of virtue. He makes morality into duty and rejects virtue as excellence. He writes:

Intelligence, wit, judgment, and the other talents of the mind... are undoubtedly good...but these gifts of nature may also

10 Immanuel Kant, *Fundamental Principles of the Metaphysic of Morals*, trans. by Thomas Kingsmill Abbott (The Project Gutenberg EBook #5682: 1785, 2004), Second Section, http://sites.birzeit.edu/dignity/index_files/kant%20-%20Fundemental%20Principles%20of%20the%20Metaphysics%20of%20Morals.php
11 Kant, *Metaphysic of Morals*, First Section.
12 Ibid.

become extremely bad and mischievous if the will which is to make use of them, and which, therefore, constitutes what is called character, is not good. It is the same with the gifts of fortune. Power, riches, honor, even health, and the general well-being and contentment with one's condition which is called happiness, inspire pride, and often presumption, if there is not a good will to correct the influence of these on the mind.[13]

H. A. Prichard explains the disjunction between Kantian morality and Aristotelian virtue. Virtue is undertaken in order for a person to enjoy some pleasure or sense of accomplishment. Morality is accomplished by following the laws of duty. Any pleasure a person might enjoy from the act would disqualify it as moral. Prichard elucidates the difference as follows:

> We must sharply distinguish morality and virtue as independent, though related, species of goodness. . . . An act, to be virtuous, must, as Aristotle saw, be done willingly or with pleasure; as such it is just not done from a sense of obligation but from some desire which is intrinsically good.... The goodness of such an act is different from the goodness of an act to which we apply the term moral in the strict and narrow sense, viz. an act done from a sense of obligation.[14]

With his usual insight into human qualities, Nietzsche raises the following problems with what we usually think as good, thereby showing the difference between virtue as excellence and virtue as responsibility towards others:

> ... we call good someone who does his heart's bidding, but also the one who only tends to his duty; we call good the meek and the reconciled, but also the courageous, unbending, severe; we call good someone who employs no force against himself, but also the heroes of self-overcoming; we call good the utterly loyal friend of the true, but also the man of piety, one who transfigures things; we call good those who are obedient to themselves, but also the pious; we call good those who are noble and exalted,

13 Ibid.
14 H. A. Prichard, *Moral Obligation* (Oxford: Clarendon Press, 1949), 11–12.

but also those who do not despise and condescend; we call good those of joyful spirit, the peaceable, but also those desirous of battle and victory; we call good those who always want to be first, but also those who do not want to take precedence over anyone in any respect.[15]

For Kant, virtue can be a bad thing if used without a moral sense. Kant denigrates virtue. He insists that a moral person can have no reward, even the satisfaction of having acted well. As Susan Schell points out, Kant not only raises the standard by which morals are judged, but he also endeavors to establish metaphysical certainty. Reason becomes not prudence or even experimental science, but logic.[16] Like mathematics, logic has certainty because it is a phenomenon within the mind. Nature does not make two plus two equal four. It does not calculate the expression: if A is larger than B, and C is larger than A, then C must be larger than A. Only human reason can devise these relationships.

Kant's effort to make the metaphysical world as orderly as logic caused Nietzsche and Heidegger to rebel against Western metaphysics. They, along with his anti-foundationalist followers, did not want to live in a world where all was known, settled, and decided.

The effect of Kant's morality has been to raise the standard of proof of a moral action so high that no one can be moral – for any taint of self-interest obviates the morality of any act:

> ... an action done from duty derives its moral worth, not from the purpose which is to be attained by it, but from the maxim by which it is determined, and therefore does not depend on the realization of the object of the action, but merely on the principle of volition by which the action has taken place, without regard to any object of desire. It is clear from what precedes that the purposes [of]...our actions, or their effects regarded as ends and springs of the will, cannot give to actions any unconditional or moral worth.[17]

---

15 Friedrich Nietzsche, from unpublished material composed during the period of *The Gay Science*, 1881–82; see XII, 81, quoted in Heidegger, *Nietzsche*, vol. 1, 157.

16 Susan Meld Shell, *The Embodiment of Reason* (Chicago: University of Chicago Press, 1996).

17 Kant, *Metaphysic of Morals*, First Section.

Kant's ideas have made virtue practically impossible since almost every act is motivated by some calculation of interest, pleasure, or happiness. Little wonder that such a strict norm caused Libertarians to question whether such a thing as morality exists.

Kant's Influence

Despite the problems with practicing the purity of Kant's principles, they have become the moral guidepost in the secular Western World. Kant's ideas are the impetus for natural rights, humanism, and a universal standard of moral conduct.[18] Exactly as Kant hoped, the simplicity and clarity of his ideas would shape moral sentiments. "Since a metaphysic of morals, in spite of the discouraging title is yet capable of being presented in popular form, and one adapted to the common understanding," it is readily comprehensible by the public at large.[19] Kant's morality is easy to understand because it is based on something quite familiar, our inner own will.

How can we recognize what actions are moral? Kant claims that this too is a simple task, such actions discerned without difficulty by every rational person. According to Kant, wrongdoing is easily understood because our minds make universal categories from particular examples. We are aware almost immediately when we are treated differently than others. We do not like it when someone jumps ahead of us in line, when a parent favors one of our siblings, when a judge makes a biased ruling, or when a political leader claims special privileges. We are especially attuned to hypocrisy. Scandals involving priests and ministers who give Sunday sermons on righteousness but engage in trysts with parishioners during the week are universally condemned.

From the inclination of the human mind to recognize hypocrisy and inequity and apply these valuations generally, Kant puts forward the categorical imperative: "Act only on that maxim whereby thou canst at the same time will that it should become a universal law."[20] To be moral, an act must apply equally to everybody. Kant would have us go beyond the dictum of "Do unto others as you would have them do unto you."[21] For Kant, an action is moral only if we have no thought for ourselves whatsoever:

18   Peter N. Stearns, *Human Rights in World History* (New York: Routledge, 2012).
19   Kant, *Metaphysic of Morals*, Preface.
20   Kant, *Metaphysic of Morals*, Second Section.
21   Mathew 7:12.

To behold virtue in her proper form is nothing else but to contemplate morality stripped of all admixture of sensible things and of every spurious ornament of reward or self-love. How much she then eclipses everything else that appears charming to the affections, every one may readily perceive with the least exertion of his reason, if it be not wholly spoiled for abstraction.[22]

Kant's moral principles have, without question, been efficacious. They have helped overcome parochialism and dogmatism. They have facilitated civil society by obliging people to apply natural rights to others. Morality no longer need be expressed narrowly in terms of defense of one's own family, region, country, race, or religion.

For example, Abraham Lincoln seems to have transformed Kant's metaphysics into homilies in order to illustrate the iniquity of slavery. He states:

If A. can prove, however conclusively, that he may, of right, enslave B. – why may not B. snatch the same argument, and prove equally, that he may enslave A? You say A. is white, and B. is black. It is color, then; the lighter, having the right to enslave the darker? Take care. By this rule, you are to be slave to the first man you meet with a fairer skin than your own. You do not mean color exactly? You mean the whites are intellectually the superiors of the blacks, and, therefore have the right to enslave them? Take care again. By this rule, you are to be slave to the first man you meet with an intellect superior to your own. But, say you, it is a question of interest; and, if you can make it your interest, you have the right to enslave another. Very well. And if he can make it his interest, he has the right to enslave you.[23]

Kant's principles have also helped establish universal concepts of human dignity. They are the foundation of the global perspective of human rights. They have weakened sectarian hatreds and ameliorated nationalist passions. Since morality cannot be derived from the phenomena of life, people cannot allege that their cultural norms or religious pronouncement

22 Kant, *Metaphysic of Morals*, Second Section.
23 "Fragment on Slavery," July 1, 1854, *Collected Works of Abraham Lincoln*, II, 222. Lincoln on Slavery: www.nps.gov/liho/historyculture/slavery.htm, retrieved June 4, 2011.

are truer or more worthy than others. Kant explains, "Nothing is more reprehensible than to derive the laws prescribing what *ought to be done* from what *is done*, or to impose upon them the limits by which the latter is circumscribed."[24]

Kant's ideas have been popularized and democratized in support of an elevated view of individual significance. After all, if morality consists of universally according every person dignity, then, as Hegel predicted, individuals must be "recognized" for their inner feeling and thoughts. What people think is important for their personal fulfillment becomes the key element in the construction of the self. Every self must be accorded dignity, a fact glaringly apparent in the age of Twitter when all people can report their every thought and action to the world.

Reverse Kantianism

If good will is the source of much contemporary morality, why is there such a heated debate among political elites about what constitutes moral policies? Why do they accuse each other of ill will? Why don't political rivals have good will towards each other? Here, too, Kant is the culprit. People engage in what might be called reverse Kantian morality. Kant holds that the sole component of morality is good will. He states:

> A good will is good not because of what it performs or effects, not by its aptness for the attainment of some proposed end, but simply by virtue of the volition; that is, it is good in itself, and considered by itself is to be esteemed much higher than all that can be brought about by it in favour of any inclination, nay even of the sum total of all inclinations.[25]

Kant insists that the *only* source of morality is a good will, and good will is only good when an action can be applied to everyone. "There is therefore but one categorical imperative" which is a universal law.[26] The universal application of the categorical imperative insures that no hidden motives of self-interest or personal hope of gain sneak into the calculation of morality,

---

24   Immanuel Kant, *Critique of Pure Reason*, trans. Norman Kemp Smith (New York: Palgrave Macmillan, 1929), 313.

25   Kant, *Metaphysic of Morals*, First Section.

26   Kant, *Metaphysic of Morals*, Second Section.

for "effects regarded as ends and springs of the will [incentives] cannot give to actions any unconditional…moral worth."[27]

Since we never use ourselves as a means to an end, we must do likewise with others. Kant writes:

> For all rational beings come under the law that each of them must treat itself and all others never merely as means, but in every case at the same time as ends in themselves. Hence results a systematic union of rational beings by common objective laws, i.e., a kingdom which may be called a kingdom of ends, since what these laws have in view is just the relation of these beings to one another as ends and means. It is certainly only an ideal.[28]

Those who accept the Kantian explanation of morality know that *they* have good will. *They* believe in universal peace, anti-imperialism, social justice, environmentalism, and tolerance for all, except perhaps for narrow-minded religious believers and business people, of course. If good will is the true test of moral goodness and they believe that their action or idea is based on good will, then they must be moral. Other people with whom they disagree and who act on a principle of self-interest must *not* have good will and therefore are evil. Rather than making moral people tolerant and moral principles universally applicable, as Kant had originally intended, reverse Kantianism makes people self-righteous. It privileges one's own moral purity and denigrates the motives of those with difference views. As Aurel Kolnai points out, Kantian morality creates a sense that good will matters and that those who disagree with this good will either must have a sinister and self-interested motive or must lack a common sense of humanity.[29]

Kant gives his followers a justification for this high-handed attitude: the moral worth of an action is determined solely by good will and not by a calculation of its effects.[30]

There is, then, according to Kant, an unbridgeable gulf between the phenomena and the noumena, what people do and what they think they should do. If the consequences of an action are not considered in deciding whether it is

27 Kant, *Metaphysic of Morals*, First Section.
28 Kant, *Metaphysic of Morals*, Second Section.
29 Aurel Kolnai, *Privilege and Liberty and Other Essays in Political Philosophy*, ed. Daniel J. Mahoney (Lanham, MD: Lexington Books, 1999), 84.
30 Kant, *Metaphysic of Morals*, First Section.

moral, it is also consistent to maintain that no matter how people act in their personal lives, their good will makes their actions moral. Thus the origin of spirituality, a system in which God helps but never harms anyone. Moreover, everyone – even preposterously rich, unpleasant, demanding people – can feel righteous in attacking the truly bad people on this planet (or any other), those who disagree with them. In spite of their personal behavior, everyone can feel indignant because they know that they have good will and that, as Kant explains "experience is not capable of determining anything about" morals.[31]

The categorical imperative holds that an action is moral only if it is free from calculation of reward or gain. To be truly moral, people must abandon all practical considerations of need or desire; they must be directed by pure good will alone. The absolutism of Kant's moral position has made people suspect the motives of others. Our own good will – which we know because we experience it – makes us feel morally superior to others. Those who disagree with our own pure good must not have good will.

Kant's philosophy has particularly been directed against business. Business people can never measure up to Kant's standard. They always make choices based on costs and benefits. Their businesses would quickly go bankrupt if they made decisions solely on the basis good will rather than interest.[32] Kant's principles have raised the moral standard so high that even the common inclination to perform an act for personal gain is looked on with mistrust. In much of Kantian-influenced popular culture, business people have been cast as the evil antagonists; they seek gain instead of the good.

David Brooks points out the attitude of the Bourgeois Bohemians, who live comfortable middle-class lives, but who denigrate the profit motive and denounce corporate greed. How can we account for such hypocrisy? Again, Kant is the culprit. Bourgeois Bohemians know that however high their incomes, they have good will. They believe in moral causes and scorn all whose interest seems in conflict with those ends.[33]

Brooks rethought his views. In *The Social Animal*, he argues that the popularization of Kant's principle is only part of the story. He also came to see – as this work endeavors to show – that virtue is a natural and therefore universal component of the human condition. It survives in every culture.

---

31 Kant, *Metaphysic of Morals*, Second Section.
32 Ruth Grant, *Strings Attached: Untangling the Ethics of Incentives* (Princeton, NJ: Princeton University Press, 2011).
33 David Brooks, *Bobos In Paradise: The New Upper Class and How They Got There* (New York: Simon & Schuster, 2001).

Despite its complexity and imprecision, the concept of virtue instructs every people in every age.[34]

Kant's ideas are the reason that the concept of virtue has fallen out of favor. Today we speak not of virtue but of values. Kant's principles dignify personal choice. People claim a right to assert their personal values. But as we have seen in Hiedegger's analysis, values are little more than the nihilistic conclusion that there is no universally acknowledged "right" or "wrong." People can believe whatever they choose.

Despite this important alteration in the ideas about metaphysical concepts, the phenomenon of virtue is still visible. Although they no longer call it virtue, people continue to admire both excellence and social responsibility. As always, people try to live up to their ideals. To better understand how virtue has and should survive in our age, we need to reexamine the principles of the Classical philosophers.

---

34   David Brooks, *The Social Animal: The Hidden Sources of Love, Character, and Achievement* (New York: Random House, 2011).

Chapter Eight
Plato & Aristotle

Virtue comes to us by a divine dispensation, when it does come….the certainty of this we shall only know when, before asking in what way virtue comes to mankind, we set about inquiring what virtue is, in and by itself. Plato[1]

The Liberal Arts and the Pursuit of Truth and Good

In our age, it is appropriate to wonder about education, particularly the status of the liberal arts. The liberal arts and the quest to understand what is true and good have been intimately connected since at least the time of Plato's academy, or perhaps since the advent of Socratic philosophy. But today, intellectuals raise serious questions about whether it is possible to comprehend the qualities of virtue or the nature of truth. The postmodern and deconstruction schools deny that "the truth" exists and that there is such a thing as the good.

If there is no truth or good, why are the liberal arts important? What is keeping higher education in business if there if nothing essential to learn, except perhaps that there is nothing essential to learn? Why should not schools offering useful Science, Technology, Engineering, and Math (STEM) classes replace liberal arts institutions? Or if, as some suggest, the purpose of a liberal arts curriculum is to make students think critically (meaning weighing alternatives), why do make them grapple with difficult and arcane texts? Surely, there must be a less painful and autocratic way to teach them to consider alternatives? For example, instead of pondering the difference between Aristotle and Hobbes' views on politics, they could consider the relative merits of the international sport of football (soccer) to the more parochial pastime of baseball, or they could debate the costs and

1   Plato, *Meno* 100b.

benefits of "hooking up" versus making a long-term commitment to a significant other.

The striking thing about the antifoundationalist position is how readily many students in some colleges – even quite conservative ones – have adopted it. Less conservative students express even greater skepticism about the status of truth or good. Most students today are not from religious backgrounds; their religion is of the easy-going "spiritual" variety. They believe that God wants them to be happy whatever they do.

If students do not believe that truth and goodness derive from religion, is it appropriate to ask them to propose another source of those qualities? Students often argue that common sense tells us what is true and false or right and wrong. But, that assumption is difficult to prove since all of our metaphysical judgments about reality may be nothing more than cultural convention. Long-held customs seem to be true because they are widely accepted and passed down from authority figures like parents and teachers. In the global postmodern age, however, such old-fashion values are losing their hold over us as an awareness of the range and number of cultural mores grow. Therefore, common sense might be a flawed basis for truth and good.

Plato's Forms

The liberal arts have traditionally attempted to produce both thoughtful and decent human beings – wisdom was thought to help inculcate all the virtues. Where do we turn to find a foundation for truth and good, and with it a reason for the continuing relevance of the liberal arts? Perhaps a review of the origin of the concept of virtue might provide a way to grasp it. We consider Plato and Aristotle, not because we accept their views on authority, but because in the beginning, they had to think through the nature of the truth and the good fully in order to be comprehensive and compelling.

Like us, Plato and Aristotle lived in an age when tried-and-true beliefs were called into question. One need only look at Aristophanes' *Clouds* to see that many of the Athenians were atheists. Plato's characterization of Thrasymachus in the *Republic* and of Callicles in the *Gorgias* affords ample evidence of the skepticism rife in the Classical age.

Partly to refute the notion that all human things are mere constructions and that existence has no substance, only continual motion and change, Plato turned his attention to the way in which people understand their lives. He discovered the forms or ideas.

The forms are easiest to understand if we begin, as Plato does, with ordinary experiences. How is it that we recognize a dog? After all, not all dogs are alike. There are all kinds of dogs – big ones, little ones, variously colored and marked ones – and hundreds of breeds. How is that we can recognize this array of seemingly different objects all as dogs? What is it that makes them dogs? Does not there have to be a peculiar characteristic that designates all these animals dogs and not horses or some other species? Is there not some attribute – call it "dogness" – that allows us to recognize all these quite different creatures as belonging to and composing the species, dogs? Plato would say what unites them is the form of dog. They are all dogs, and we perceive them as such because our minds are attuned to creating categories of things into which all particular instances of the category fit – in this case, dogs.

Another example might help. If we look around a room, we might see a wide range of objects of very different sizes, colors, and shapes. Even though they really do not look alike, we recognize them all as chairs. Do we not have to have some notion of "chairness" that makes it possible for us to understand all these dissimilar objects as chairs?

Of course, it might be argued that we know what chairs are because we sit in them. But did not some artisan or designer have to make the different types of chairs? What model would crafts-people use in constructing a new type of chair? Again, these people must have had a conception of a chair and what it does in order to deviate from any actually existing chair they have experienced.

If we take the example of a circle, we can see that the forms actually construct our conception of reality. When I am making this point to students, I draw a circle on the blackboard. They quickly recognize it as a circle even though it is usually badly drawn. They see my poor representation of a circle, correct its flaws, and fit it into the category of circle. They know that a circle is a line equidistant from its center point. Where did they learn that? From their math teachers, of course, but where did the math teachers, and their teachers, learn it? Plato argues that in order not to have an infinite regression, there must have been a first instructor. And he posits that the first instructor was the forms. The form of the circle taught us how to understand a circle.

How do the forms apply to the human good, what Plato called the virtues? At this point, I usually ask my students, who have been studying the *Republic*, what is justice? I give them an incentive to answer the question: Whoever answers the question and gets it wrong receives one full letter grade off their final tally in the course. But anyone who fails to answer the question at all is penalized *two* full grades.

Someone almost always responds: That's not fair!

How do they judge the threat of grade reduction to be unjust unless they have some idea of what justice is? They have never been confronted with this exact problem before, yet they are able to fit my conditions into the category of unjust things. No one instructed them about the case in point; rather they had an abstract notion of justice, and, hearing my proposal, realized that it was unjust. It could be argued that they knew only that it was unjust, not what the just is. Yet they could not have had an idea of injustice unless they also had a vague conception of its opposite.

Despite the ease with which students solve the problem posed to them about justice, it would be a mistake to think that the forms are simple to understand or readily applied to everyday life. The problem with seeing natural virtue as spontaneous is that people experience virtue culturally or socially, and each particular culture has its own understanding of virtue. People in one place might accept a notion of virtue that contradicts another society's understanding of the word. We are greatly influenced by our customary way of life.

Plato understood this problem perfectly. In a dialogue about justice, he recommends that his perfect city practice a cruel foreign policy towards it nearby states. How could undermining a neighbor be just? Plato accepts that justice is possible only in domestic affairs, not international relations. Kant understood the problem as well, which is why he advocates a cosmopolitan state based on universal ideas of morality.

Plato is also aware that people are immersed in the way of life of their culture and often accept its principles without question. The characters in his dialogues almost always begin with a clear idea of what a particular virtue is. Cephalus knows that justice is paying back what is owed. Polemarchus is sure that justice is helping one's friends and hurting one's enemies. The cynical Thrasymachus is convinced that justice is the interest of the stronger. What seems common sense to them, might be a Greek prejudice.

In almost every dialogue, Socrates overthrows the convictions of his audience. Socrates' questions obscure rather than clarify the virtues. Readers are confused about what they know. Socrates in this sense is "antifoundationalist." He knows only that he does not know. However, Socrates would have had nothing to discuss if there were no forms. He surely would not have continued to debate the nature of the virtues with his companions if some form of the truth did not exist.

We can most clearly see the way Plato attempts to solve the Socratic problem in *Lysis*, a dialogue about friendship. Although they make a spirited attempt, Socrates and his young friend cannot discover what friendship is. The dialogue ends with both more confused than when they started. Socrates' questions serve only to befuddle us as well as the people he is talking to. Despite the confusion, however, friendship is evident in *Lysis*. The dialogue is not, as Paul W. Ludwig argues, "without foundation."[2] Plato's literary structure shows the reader the phenomenon of friendship through the gentle, caring, and thoughtful way Lysis and Socrates interact. If friendship had no foundation, there would be no question about what it is. It is only because we experience friendship, as Lysis and Socrates did, that we know it exists. It is only through a dialectic inquiry that we understand the complexity of the phenomenon – its presence and absence in our understanding.

There seem to be certain phenomena in life that are real despite there being no material manifestations or thorough-going explanations for them. We know that we experience love, joy, pride, hate, and doubt. We feel the sting of unfair treatment. But often when we try to give an account of these all-too-human experiences, we cannot point to a material object or provide an adequate explanation. Still, we have the experience. Anyone who has suffered a broken heart or whose loved one has passed away knows that the experience is as agonizing as a physical injury.

Although Heidegger is often considered the father of anti-foundationalism, his lectures on the allegory of the cave in the *Republic* provide one of the clearest accounts of Plato's theory of the forms. Heidegger argues that language stands between perception of what is real. Language keeps us from perceiving what is real, but it does not create what is real – a most significant difference. Heidegger's position is not unlike Plato's. People's immersion in their culture obscures the truth. "When the familiarity of beings in their immediate power is uprooted...it is certainly difficult to awaken a real understanding for the unmediated perception of beings and their immediacy."[3]

---

2   Paul E. Ludwig, "Without Foundations: Plato's *Lysis* and Postmodern Friendship," *The American Political Science Review* 104:1 (February 2010): 134-150.

3   Heidegger, *The Essence of Truth*, 150–51.

Heidegger recreates Plato's theory of the forms using Plato's *Theaetetus* as his guide. He argues that we mentally make perceptions comprehensible. Sometimes what we organize is different from the perception of a phenomenon. Sometime we add things to our perceptions that are not there. I see Theaetetus (what Heidegger calls "being-present") and mistake his features for Socrates' face. I form Socrates in my mind with a perception that is not Socrates. I construct (what he calls "making-present") the missing Socrates with the bits of perception from Theaetetus (being-present) that are similar to Socrates. The form or idea of Socrates exists independently of the real Socrates – as is the case with all the other beings.

Theaetetus investigates how the human mind both understands and misunderstands experience. Plato raises the question of the relationship between knowledge and humor or jokes. For instance, when Theodorus praises Theaetetus for being of good character, Theaetetus remarks that the compliment could be a joke: Theodorus could be placing Theaetetus in the category of good character when he belongs in the opposite category since jokes are often based on placing (misplacing) a phenomenon in the wrong category or form.[4]

Heidegger gives an illustration from Hegel to show the difficulty of characterizing Being, an example apropos to the forms. Someone asks for fruit, and apples, pears, cherries, peaches, and grapes are provided. The person rejects them all. None are not actually fruit, but merely examples of fruit. Does this mean that fruit does not exist? Perhaps humans merely constructed this category, fruit, to explain a variety of perceptual phenomena. Apples, pears, cherries and the like exist, but fruit is – as deconstructionists would say – a literary-linguistic construction.[5]

Yet people, despite never having seen fruit, are perfectly capable of understanding what fruit is, and of placing particular varieties of edible items in the proper category – spinach is not fruit, but blueberries are. The forms are a human creation, of course (although animals comprehend perceptual categories as well), yet they exist. The forms are the way we understand the beings. The forms are the method by which the beings (and therefore Being itself) become knowable to humans. The forms make humans rational.

Heidegger argues that somehow we have a conception of whether a thing is true even before we are *sure* it is true:

---

4   Plato, *Theaetetus* 145c.
5   Martin Heidegger, *Identity and Difference*, trans. Joan Stambaugh (: Press, 2002), 66, 74. Heidegger makes a joke. He points out there is no such thing as fruit, and yet he hopes that his seminars will bear fruit.

With regard to the definition of the essence of the human being, however one may determine the ratio of the animal and the reason of the Living being, whether as a "faculty of principles" or a "faculty of categories" or in some other way, the essence of reason is always and in each case grounded in this: for every apprehending of beings in their being, being in each case is already cleared, it is appropriated in its truth.[6]

Plato might say to Heidegger that the forms make thinking possible. They are as prevalent as Dasein. The forms are the means by which Dasein gains awareness. Without forms, we would experience unorganized perception, and our consciousness of Being would disappear. We know what is true by fitting a perception into a form or idea – that is blue, it is a chair, that fellow is tall. Plato's forms or ideas are the way we categorize and understand perceptions. Without categories, we would merely experience an undifferentiated mass of images, sounds, and tastes.

Heidegger asks where this ability to make a category of things arose. What makes a true idea true? We could say that the truth is not false. Sometimes, however, what is true is neither true nor false: it is unknown. We even have an intermediary position when we do not know something. But somehow, we know that we do not know. How do we have the ability to distinguish among the true, the false, and the not known? How is it that things move from unknown to being true or not true?[7] We also know that it can be difficult to understand just how we make a judgment about what is true and false.

What is the truth? The answer is not clear, yet we can no more deny that the question is part of the human quest than we can ignore Being itself. Plato tries to solve this problem by analyzing the divided line. At some point, we must trust our judgment about reality, for to doubt that we can understand what is real would logically lead to distrusting even our own doubt. First, we learn things from opinion: our parents and teachers explain to us what things are and how they work. We then become more experienced and have our own sense of the world's processes. Yet, suppositions about what causes what may be incorrect. At the next level, we test ideas as hypotheses, trying to clarify situations using mathematical models. Finally, there is knowledge

6   Heidegger, "Letter on 'Humanism,'" *The Basic Writings*, 203.
7   Heidegger, *Being and Time*, 55–63.

– we know the form of the thing and can give concrete examples to demonstrate our understanding.[8]

As well as Plato's scheme might work in the physical world, it could be argued that it has little applicability to the metaphysical. Justice is not like a triangle, and courage has no square root. But it is undeniably true that we experience love, friendship, a sense of duty, and an understanding of what is just. These things are not like tables and chairs, and therefore they cannot be reduced to formulas. Plato seems to admit this, because at the highest level of understanding, he claims that dialectic will still be needed. In other words, every hypothesis about virtue must be challenged. The Socratic method of questioning attempts to disentangle opinions about the virtues from what is true. In Heidegger's terms, Plato's divided line examines the veracity of the views of the "they."

The forms coexist with Being. While it is true, as Heidegger insists, that there would be no awareness of Being absent Dasein, it is equally true that there would be no Dasein, no understanding of beings or Being, without the forms. Although Being is not one of the beings, it is still a concept, and, as such, has a form in the human mind. In order for humans to understand Being, it must be a form – for humans understand every abstract concept as a form. After all, Heidegger spent his life trying to explain the character of Being.

We can only speculate why the forms exist for humans. Other animals can distinguish one object from another. My dog knows the difference between a squirrel, which he loves to chase, and a ball, which he does not. He even knows the difference between the word *squirrel*, at which he perks up his ears, and the word *ball*, which he mostly ignores, although he knows what it means (sometimes).

Human beings understand the forms in a far more complex way. The forms themselves can construct reality independently of the phenomena. Animals have neither art nor humor. Art is a form. It makes the idea of a thing clearer than the experience of the thing itself. The form comes alive in art. We can see virtues such as the heroism of Homer's Achilles or Shakespeare's Henry V far more clearly in a work of art than in real life. Art attempts to bring into being the form itself, working backwards from the form to particular characters. In real life, individuals reach toward the form but

8   Paul Stern, "The Philosophic Importance of Political Life: On the 'Digression' in Plato's *Theaetetus*" *The American Political Science Review* 96:2 (June 2002), 275–289.

never finally arrive at it. Socrates claims to speak about virtues, even rec-ommending them as a way of life, yet he also insists that he is ignorant of what the virtues are. He knows only that he does not know.

Heidegger attempts to show why the Platonic understanding of exis-tence might be inadequate. If humans have the ability to mistake one set of perceptions about a being (Theaetetus) for something that is not present (Socrates), then perhaps they can also mistake one perception of Being for another. Perhaps our common sense, cut-and-dried judgments about true and false are too simplistic because our minds (making-present) organize so much of the "truth." Moreover, what we know to be "truth" (things are either true or false against the test of common sense perception) is too lim-ited. Our minds "make-present" what is true, almost as much as our per-ceptions do, although we do not notice this fact because Plato's conception of reality has constructed and influenced everyone else's. For humans, Hei-degger maintains, art is as proper a method of organizing life as is logic or science – Homer is as "truthful" as Descartes, and Hölderin's poetry can make us just as happy as a new BMW.

This ability to construct reality from pieces of perception makes art possible, since art is a way of making what is not present "there." It makes Being present to us without our actually experiencing it (being-present). Animals do not seem to need art – evidently they are happy perceiving what is present to them.

Heidegger's anti-foundationalist followers argue that we cannot know the true nature of things because we make the objects of experience present through language. What we know is not the object, but our account of the object. Language gives us understanding. The Classical Greek philosophers devised a manner of explaining the world that has been passed down to us as the proper understanding of the phenomena. If we deconstruct language, we become aware that the Western version of the "truth" is no more than a long-standing custom. As Rorty puts it, there is no truth, but only "sen-tences."[9]

However, there is a difference between the existence of a thing and its form, or what the medieval philosophers called its essence. Even things that are entirely human constructions –created by people – have a form inde-pendent of that creation. Take, for example, the sport of basketball. It is easy to discover the origin of the game, its inventor, development, and equipment. It could be argued, therefore, that basketball has no natural foundations. It

9   Rorty, *Essays on Heidegger*, 110.

is entirely constructed. Yet in order to *be* the game of basketball, basketball must conform to its rules. If we began kicking the ball rather than bouncing it, or score with a goal instead of a basket, we are no longer playing basketball, but soccer. Of course, it could be argued that we can alter the form of basketball by changing the rules, but then basketball will have an altered form that we and the players will have to follow.

Thus, even humanly created activities must have a distinctive character or essence to be seen, understood or engaged in. Anti-foundationalists are mistaken about language constructing reality. Language can make things come to life that do not exist in the phenomenal world, such as art. But language also explains the form of things, and that form defines or categorizes the nature of the things.

The Forms Applied to Virtue

Heidegger quotes a passage from Plato's *Theaetetus* to explain how our ideas are constructed. Socrates asks Theodorus to name a person with a good future. Theodorus responds that he knows such a person, but he "hesitates" to call him beautiful "lest I give the impression to anyone that I bear a passion for him." Heidegger says this example shows that we are able to view ourselves as if we were others. We become the other to judge ourselves. He says:

> the Greeks say… 'lest I appear before someone as such and such', 'who gives the impression'…. I appear to others or to myself as …; I seem to myself to be such and such…. 'I appear to myself as someone who believe of myself, I have the opinion that, I shall defeat Hector.' The state of affairs is no longer seen from the standpoint of *that which* shows itself, from the object, but from those who are looking at it, i.e. from this comportment; from those to whom something is shown and presented (this is himself: he presents himself to himself, he holds himself for such and such) and who thus have a *view* of what shows itself. Thereupon: what one *represents to oneself in* such self-showing.[10]

The human capacity to put ourselves in the place of others makes virtue possible. By looking at the world through our own eyes as well as the eyes

10 Heidegger, *The Essence of Truth*, 182.

of another, we see the consequences of our behavior and how our actions might affect others. We are aware of others' situations. We see our own strengths and weaknesses in relationship to others. From these experiences, we become aware of general rules of conduct. Virtue exists in that space between what we perceive and what we categorize with our minds. Virtue is our capacity to make present norms of behavior. This same capacity to look at ourselves as others might, is Smith's impartial spectator in *Theory of Moral Sentiment*.[11]

The antifoundationalists might have misunderstood Heidegger. Because Heidegger was reticent about constructing a *political* philosophy, he failed to take the next step. Human beings have the capacity to comprehend the forms since making them present in our minds is the essential element in turning perceptions into understanding. It follows, then, that our ability to make the virtues present is not merely chimerical. We experience the phenomena by making them present in our lives. They are "natural" because human relationships make consideration of virtue inevitable. We experience friendship, love, and anger, even though they are not present as *physical* phenomena. Yet we perceive them almost as if they were. We make them present, as part of comprehension, just as we do with all other categories.

As we have seen, Plato banishes the poets. He bans them from his ideal city because their portraits of extraordinary adventures and beautiful characters might make people unhappy with their everyday lives and responsibilities. He also expels them because the images of perfect virtue they construct are impossible in actual life. The *Republic* attempts to guard against the overly optimistic hopes for reform of young men like Glaucon. Plato is aware that what we now call ideology is possible because people construct (make present) reality to fit their experiences.

Heidegger argues that we encounter Being as presence – that is, as the present in a particular time. Truth is experienced in a temporal way, as being there – Dasein – not just being true. The truth is the thing *there* – something which is now but was not in the past and will not be in the future, although strangely it was true at another time and may be again.[12] Does this temporal limitation really matter as much as Heidegger and his followers argue? They claim that because the truth is experienced only in the present, all ideas are

11 Adam Smith, *The Theory of Moral Sentiments* (Amherst, NY: Prometheus Books, 2000).
12 Martin Heidegger, *The Basic Problems of Phenomenology*, trans. Albert Hofstadter (Bloomington, IN: Indiana University Press, 1982), 227–318.

true only for their time and place in history. The truth is different at different times because the truth can exist only in the present. However, are not human beings capable of projecting their ideas back to the past and into the future? For example, we learn algebra; in Heidegger's terms, the truth of its mysteries is unhidden from us. Then, no longer enrolled in algebra classes, we forget it. We remember, however, that there was a truth or symmetry to algebra that we can rediscover if we apply ourselves to relearning it. The truth of algebra has not changed because our relationship to it has changed (we knew nothing, we learned it, we forgot it, we relearned it). Is it not the form of algebra that informs each age, not the age that informs how we comprehend algebra?

In a sense, people can experience Being in the past, present and future. We can remember our experiences. We often assess and judge our past behavior by our present standards: "I wish I had done that differently"; or "I wouldn't have changed a thing." We can also project ourselves into the future: "I hope to be on time for class" or "I will become a lawyer." When we envision an action that does not yet exist, we say it *should* happen. We even have a way of expressing that a future action would be desirable – the subjunctive mood. Although the subjunctive is a state of mind, it expresses a hypothetical reality that we hope might take place. (The Greeks take the idea further with the optative mood, which is counter-factual. If only I had had studied algebra in school, I would have been successful).

The "should" is similar to "should" that is the basis of judgment about the virtues. Things *should* be this way. As Heidegger argues, Dasein is always running "ahead-of-itself."[13] Despite all the self-help books that counsel us to live in the moment, we never do. Rather, we exist in the present but constantly think about what we should be doing the next moment. The "should" is always present in the very structure of Dasein. Without the "ahead-of-itself," we would not have forethought. "Being there" requires that we look upon our present situation from the perspective of what should be done in the future. If running ahead of ourselves is a key element of Dasein and always expresses itself as a *should*, is it not correct to conclude that Dasein (there being) is the same as Dasollten (there should)? We are, therefore, not only the beings who are "there"; we are the beings who make judgments about what *should be* thereafter.

As Solzhenitsyn claims, moral evaluations are intrinsic to consciousness. He states that, "Even without a religious foundation" all

13   Heidegger, *Being and Time*, 236– 40, 303.

people, "even the most extreme economic materialists," make judgments about "our spiritual values: noble, base courageous, cowardly, hypocritical, false, cruel, magnanimous, just, and unjust...since they remain human beings."[14] Human aspirations, longings, and valuations are inevitable to the human condition exactly because we have consciousness (Dasein). We must make decisions about how we *should* behave rather than just living in the moment. The capacity to comprehend morality, Solzhenitsyn says, began when the "human race broke away from the animal world through thought and reason."[15]

Heidegger argues that speech is the source of our understanding of the world. The same constructed capacity that makes speech possible – the very capacity for mediating all objectives and perception – means that humans can make non-perceived phenomena into something real for humans. Thus, Socrates' questions about the phenomena of courage, justice, and the other virtues is not an effort to make the virtues into objects, but rather to investigate how people perceive these quite human phenomena.

Virtue and Morality

The concept of virtue originally described by the Greek philosophers is a better way than the theory of morality to understand why people act for the good. Because of the influence of Kant's ideas, morality has been associated with utter selflessness, a standard of almost inhuman detachment in which the actions of a moral person cannot result in personal benefit in any way – even in the hope of a final reward in the afterlife. The concept of virtue takes into account the sense of accomplishment we feel when we act for the good. We overcome our inclinations for the sake of something higher. Yet our mastery over ourselves is never complete because we always live with desires and passions that make us self-directed and even selfish. Of course, we are fated to suffer, experience loss, and die, so our mastery is only temporary and ephemeral. It is probably because virtue is so difficult and rare that we take such pride in it and feel such happiness when we are able to practice it. Indeed, virtue can make us so proud of ourselves that it can readily turn to arrogance. It is little wonder that the

14 Solzhenitsyn, "Repentance and Self-Limitation in the Life of Nations," in *Solzhenitsyn Reader*, 529.
15 Solzhenitsyn, "Open Letter to the Secretariat of the RSFSR Writers' Union," in *Solzhenitsyn Reader*, 509.

term virtuoso is often associated with extraordinarily talented, yet high strung and self-centered artists.

As we have stated, we need to reconcile our physical requirements, the desire for distinction in our spirit, and the need for stimulation of our minds. These things do not fit readily together. Satisfying only one part of our being is not fulfilling. Virtue as excellence and decency is perhaps a compromise needed to address the dilemma. Paul Stern puts the problem succinctly:

> Were man absolutely determined in the manner of either body in motion or rational necessity – as say the law of non-contradiction – guilt would be a nonsensical notion. Indeed, the very idea would not arise. Man can be understood to be responsible for action, then, only insofar as he is not either incorporeal intelligence alone or body alone.[16]

Virtue is an effort to attain excellence, to satisfy the longing for personal fulfillment without abandoning concern for others.

Aristotle and Teleology

Aristotle seems to understand virtue, or the highest virtue, as a kind of freedom from the worries, anxieties, and fears of life. The magnanimous man who is unmoved by things exterior to himself seems to be the ideal or teleological model towards which "human nature" is pointing. Aristotle states that the virtuous person wants to control his destiny. Indeed, insofar as virtue is the manly assertion of one's demand for recognition or honor, then virtue becomes a claim of superiority – thus independence – from others. Yet Aristotle argues that the desire for autonomy can be taken too far, for "he who is unable to live a city, or who has no need because he is sufficient for himself, must be either a beast or a god."[17] But it is not as easy to become a god as it is to become a beast. A god must utterly control his beastliness; he must be beyond the temptation of pleasure and the woes of pain, fear or anxiety. To be beastly, one need only give in to one's strongest inclinations and passions.

Feminist critics have noted with disfavor Classical philosophers'

---

16   Paul Stern, "Antifoundationalism and Plato's *Phaedo,*" *The Review of Politics* 51:2 (Spring, 1989), 200.
17   Aristotle, *Politics*, 1253a19.

relegation of women to secondary roles. Plato has Meno succinctly describe the patriarchal dichotomy, applying different virtues to men and women:

> First of all, if you take the virtue of a man, it is easily stated that a man's virtue is this—that he be competent to manage the affairs of his city, and to manage them so as to benefit his friends and harm his enemies, and to take care to avoid suffering harm himself. Or take a woman's virtue: there is no difficulty in describing it as the duty of ordering the house well, looking after the property indoors, and obeying her husband.[18]

Feminists argue that Aristotle is particularly to blame for fostering traditional Greek patriarchy. They maintain that Aristotle's ideal proposes that men seek mastery and self-determination while women address more basic bodily and physical needs of the household. Men are the achievers and women the caregivers.[19] But the superiority that Aristotle seems to extol in the *Ethics* can quickly turn into blind assertiveness. Aristotle apparently champions the assertiveness of traditional Greek patriarchy in the *Politics*:

> Hence the ruler ought to have moral virtue in perfection, for his function, taken absolutely, demands a master artificer, and rational principle is such an artificer; the subjects, oil the other hand, require only that measure of virtue which is proper to each of them. Clearly, then, moral virtue belongs to all of them; but the temperance of a man and of a woman, or the courage and justice of a man and of a woman, are not, as Socrates maintained, the same; the courage of a man is shown in commanding, of a woman in obeying.[20]

To shore up his point, Aristotle employs an argument from authority. He quotes Sophocles' *Ajax*: "Silence is an ornament to woman." Taken out of context, this passage supports the claim that Aristotle believes in the superiority of male judgment. However, the quote comes from a scene where

---

18   Plato, *Meno* 71e.
19   Ruth Greonhout, "Aristotlian Virtue and the Contemporary Virtue of Care," *Feminist Interpretations of Aristotle*, ed. Ruth Greonhout (University Park, PA: The Pennsylvania University Press, 1998), 170–200.
20   Aristotle, *Politics*, 1260a.

Tecmessa (whom Ajax has taken as a concubine after destroying her home-land) is giving Ajax prudent advice – counsel which he impetuously ignores, resulting in his humiliation:

> At some point in the night, when the evening torches had stopped burning, Ajax took up his two-edged sword, resolved to set off on a senseless expedition. I challenged him and said, "What are you doing? Ajax, why are you going out like this? There's been no summons, no messenger, nor any trumpet call. All the army is now sleeping." His reply to me was brief, that old refrain, "Woman, the finest thing that females do is hold their tongues."[21]

Aristotle's point seems to be that our contingency makes us aware of the need for virtue, and we ignore it at our own risk. Aristotle disguises his feminist argument, perhaps because it would have seemed too radical in patriarchal Greece. He agrees with feminists that our contingency compels us to consider the need for familial and communal action if we are to survive and live well. Men must listen as well as speak. Following the demands of virtue is difficult. Being virtuous gives us a feeling of accomplishment. Achieving virtue is a source of pride, and pride misleads men into thinking that virtue can be independent of human needs and defects.

Of course, it is true that different kinds of virtues are stressed in different societies, demonstrating the different attributes found in human beings. Still, all societies share some sense of both human vulnerability and capacity for achievement. Even the most aristocratic societies recognize the need for humane treatment of the weak. For example, in Sophocles' *Oedipus,* a shepherd of the flocks of the king of Thebes takes pity on a baby whom King Laius has ordered exposed. Instead of leaving the infant to die, the shepherd gives the boy to another shepherd from Corinth on the other side of the mountain. There the child is adopted by Polybus, Corinth's childless king. And the rest makes for quite a tragic story.

Aristotle begins the *Politics* with the words, "We see." What we see is partly natural and partly culturally determined or meditated, because, as noted above, humans must create societies to live in. Nature directs that we live together as social animals, but it does not give us universal codes of

---

21   Sophocles, , trans. Ian Johnston, 340–350, http://www.mala.bc.ca/~johnstoi/sopho-cles/ajax.htm#n15.

conduct to live by. It is difficult to disentangle what is natural from what is conventional. For instance, it might be surmised from examining contemporary American culture that men generally have shorter hair than women; that although most people want to be thin, most adults tend to be plump; and that everyone complains about people texting and paying no attention to their surroundings. We know, of course, that these practices are mere conventions. Yet it might also be true that there are natural differences between the sexes that tend to be conveyed through fashion; that the desire to see and to be beautiful is a common human longing, although the beautiful is usually rare; and that humans are naturally sociable, although aimless chatter and gossip often characterize that sociability.

Still, we have not discovered how natural virtue might be distinguished from its expression in particular social situations. Aristotle makes the problem even worse by suggesting that each person has a distinct view of virtue. He explains:

> That wish is for the end has already been stated; some think it is for the good, others for the apparent good. Now those who say that the good is the object of wish must admit in consequence that that which the man who does not choose aright wishes for is not an object of wish (for if it is to be so, it must also be good; but it was, if it so happened, bad); while those who say the apparent good is the object of wish must admit that there is no natural object of wish, but only what seems good to each man. Now different things appear good to different people, and, if it so happens, even contrary things.
>
> If these consequences are unpleasing, are we to say that absolutely and in truth the good is the object of wish, but for each person the apparent good; that that which is in truth an object of wish is an object of wish to the good man, while any chance thing may be so the bad man, as in the case of bodies also the things that are in truth wholesome are wholesome for bodies which are in good condition, while for those that are diseased other things are wholesome- or bitter or sweet or hot or heavy, and so on; since the good man judges each class of things rightly, and in each the truth appears to him? For each state of character has its own ideas of the noble and the pleasant, and perhaps the good man differs from others most by seeing the truth in each

class of things, being as it were the norm and measure of them. In most things the error seems to be due to pleasure; for it appears a good when it is not. We therefore choose the pleasant as a good, and avoid pain as an evil.[22]

Aristotle employs teleology to solve this problem. Teleology attempts to judge things by their end or goals. For instance, the teleological end of an acorn is to become a fully grown oak tree. All acorns aim at achieving this purpose, although some are eaten by squirrels, others fall into unproductive soil and do not sprout, and still others send up shoots, only to have them trampled or gobbled by hungry deer.

For human beings, the goal is full use of their peculiar attributes of speech and reason. Humans develop their full capacities in two pursuits: philosophy, which engages the mind to the fullest, and politics, which forces those in authority to develop their capacities for judgment, action, and rhetoric, the art needed to persuade others of the value of one's ideas.

How do we know if a person is acting virtuously? Aristotle uses one of his circular arguments to provide an answer to this question. The virtuous man chooses virtuous actions because they are virtuous, and actions are virtuous because the virtuous man chooses them. Aristotle attempts to make us more certain about what virtue is by showing us living examples of a particular virtue. In effect, he argues that virtues can be experienced (being-present) as well as known through categories or forms (making present).

What if the virtuous man deviates from virtue? Is he still the model of virtue? How does he know what is virtuous if he himself is the standard? The insufficiency of Aristotle's argument has been noted for millennia and is especially evident in a democratic age when few people accept the idea that there are "better men." How can we tell who the better man is if no standards of conduct exist except the virtuous man's behavior? But if the better man is not the standard for virtue, what is? We are back to the skeptics' criticism that virtue is in the eye of the beholder.

The ideas or forms are ubiquitous, and so we hardly notice them. For instance, most commentators accept that Aristotle's standard of virtue is the virtuous man. Who is teaching Aristotle about the virtues? Although Aristotle claims that the good man is the standard of virtue, he hardly ever mentions real men. He seems to have abstract standards or ideas about the

---

22   Aristotle, *Nicomachean Ethics*, 1113a 18–34.

virtues, as does Plato. Aristotle's analysis does not merely come from practical observation, because it not only explains, but corrects the actions of practical men. Aristotle teaches the rash that spiritedness is distinct from courage, and that justice cannot be reduced to mathematical formulas.[23] As Socrates suggests, we know about virtues but do not know about them. Without knowing something, we cannot know that we do not know.

Although Aristotle attacks Plato's forms, he seems to use the forms himself in describing people's actions. The circular argument that the virtuous man is the standard of virtue is only partially true, since Aristotle himself is not simply the virtuous man. Rather, Aristotle explains what the virtuous man is by using an elaborate set of examples, categories, qualifications, and ideas.[24]

It could be, as Tessitore argues, that Aristotle constructs the virtues, and the rest of us live in a reality mediated by Aristotle's genius. But, where did Aristotle get his ideas about virtue? One could argue the answer is that in politics or in matters concerning ethics, Aristotle's influence has been so pervasive in Western civilization that what was originally Aristotelian instruction has now become something like second (or even first) nature. But if we consider Aristotle's discussion of generosity, a virtue for which Aristotle is hardly famous, we discover that the phenomena – common sense experiences – teach as well as does Aristotle. Aristotle argues, of course, that generosity sits between parsimony and profligacy, and that it is often more appreciated by the donor than the recipient. Anyone who has given money to a wasteful relative knows that at some point the largesse ceases to be generosity and can do the recipient more harm than good.[25]

Forms give a better understanding of the virtues than does teleology because the forms do not attempt to dictate a specific way of life as teleology claims to do. While there is something noble about Aristotle's magnanimous man, people who cannot achieve such heights are left wondering what standards they should apply to follow virtue.

Aristotle employs teleology as a way of making people more certain about what virtue is. They do not have to ponder complex arguments, as Socrates does, to understand what is proper and fitting. They can aim their actions at a specific goal, a form of excellent behavior visible in their own lives.

23 Delba Winthrop, "Aristotle and Theories of Justice," *American Political Science Review* 72 (December 1978): 1201–16.

24 Tessitore, *Reading Aristotle's Ethics*, 62–65.

25 Aristotle, *Nicomachean Ethics*, 1121b 20–30.

Yet contemporary authors who employ a teleological view of human nature do not agree about what the goal of human life is. For instance, Arnhart argues in favor of traditional family values and conservative politics.[26] Ridley maintains that teleology leads to libertarian politics and free-market economics.[27] MacIntyre claims that we should take our bearing from the weak and vulnerable. Thus a welfare state with a social safety net for all is the prober purpose of human society.[28] But if teleology provided a sure ground from which to assess the purpose of human life, those who accept its principles would not disagree so profoundly. If there were really an end towards which action aims, people would be guided toward similar ends.

The problem with a teleological view of nature is that we must chose among the desires. Which desire can tell us which desire is correct? While animals can make choices about how to fulfill their desires, people wonder about why they have desire and whether desire is an appropriate motivation for human conduct. Moreover, teleology does not fully account for the enormous diversity of human behavior.

Platonic philosophy does not, as some argue, present the forms as a contradiction of common sense. Rather, the forms give meaning to common sense. We use our minds to comprehend what we should do. However, we are never fully certain – as an animal guided by instinct would be – that what we are doing is good. The forms comprehend virtue as neither spontaneous nor fully graspable. The forms are a better way to comprehend virtue because they exist only as a human possibility. We can know the forms, but we can choose not to follow them – thus the diversity and complexity of our behavior.

---

26 Arnhart, *Darwinian Conservatism*; Larry Arnhart, *Darwinian Natural Right: The Biological Ethics of Human Nature* (Albany, NY: State University of New York Press, 1998). See also Timothy Sandefur's review of *Darwinian Conservatism* at the for Science Education webpage: http://www.ncseweb.org/resources/rncse_content/vol26/3621_idarwinian_conservatismi__12_30_1899.asp.

27 Ridley, *The Origins of Virtue*.

28 MacIntyre, *After Virtue*; MacIntyre, *Dependent Rational Animals*.

Chapter Nine
Nature's Virtue

Shibumi: "being without the angst of becoming." Trevanian[1]

Virtue and Its Critics

Few people use the word *virtue* today. I do not think I have heard the term used in colloquial speech in twenty years. People in the media never talk about virtue. In 1996, Jeb Bush wrote an article asserting that popular culture should articulate and promote virtue.[2] But evidently no one in show business listened. It is entirely absent from popular culture, as a Google search of "virtue" and "popular culture" shows.

If there is a general neglect of the concept of virtue in popular culture, there is outright hostility in academia. A strange coalition exists in the current academic debate that denies or discounts the capacity of reason to discover virtue. On the one hand, postmodernist thinkers and their intellectual cousins, deconstructionists, maintain that virtues are little more than "narratives" reflecting the social setting of the culture in which they arise. For postmodernists, language alone mediates reality. Virtues are not grounded in timeless principles, but are reflections of the most common cultural ideas, usually put forward to support a privileged group. Postmodernists – who are, without exception, liberals and progressives, like Rorty – argue that people should be good to one another. But they cannot offer a reason why this is good advice.[3] To be fair, Rorty says that people are enframed by the

---

1   Trevanian, *Shibumi* (New York: Ballantine Books, 1980), 74.
2   Jeb Bush and Brian Yablonski, "Virtuous Reality: Character-Building in the Information Age," *Policy Review: The Journal of American Citizenship* 75 (January-February 1996), http://www.leaderu.com/common/virtuous.html.
3   Rorty, *Philosophy and Social Hope; Objectivity, Relativism, and Truth; Achieving Our Country: Leftist Thought in Twentieth-Century America* (Cambridge, MA: Harvard University Press, 1999).

culture in which they live.[4] Happily, our Anglo-American society is liberal, so it has taught us to be good – although our actions have often not matched our ideals.

On the other hand, free-market conservatives maintain that we cannot discover virtue because there are no objective standards of conduct beyond our individual desires. Free-marketeers claim that we are autonomous individuals – or at least should be – who make choices based on personal preference. Even if there were objective standards of conduct, no one person or group of people has enough information to make a rational judgment about the good of the whole. Better to leave individuals free to choose what is good for them, because at least then they are not forced to do something against their interests.[5]

Finally, a small number of traditional religious thinkers (rare in academic circles) speak to, and in some ways for, the wider religious community. The religious view is not so much antithetical to virtue as doubtful about the capacity of reason to recognize it. For religious people, virtue can be based on reason, as St. Thomas Aquinas argues, but ultimately reason must defer to revelation. Reason uninformed by faith is incapable of grasping what is good.

Despite the current prejudice against the concept of virtue, and although the word seems to have fallen out of favor, the phenomenon of virtue is still clearly visible even in our cynical age. To play out the scenario presented in the Introduction: What if a person of temperate yet charming personality really was a candidate in the New Hampshire primary? What if the person was courageous, fair, generous, and forthright? Wouldn't such a candidate gain respect and perhaps even garner votes? Wouldn't the citizens of the Granite State find the attributes of such a person attractive, perhaps even compelling? In fact, aren't we always looking for such people in politics and even more in life generally? What makes us so drawn to virtue? What is its strange allure? Is virtue merely something that we hope for but which is never attained in real life?

The question raised by this book is whether virtue is grounded in nature. Or is virtue, as Heidegger and his followers claim, merely a discredited metaphysical principle? A defense of the natural ground of virtue rests on

---

4   John Rawls, *Justice as Fairness: A Restatement*, ed. Erin Kelly (Cambridge, MA: Belknap Press of Harvard University Press, 2001).

5   Nozick, *Anarchy, State and Utopia*; Milton and Rose Friedman, *Free to Choose: A Personal Statement* (New York: Harcourt Brace Jovanovich, 1980).

observation. Many liberals have a strong sense of social justice. They often criticize their Anglo-American society, contrasting it to a better, more just, political and economic arrangement. If our ideas come from our society, how is it that liberals have been in the forefront of attempts to change society? Where did their notions of justice come from?

In the same vein, many free-market economists take good care of their children and even their parents. If we are all autonomous individuals who think only of our own needs and desires, how can their concern for others be explained? Why, after all, does a fully autonomous person need love? Are human beings needier than advocates of the free market suggest? Moreover, although economists argue that self-interest is the only motive directing human conduct, almost every free-market advocate wants to reform economic policies to better reflect market forces. Why do economists care about whether other people thrive? Actually, what they really believe is that free-market economics is the most efficient, and that such an economy is better or more just. If there were not some form of "good" or "just" in their calculations, they would not bother attempting to reform society to make it better.

My skeptical students often revolt when they study Plato and Aristotle. They do not like being told what to do, and they cannot accept that the wise have a claim to rule over them. They insist that no one has a right to tell someone else what is right and what is wrong. What they mean, of course, is that it is *unjust* for one person to tell another what is right and wrong. They are thus admitting their own reliance on a form of justice, one that is abstract, universal, and not self-constructed.

Religious people claim that revelation is the ultimate authority for deciding what is good, but they almost always forget just how demanding a strict adherence to divine commands can be. Most religious people in the West behave a lot more like the autonomous individuals of free-market theory than like faithful disciples who supinely accept the word of God. Moreover, almost every person of faith cherishes equality of opportunity, personal freedom, and natural rights – principles almost completely absent in the Bible. In fact, although a small and passionate faction of devotees are radical fundamentalists, most religious people distrust fanatical attachment to dogma. In addition, it is not entirely clear whether true believers are motivated by fidelity to God or by a sense that injustice has been done to their faith, culture, and way of life.

Religious people do not get their ideas about virtue solely from sacred texts. Free-market conservatives in their personal lives do not act in concord

with their academic theories. Liberals are always reaching beyond the principles of their society in order to make it better. Postmodernists believe in
social justice, but they deny the existence of justice or virtue. Where do our
ideas about what is good and virtuous really come from?

Of course, we are all tempted to misbehave. Almost every society has
acknowledged this dark aspect of human nature and has devised legal codes
to combat it. Once the rule of law is established in a normally functioning
society, people are more often good than bad; honesty and law-abidingness
are the rule, not the exception.

Why are people usually law abiding? Fear of punishment is the most
obvious answer. Perhaps what people call "conscience" is also at work. The
phenomenon of decent behavior is complicated. It could be argued that
morality is merely a human construct passed down from one generation to
the next, but whose origins have been lost in the mists of time. This argument just pushes the question back further. Why did all societies establish
rules of conduct for citizens? Why are narrow self-interest, dishonesty, theft,
and, gratuitous cruelty, especially to the innocent, proscribed in almost every
culture known to us? It could be that something in the nature of experience
dictates these principles. Maybe people discovered, rather than invented,
virtue. Perhaps we are not merely selfish or subjective; maybe we act for
the sake of others. Compassion, love, unselfish concern for our neighbors
are as much a part of human history as war and evil, although they get far
fewer columns in history texts.

A skeptic might respond that while people of good character might be
successful in private lives, they cannot survive in politics. A virtuous president is possible only in a work of fiction or on a television show. Politics is
too tough a business for those with scruples.

Moreover, are not some societies cruel? The Incas practiced human sacrifice; the Roman gladiatorial spectacles killed thousands; there is no need
to mention Nazi Germany and the Soviet Union during Stalinism. Do not
these examples show that virtue is ephemeral?

The father of all skeptics regarding moral virtues is Niccolò Machiavelli, who uses the word *virtue* (or *virtù*) playfully, stripping its moral
component and keeping the idea of prowess. Before Machiavelli, virtue
was defined as the use or function of a thing, plus its excellence. So, for
example, the virtue of honorable people was their ability and the pride
they took in stooping to cheat, lie, or steal. Since human beings are social
animals who almost universally live in communities that require upright
behavior and sacrifice for the group, it was thought that standards of

conduct required to maintain the community – judgments such as good or bad, noble or base, courageous or cowardly – were natural. Therefore, people who fulfill their social responsibilities and live in upright lives are virtuous.

Machiavelli did not doubt that virtues are needed to establish and maintain political communities, what he called "modes and orders." However, he did not believe that rules of conduct are natural. For him, virtues are little more than political tactics ambitious princes use for personal aggrandizement. Machiavelli cares about the civic responsibilities of ordinary citizens only insofar as they lead to a stable political order; there, citizens' virtues are instrumental. True virtue is seen in the creative exploits of shrewd, spirited, cunning princes who are not bothered by moral qualms. A prince must trust no one fully and must be able to foresee – so as to forestall – the actions of others. The prince must "be alone" if his schemes are to bear fruit.[6] Machiavelli judges virtue from the perspective of an autonomous prince whose first responsibility is to his own success, regardless of how his schemes affect others. If a prince can secure modes and orders that promote the good of the community, so much the better for his reputation and accomplishments.

Thomas Hobbes expands the idea of the solitary individual alone against the world even beyond the scope of Machiavelli's indomitable prince. Rather than being social animals, Hobbes explains, "men have no pleasure (but on the contrary a great deal of grief) in keeping company."[7] People despise and fear each other because in a world where resources are scarce their physical needs compel them to struggle to survive. Conflict is the rule, not the exception. Human beings are so antisocial in their natural condition, Hobbes famously states, there is:

> no place for industry, because the fruit thereof is uncertain: and consequently no culture of the earth; no navigation, nor use of the commodities that may be imported by sea; no commodious building; no instruments of moving and removing such things as require much force; no knowledge of the face of the earth; no account of time; no arts; no letters; no society; and which is

6   Harvey C. Mansfield, *Machiavelli's Virtue* (Chicago: The University of Chicago Press, 1966), 6–52. See also Leo Strauss, *Thoughts on Machiavelli* (Chicago: University of Chicago Press, 1958).

7   Hobbes, *Leviathan*, Ch XIII.

worst of all, continual fear, and danger of violent death; and the life of man, solitary, poor, nasty, brutish, and short.[8]

In this condition of universal conflict, it is little wonder that there is no virtue, and fear and force are the only mechanism for controlling behavior. Hobbes argues that:

> Good and evil are names that signify our appetites and aversions, which in different tempers, customs, and doctrines of men are different: and diverse men differ not only in their judgment on the senses of what is pleasant and unpleasant to the taste, smell, hearing, touch, and sight; but also of what is conformable or disagreeable to reason in the actions of common life.[9]

For Hobbes, security is the most important commodity; it makes possible the satisfaction of all other desires. Virtue is thus reduced to obedience to an established government.

David Hume disagrees with Hobbes about the origin of virtue, arguing that every society must inculcate certain kinds of beliefs in citizens in order for the community to survive. For example, societies must habituate the primary political virtue – a sense of justice – in order for its members to coexist. Hume reasons that "those impressions, which give rise to this sense of justice, are not natural to the mind of man, but arise from artifice and human conventions."[10]

Hume creates an even more elaborate thought experiment than Hobbes to prove that virtue is not innate. Not only are people fearsome and hateful to one another in a situation of scarcity, but they are also unnecessary to one another in a condition of abundance. "Let us suppose," he conjectures:

> that nature has bestowed on the human race such profuse abundance of all external conveniences, that, without any uncertainty in the event, without any care or industry on our part, every individual finds himself fully provided with whatever his most voracious appetites can want, or luxurious imagination wish or

---

8   Ibid..

9   Hobbes, *Leviathan*, Ch XV.

10   David Hume, *A Treatise of Human Nature*, ed. L. A. Selby-Bigge (Oxford: Oxford University Press, 1978), Section II, Part II, emphasis original.

desire….No laborious occupation required: No tillage: No navigation. Music, poetry, and contemplation form his sole business: Conversation, mirth, and friendship his sole amusement. It seems evident, that, in such a happy state…the cautious, jealous virtue of justice would never once have been dreamed of…
…Justice, in that case, being totally USELESS, would be an idle ceremonial, and could never possibly have place in the catalogue of virtues.[11]

Although Hume claims that in a state of abundance "every other social virtue" but justice "would flourish," it is unclear why virtues such as temperance and generosity would be practiced. Moreover, if we assume that a luxurious life is available to everyone, it is doubtful that the virtue of courage would be needed. People could share their wealth by bribing outsiders instead of fighting against them in order to defend the community.

Hume's thought experiment – like Machiavelli's lone prince and Hobbes' solitary individual in a hostile world – makes virtue irrelevant to the human condition.

Should the individual be the starting point from which we survey the human condition? Should virtue be discounted because it is so often at odds with individual self-interest? For all his skepticism, Machiavelli seems to acknowledge that virtue exists. He counsels princes to take advantage of other people's virtue in a number of ways. First, the compunctions associated with the moral component of virtue limit or restrict most people's capacity to carry out the sometimes dirty business of politics. Princes – not burdened by such qualms – can easily get the best of others. Second, most people are so enmeshed in the moral constraints of their culture that they cannot even conceive of certain kinds of evil deeds. Princes can easily take advantage of this naivety – they are wolves (or perhaps foxy lions) among gullible sheep.

Finally, virtues are necessary, indeed essential, once princes establish modes and orders. Force, fraud, and fear are not the primary basis of communal life – dedication to the community is. Citizen-soldiers are needed to protect the community. Mercenaries are not dependable, but well-trained, self-disciplined, dedicated citizens can conquer the world, as the Romans did. One could almost say that it was the example of the Roman people's

11 David Hume, *An Enquiry Concerning the Principles of Morals*, ed. Schneewind, J. B. (Indianapolis, IN: Bobbs-Merrill, 1983), Section III, Part I.

virtuous dedication to their community that inspired Machiavelli's effort to remake the enervation and indolence he saw around him.

In order to discover human nature, Hobbes strips away all political institutions, social customs, and conventional mores. What is left (and cannot be removed) is human nature. Since we all have bodies, desires, passions, needs, fears, and ambitions, there is some truth to the individualism that Hobbes reveals. Hobbes' extremism is the result of a thought experiment that focuses death – or fear of death, the most definitive human emotion. Death, Hobbes says, shows that we are alone in the universe with only our desires and ability to calculate how to fulfill the desires to protect us from extinction. The human condition is one of perpetual effort to avoid death and suffering while seeking longevity and pleasure.

Hobbes' assertion that we seek "power after to power" to gratify our desires seems overstated. As we have seen, temperance is natural to humans. Temperance is so common that it is an almost forgotten virtue. Without temperance, we would be little more than mindless beasts seeking to gratify the most immediate bodily sensations. As Rousseau shows by the example of feral children, people who seek to indulge passion after passion are neither happy nor human.

People who are perpetually intemperate feel terrible about themselves, as if their lives were not their own. People recovering from addiction go to meetings to share stories about their unhappy situation under the influence of drugs or alcohol. They are happy when they become temperate because intemperance means that their desires, not themselves, are in command. Nature seems to direct us away from mere gratification and makes us unhappy when we are enslaved by our desires. Since human beings are the only species that can resist its physical desires, every society places restrictions on them and trains people to discipline themselves. To be human is to feel more than animal desires. ·

Death may be the signal event in human existence, but anyone who has been close to death knows that Hobbes' description of the way it influences the human psyche is only partly correct. If sickness is to be what sends us to our final rest, most people are more worried about pain and suffering than about their actual demise; illness robs us of our spirit. Infirmity also fills us not so much with anxiety as with a kind of torpor. When we are ill, we do not seek the company of others, either in fear or joy – we are miserably alone in our suffering. We give almost no care to our appearance; bathing, combing our hair, or brushing our teeth seem to be too much effort. But as soon as we start feeling better, we quickly want to become presentable. In fact, experienced nurses force their patients to practice what they call "the activities of daily living," knowing that normal routines make patients feel better. It is almost as if our personal sense of well-being is tied up with how we are perceived by others. Making ourselves presentable gives us a sense that we are back in command of our lives. Our concern for how we appear to others in part constitutes how we feel about ourselves.

Awareness of death also reminds us of our contingency and vulnerability. As Heidegger argues, human beings represent their "throwness" in tragic theater. Hobbes may be right that anxiety over scarcity causes people to compete and even clash, but the awareness that death is part of the human condition is also the source of compassion and a sense of limits. Because people have the capacity to put themselves in the place of others – to comprehend, if not experience directly, the travails of others – they can understand why they should limit their self-interested behavior. Even more, we perceive why there should be general rules of conduct against harmful behavior, such as laws against murder, theft, and unnecessary cruelty. Our attentiveness to our own fragility – and by extension to the contingency of others – is the reason why every community, almost as a definition of the term, makes such actions a crime.

Hobbes maintains that fear of death leads to all-out war. However, as Rousseau argues, individuals hardly ever struggle over necessities – or if they do, the battle is brief and rarely deadly. The root of intense conflict is pride and commitment to principles such as patriotism or religion. Human beings are much more apt to battle unto death when they believe in something worth fighting for. Conflict is lethal when people commit themselves to a principle beyond their physical well-being.

Lawler imagines a condition just the opposite of Hobbes' thought experiment, one based on the full conquest of death by biogenetic technology. Would Socrates have behaved virtuously, or even contemplated virtue, Lawler asks, if he knew he would not die? Quoting Francis Fukuyama, Lawler answers, "Probably not." Even Socrates would desperately cling to a life that could be terminated only by foolish or reckless behavior.[12] Since philosophy is based on the wonder of Being and non-Being, without the looming presence of death, there would be no wonder and no need for philosophy.

---

12 Lawler, *Stuck with Virtue*, 127. See also Francis Fukuyama, *Our Posthuman Future: Consequence of the Biotechnological Revolution* (New York: Farrar, Straus, and Giroux, 2002), 71.

It is not altogether clear whether an immortal Socrates would have given up philosophy, since he might still have felt compelled to wonder about the meaning of a long life. It might be true that a deathless Socrates would have submitted to Athens' demand that he stop philosophizing at age 70. However, it is doubtful – in line with the spirit of the thought experiment – whether the deathless citizens of would care what Socrates did at 71. The more important point is that human beings *are* contingent. They want to be part of, or participate in, something lasting, exactly because they are impermanent. For most people, as Lawler points out, the human longing for eternity manifests as religious belief, and along with religion come moral dictates. Other people find it enough to lead a good life of virtue. For a very few, the quest to understand the meaning of life makes them behave in a virtuous manner. We are stuck with virtue.

As for Hume, perhaps one good thought experiment deserves another. As I have written elsewhere, the absurdist playwright Havel constructs a society without morals or virtues.[13] Havel based *The Beggar's Opera* on a 1728 play of the same name by John Gay. In Gay's work, the main character, Macheath, is an amoral manipulator who uses charm to deceive his lovers for lewd and reprehensible ends. The young women he seduces are disgraced in the eyes of society.[14] In Havel's play, everyone is amoral. Fathers counsel daughters to use sexual wiles to spy on foes. Mothers encourage daughters to conceive out-of-wedlock children in order to manipulate opponents. Everyone steals and cheats. The police are more corrupt than the criminals; in fact, they are the leaders of the underworld syndicate. All the characters are motivated exclusively by self-interest. They think nothing of morals, because morals do not exist.[15] As Havel's biographer, John Keane, explains:

> ...selfishness is 'reality,' and...the system encourages and depends upon chronic lying, double-crossing, back-stabbing, trickery, the greedy pursuit of self-interest as it is defined at that particular moment. To act in contrary ways – for instance,

13 James F. Pontuso, *Václav Havel: Civic Responsibility in the Postmodern Age* (Lanham, MD: Rowman & Littlefield, 2004).

14 John Gay, *The Beggar's Opera*, Electronic Text Center, University of Virginia Library, http://etext.lib.virginia.edu/modeng/modeng0.browse.html (first published 1728) 1765 Edition.

15 Václav Havel, *The Beggar's Opera*, trans. Paul Wilson, intro. Peter Steiner (Ithaca: Cornell University Press, 2001).

to embrace precepts like honesty or care for others – would amount to pure foolishness.[16]

If there really were no virtues, and if self-interest were the only human motivation, the intrigue in Havel's play would be an accurate depiction of the real world. But Havel's work is absurd and is intended to make the audience wonder why people are not always self-interested. The play is a thought experiment intended to show the unreality of an amoral world. No human society has ever existed or could ever exist under the conditions in *The Beggar's Opera*. The simplest communication between people would be impossible, because language is an agreement that words have a particular meaning. Parents' self-interest would lead them to abandon their children. Without nurture, children would die an early death.

Even the worst totalitarian societies required that the populace practice moral restraint. Since we have no example of a thoroughly amoral society of the sort Havel imagines, can we surmise that moral virtue is somehow natural. Can we not say that human existence is constructed in such a way as to give humans an awareness of virtue? Havel's absurd play is not:

> an expression of a loss of faith....Quite the opposite, only someone whose being thirsts after meaning…can experience the absence of meaning as something painful…. The experience of absurdity is inseparable from the experience of meaning; it is merely, in a manner of speaking, its obverse."[17]

Hume is perhaps correct to point out that if we lived in a condition of uninterrupted plenty or unremitting scarcity we would not practice virtue. But almost everywhere people live in a middling condition between poverty and plenty. In the actual world, virtues are needed and therefore practiced. Moreover, the history of societies where law and justice have broken down shows that it is precisely in extreme cases where people go to extraordinary lengths to reestablish some order and some form of justice.

16 John Keane, *Václav Havel: A Political Tragedy in Six Acts* (New York: Basic Books, 2000), 235–36.
17 Václav Havel, *Letters to Olga*, trans. Paul R. Wilson (New York: H. Holt, 1989), 177.

Nature and Virtue

What do we mean by human nature? How is nature a guide for human conduct? People are not like the rest of nature because the rest of nature cannot reflect on the naturalness of its behavior. Natural does not mean spontaneous, for human beings usually consider what to do before they act. The fact that humans wonder about their nature means that they are free from the arrangement that determines the behavior of all other things. As Aristotle says, humans are not like bees, although they are social.[18] Nature does not act on humans the way it does on other animals. We can defy even our most powerful urges. Human nature cannot be grasped the way scientists understand the laws of nature – as something invariable or governed by mathematical regularity. Humans have free will and can choose not to follow rules. Even if we could discover laws governing human conduct, once they became known, people would be free to ignore or in some way alter them. We always remain above and beyond nature's control. As Lawler suggests, scientists hoping to unlock the mysteries of human existence by figuring out the human genome will succeed only at giving human beings more power and command over their lives, making the issue of what to do with life all the more difficult.[19]

For the most part, contemporary opinion concerning human nature is divided among those who believe that humans are (1) determined by their interests and desires; (2) formed by their social milieu; (3) free to choose what they will make of themselves, and thus, capable of constructing their own identity through an act of will; or (4) unable to decipher the "truth" about the meaning of life and required to decide their own destiny. Economists simultaneously hold the first and third of these propositions, and postmodernists the second and fourth, but this fact does not seem to bother their respective proponents. How can human beings be both determined *and* free?

Aristotle might be assumed to agree with those who argue that humans are determined when he states that the city "is prior by nature to the household and to each of us."[20] Human beings have long gestation periods and vulnerable toddler years. They do not have fangs or claws. Human survival relies on group action. Since individuals are incapable of surviving on their

---

18 Aristotle, *Politics*, 1253a 8. See also James Bernard Murphy, "Nature Custom and Reason as the Explanatory and Practical Principles of Aristotelian Political Science," 64, *The Review of Politics* (Summer 2002): 469–95.

19 Lawler, *Stuck with Virtue*, 45–71.

20 Aristotle, *Politics*, 1253a 19.

own, the group must have preceded the individual. At some point, primitive people developed speech to help coordinate their actions. Along with speech came rules necessary for communal living.

Yet this social origin does not fully determine our human trajectory. Speech gives humans the capacity to reason, making it possible for them to think outside, even contrary to the norms of their group. Humans are both molded by their social setting and free to alter or escape it. Aristotle calls humans political, not social, animals, meaning they control part of their fate.

The latest social science studies seem to support Aristotle's view that humans are inclined toward sociability, not individualism. Studies done by Felix Warneken at the Max Planck Institute of Evolutionary Anthropology indicate that toddlers as young as 18 months understand other people's goals and seem to enjoy helping fulfill them, especially when another person is in need. This concern for others seems to be part of the human condition even before a child has fully acquired either a language or the ability to demonstrate complex moral reasoning. Warneken explains that children's capacity to empathize is a "pro-social motivation," a desire to be part of their community.[21] Put more simply, children think it is fun to help adults.

Social life defines certain categories of behavior that individuals must internalize if they are to become human. Children who are not socialized never seem quite human. Some loners who cut themselves off from others exhibit a tendency to commit heinous crimes, as is predicted in stunning fashion in Fyodor Dostoyevsky's *Notes from the Underground*.

Codes of human conduct are not like physics, so strict rules cannot be unalterably applied. Humans have volition and are able to accept or reject requests. If the demands of virtue were absolutely clear, people would stop being human, since there would be no choices. The best we can expect is that through interaction with others, nature makes people aware of virtue, and perhaps, as Aristotle suggests, gives them a sense of accomplishment or happiness when they live up to nature's requirements.

People usually learn about virtue as children, a time of weakness, dependence, and need. Our vulnerability at such times makes us aware of the need for standards of conduct since we are the ones most likely to be hurt

---

21   Felix Warneken and Michael Tomasello, "Altruistic Helping in Human Infants and Young Chimpanzees," *Science* 311 (3 March 2006): 1301–03. See also Nigel Barber, *Kindness in a Cruel World: The Evolution of Altruism* (Amherst, NY: Prometheus Books: 2004) and Leonard D. Katz, ed., *Evolutionary Origins of Morality* (Bowling Green, OH: Imprint Academic, 2000).

by their absence. It should not be surprising that teenagers, feeling less at risk, discard the lessons of youth to test their independence or power. Children born into a culture of privilege and wealth who do not feel vulnerable sometimes have more difficulty adjusting to social constraints than do children from poorer circumstances. Mistreated children, regardless of class, can spend their lives confused and anxious, as if they do not know how to live well. They seem always to be searching for some formula – a better self-help book, perhaps – to guide them through life. Humans want to be trained in virtue.

Alan Dershowitz posits an interesting theory about how the human race learned right from wrong. He argues that although it is often difficult to know exactly what is right, we do seem to have a sense of things that are wrong. Even more, we are acutely aware when an injustice or slight is done to us. From our experience of past wrongs, we derive rules to protect ourselves from further injustices or injury. Despite the fact that "few people really care whether *other* people or groups are treated equally so long as they themselves come out on or near the top," Dershowitz maintains that some events in our lives have gone so horribly wrong that we learn the wisdom of protecting ourselves from them.[22]

Dershowitz argues that the only yardstick of right and wrong is experience; we keep what works and discard what does not. This is an odd supposition. We would not know what to keep and what to throw away unless we already had some idea of what was good and bad. What makes us capable of making such judgments is a capacity to understand the meaning of our own experience. We know when injustice is done to us, and we generalize from this experience to others.

Abraham Lincoln claimed, for example, that he could prove slavery was wrong, not because white people had experienced the practice, but on principle. No one, he would say, addressing a pro-slavery audience, wants to be a slave. A universally held opinion must have some truth. Lincoln attempted to show the injustice of slavery by putting defenders of the peculiar institution in the position of slaves.

Perhaps self-interest is the strongest motive in the human species, but generosity and responsibility are present, too, exactly because we can put ourselves into the position of other people. Why, after all, does Dershowitz care enough to write books about protecting rights if he does not think it necessary to influence other people about what is right?

22 Dershowitz, *Rights from Wrongs*, 25.

Practical experience alone is never sufficient for making qualitative judgments. As is the case with all progressive historicists, Dershowitz commends the things he likes about contemporary society; he calls them an inevitable development of social advancement. And he rejects things he does not like, insisting that evolution will triumph over backward practices. Unless Dershowitz is capable of knowing what future generations will decide is beneficial, he has no idea what customs they might choose to maintain and which they will discard. If we follow the logic of his argument, some future society might abandon Dershowitz's cherished natural rights, finding them and the democracy in which they developed disruptive to public order. Would Dershowitz accept this future as good simply because a future society found it functional?

Dershowitz, like most people, has an idea of what is proper. As puts it, "Face to face with the distillation of evil, man might well recognize what is good."[23] What creates these ideas about the proper, good, and virtuous is not fully clear. It seems to be a combination of our vulnerability, our sociability, our ability to put ourselves in the place of others (empathy), and our capacity to make and comprehend general of rules of conduct.

Virtue is practiced both for ourselves and for others. If we ignore either part of the equation, virtue becomes a self-gratifying show or a self-abnegating and unwelcome burden. In any case, living up to high standards of conduct makes us pleased with ourselves. To paraphrase Benjamin Franklin, if we were humble about our virtues, we would be proud of that.[24]

Harvey C. Mansfield argues that manly virtue wants to be admired and looked up to; the manly assertion of strength or valor seeks not merely to be recognized but singled out. "Admiration is quite different from sympathy or compassion for someone's suffering. Admiration makes you look up to someone in control, compassion makes you look down to someone in distress," he says.[25] Yet it is a strange element of virtue that it contains aspects

---

23 Václav Havel, *Disturbing the Peace: A Conversation with Karel Hv   ala*, trans. and intro. Paul Wilson (New York: Knopf, 1990), 199.

24 Jerry Weinberger, *Benjamin Franklin Unmasked: On the Unity of His Moral, Religious, and Political Thought* (Lawrence, KS: University Press of Kansas, 2005), 133. According to Weinberger, Franklin believed that God did not exist, religion was superstition, and moral principles were merely longings of the human psyche, unfulfilled in this life or the next. Weinberger's biography argues that neither God nor nature support the human good; all evaluative judgments are assertions of the will; and virtues do not exist. Things just happen, as in physics.

25 Harvey C. Mansfield, *Manliness* (New Haven, CT: Yale University Press, 2006), 18.

of both selfish assertion and selfless sacrifice. Mansfield uses the Gary Cooper character in the motion picture *High Noon* as an example of manly virtue. However, if Marshal Will Kane were only to assert his strength, he might be admired and feared, but he would be no different from the hired killers menacing the town. Kane feels a sense of compassion for the defenseless townspeople, even if they do not deserve it. Even more, his manly virtue makes him feel responsible for the safety of his young wife, who is especially at risk because of her breath-taking beauty.

As Shakespeare dramatically shows in *Coriolanus*, even the most courageous man has no place to exhibit his virtue without a community. Coriolanus wants the Romans' admiration, but he cannot abide their pettiness. Once he breaks with , he is left with manly assertion but with neither admiration nor virtue. The Romans hate him because he is a traitor, and the Volscesans hate and distrust him because he is a traitor *and* an enemy.

Virtue derives from the awareness of standards of human conduct. If we strive to live up to those standards, we can act for the good of others even as we feel good about ourselves. It is like "taking one for the team." We sacrifice ourselves for the good of the organization, but we feel a certain pride in having done so.

Nature and Convention

Since people must be socialized to become fully human, whatever nature they have is expressed through the particular family, region, religion, country, and culture in which they are raised. Even the most basic human activities are structured by social rules. Humans eat, but what they eat and the manners surrounding how they eat are influenced by the society where they eat. Rituals accompany birth, mating, marriage, and death. It is a common human practice for people to greet each other. But specific greetings differ. Americans shake hands, the French kiss lightly on both cheeks, and the Japanese bow.

Virtues are expressed differently in particular cultures. Sparta's lawgiver, Lycurgus, had a different conception of virtue than did Solon, the founder of Athens' democracy. Cultures differ about which virtues are most important and what specific actions are considered virtuous. But this should not be surprising, since societies evolve under different material, economic, political, and military conditions. To observe the same conventions under different conditions would not only be imprudent, it would not be the most efficient way to foster virtue. Moreover, volition is always involved in implementing virtues.

Historically, the most influential factor in defining virtue is religion because religion defines what is right and wrong. For its followers, any religion is unconditionally true. God created the world and provided people with instructions through acts of merciful revelation. Religion is foundational; for a true believer there can be no compromise of principles. This is how religion causes conflict between people. God seems to have revealed different truths to different religious groups at different times and to have given conflicting information about which one He prefers – which one is "the true religion."

To use the most obvious example: A pious Muslim – imitating Mohammed rather than following a mandate of the Koran – can have up to four wives. A pious Jew or Christian can have only one. The effect of this practice influences the status of women in a society and, in fact, the dynamic of the whole culture. As Tocqueville argues, equality of conditions does not contradict the fundamental tenets of Christianity, although it does undermine the social practices of the Old Regime. The Old Regime was a patriarchy in practice, but Christianity is not necessarily patriarchal in principle. In order to maintain polygamy, however, Muslim countries that have modeled their customs on Mohammed's example cannot admit the equality of human beings so long as they maintain polygamy. Men must have authoritative status to control the dynamics of plural marriage. Moreover, plural marriage inevitably creates a shortage of marriageable women and thereby a pool of unmarried and unattached young men. Men without familial connections tend to join a cause that gives them a sense of belonging. It is little wonder, then, that Islamic countries are home to fundamentalist religious movements. Membership in these groups is made up overwhelmingly of young men who are hostile – sometimes violently so – to the principles of equality of condition and individual freedom practiced predominantly in Western (Christian) societies. By banning polygamy in Turkey, Mustafa Kemal Atatürk established the most successful liberal democracy in the Islamic world.

We almost always think of the Enlightenment as an intellectual movement aimed at liberating people from superstition, ignorance, and poverty. But the more immediate motivation of the philosophers who launched the Enlightenment was to rid the world of sectarian violence. The religious wars of caused innumerable deaths, displaced whole populations, and almost destroyed the fabric of society. If Hobbes and John Locke were not openly hostile to religion, it was because they realized that people inevitably make value judgments about their own and others' actions. The philosophers hoped to displace notions of right and wrong with the concept of rights. The word *rights* is a brilliant stroke of misdirection, for it means that it is right to believe anything you want and wrong to deny others the same latitude. The concept of natural rights was intended to stop the battles over right and wrong. If taken to their logical conclusion, rights would have become the mechanism for eliminating conflict among different cultures over the concepts of virtue and morality. Locke especially wanted to make protecting rights a virtue. He hoped to make people take the primacy of rights so seriously that they would make a spirited defense of their own and other people's life liberty, and property.[26]

The effort to ground codes of conduct in natural rights has resulted in the contemporary view that there are no standards of right and wrong. Moral codes are decided by each autonomous individual. As Vigen Guroian points out, when people begin with the supposition that the self is the center of the universe, they have already concluded that all communal relationships and practices are merely conventional – or "epiphenomena at best."[27] Therefore, rights-based societies tend to think of individuals as detached from the myriad social relations in which they live. Such societies are reluctant to grant authority to any entity that limits citizens' autonomy. Rights-based societies dismiss the pull of virtue, which almost always limits the self in relation to others.

But this explanation tells only half the story. Most people believe that right and wrong exist. Common sense tells them that there is a difference between courage and cowardice. People know when those around them fail to fulfill their civic or familial responsibilities. What Enlightenment principles have done is slowly erode the *intellectual justification* for nature's virtue. The Enlightenment raised the standard of proof for providing a justification. Something is true only when it passes scientific muster. Scientific truth is based on laws and on a regularity of behavior best expressed in mathematical formulas. But human behavior is ultimately grounded in volition and choice. While the rest of nature follows regular laws, humans must choose the laws that regulate their behavior. Those who best understand the principles of the Enlightenment – intellectuals – are most dubious about the "foundation" of

---

26 John Locke, *A Letter Concerning Toleration*, ed. James H. Tully (Indianapolis, IN: Hackett Publishing, 1983). See also Robert P. Kraynak, "John Locke, from Absolutism to Toleration," *American Political Science Review* 74 (March 1980): 53–69.
27 Vigen Guroian, *Ethics after Christendom* (Grand Rapids, MI: William B. Eerdmans, 1994), 19.

virtue. Those less affected by the ideas of the Enlightenment are more apt to give credence to the "natural," but not scientific, inclination to virtue.

Skeptics argue that deciding what is right is too complicated. There are always competing goods that must be considered. This is true enough. Yet it is also true that virtues can be recognized. For example, no one would call people courageous if they run away from danger, leaving their family or compatriots in harm's way. We might understand what they did. We might even condone it. But we would not call it courage. No one would call a father who spends his children's college funds on drugs responsible. We may pity him. We may recognize his compulsions. But, responsible – never.

Virtues are practiced in many different ways. For example, it is hard to imagine two societies more different than Homer's Greece and modern America. Achaeans were war-loving people whose primary occupation was plunder. Martial valor was esteemed above all other human qualities, and almost no distinction was made between reckless spiritedness and prudent courage. Americans are a commercial people who believe that wars are fought to maintain the peace and who would rather make a deal than make a fracas. There were, of course, commercial Achaeans, as there are soldierly Americans. But the societies esteem different types of people. Achaeans and Americans are unlike, but this does not mean that they have no virtues in common. Most Americans think it unfair that CEOs make 262 times more than average workers.[28] Achilles thought it unfair that Agamemnon stole his prized concubine, Briseis. To judge something unfair, it is necessary to have some idea of what fairness is. The definition of justice may be different, but the desire to achieve justice and its importance as a motivator in human life are the same. Justice exists as an idea, as much a part of the human condition as love, hate, envy, pride and other emotions.

There are many examples of the forms/ideas influencing our judgment as to right and wrong, noble and base, just and unjust. To point out just a few:

The Biblical story of Abraham and Isaac is dramatic because it seems unnatural for God to ask a virtuous man to kill his son. It is as if we know innately what is *natural;* it precedes God's commands.[29]

---

28   MSN Money staff, "CEOs near record on pay ratios," *MSN Online,* 7 July 2006, http://articles.moneycentral.msn.com/Investing/Extra/CEOsNearRecordPayRatios.aspx?GT1=8380.

29   Thomas L. Pangle, *Political Philosophy and the God of Abraham* (Baltimore, MD: The Johns Hopkins University Press, 2003).

The media uses examples of parents killing their children to show that no outrage is beyond human doing. The widespread news coverage that usually follows such acts also indicates that there is an intrinsic revulsion at this heartless "unnatural" behavior.

The quest for "social justice" is a kind of virtue for people who do not believe in virtue. The social justice doctrine holds that people are equal not because they share an understanding of the metaphysical principle of human dignity, but because no one has a claim to be treated differently than anyone else.[30] Most contemporary advocates of social justice reject any principle that privileges one group or person's values over another. They repudiate the idea of virtue, especially the principle that justice is giving all people their due. To admit such a principle would suggest that the inegalitarian social arrangements prevalent in every known society might be natural and perhaps, at least in part, an indication of merit. But advocates of social justice are not interested in what they perceive in the present, including the range of abilities among individuals and groups. They are interested in the past and the future. The past is important because it is full of injustices that justify – indeed, mandate – reforms in the future.

Post-colonial studies make a virtue out of weakness or perceived past injustice. While advocates of post-colonial studies nearly always attack foundationalism as a surreptitious effort by the dominant group to assert the power over the dispossessed, they also assert a form of justice. It is unjust that white European men seem to have all the power.

Skeptics always say that justice does not prevail because people are self-interested, culturally biased, and prejudiced by their class, region, or gender. But how do they know what is unjust without a concept of the just? Did not the skeptics offer a perfect form of justice? To make a just decision, a person should not be self-interested or biased by culture, class, region, or gender. The form of justice is quite clear, but the particulars depend on the circumstances. Ironically, the people most pessimistic about human virtue have the strongest sense of virtue – no one can live up to their high standards. Pessimists are the most idealistic naysayers.

Aristotle's *Ethics* emphasizes (*kalon*) the noble or beautiful as the goal of moral virtue. We come close to Aristotle's sense of the word in sports reporting when we say, "What a beautiful play!" We mean that the athlete, in playing the game as it is meant to be played, did something extraordinary

---

30 See Weinberger, *Benjamin Franklin Unmasked*, 251 for an analysis of Franklin's non-foundational egalitarianism.

that stands out. We have an image or idea of what is supposed to be done, even though we have never seen a specific example. In the modern world, we hardly ever apply this concept to the virtues, because our culture, the mediated reality in which we live, no longer accepts the ideas that humans have a particular purpose or that some people achieve that purpose more successfully than others. Yet when we see extraordinary acts of virtue, we cannot help but respond– as if our nature rebels against our heartless and unnatural ethos.

Virtue and Philosophic Distance

Machiavelli presents the virtues from the perspective of a prince intimately and personally involved in a political struggle. It is little wonder that he dismisses virtue, for it is hard to judge fairly when one's interests are at stake. In order to discover human nature, Hobbes imagines a battleground in which only one's self interest is at issue. Our rights-based culture places the self-regarding individual at the center of reasoning about values. On the other hand, Aristotle looks at the virtues from the perspective of an observer uninvolved in the issue at hand. This distance makes it possible for people to deliberate fairly in particular cases. We would not expect the relatives of a defendant to sit on a jury and administer unbiased justice.

Adam Smith attempts to encourage a philosophic distance by proposing that human beings judge their actions as if an impartial spectator were observing their behavior. He claims that if self-interest were the only source of motivation, people would never care about their fellow human beings. Although self-interest is the source of most human behavior, it is not the only one. Smith reasons that people worry about the opinions of others. When they act, they calculate how their action will be viewed by others. It is as if our minds look at our actions as unbiased outsiders would. We calculate the costs and benefits of how an action might be perceived.[31]

Smith's account of virtue has a few problems.[32] We cannot know what an impartial observer expects of us unless we have some idea of what virtue and morality are. It is difficult to apply virtue in a particular circumstance

---

31 Adam Smith, *The Theory of Moral Sentiments* (Amherst, NY, Prometheus Books, 2000), 192.

32 Joan Tronto, "Adam Smith on Natural Liberty: Social Distance and the Sublimation of Politics," paper delivered at the American Political Science Association Convention, New Orleans, 1985.

because to do so it is necessary to know what all the attributes of the virtue, including the qualifications and difficulties of the pure form of the thing. We must abstract from the mediated, socially conditioned expression of the virtue of our own culture. We must then understand the particular circumstances to which the virtue is being applied and how best to apply it. Finally, we must understand how the mores of the society inhibit our ability to apply the pure form of virtue if doing so might create a social harm.

As Smith suggests, we need distance or perspective to judge the phenomenon fairly. First, if we are a party to the event, our self-interest clouds our judgment. Moreover, our understanding of what is noble, just, and proper is partly constructed by the society and laws where we live. To know what truly is virtuous, we must overcome our cultural bias. For example, Smith laments that some customs perpetuate cruelty toward others. He is particularly critical of ancient societies that regularly practiced infanticide, which he labels a "dreadful…violation of humanity…so gross it cannot be tolerated."[33] This condemnation contradicts Smith's assertion that people receive their moral compass from the praise of the wider society. If a society adopts such customs, why would not they praise those who follow them? Would not the influence of custom be the arbiter of whether these practices are considered dreadful?

Socrates' constant questions are an effort, in the language of our time, to "deconstruct" the mediated reality of Greek culture. Socrates attempts to unravel what is true from what is true only for Greeks. He also examines the pre-philosophic notions that we all have about non-material principles (love, friendship, justice, courage) to explore the contours, qualifications, and complexities of the phenomena.

Heidegger, too, sought distance from convention, to break free of the tradition of Western metaphysics:

> But suppose that denial itself had to become the highest and most austere revealing of Being? What then? Understood from out of metaphysics (i.e., out of the question of Being, in the form What is it to be?), the concealment essence of Being, denial, unveils itself first of all as absolutely not-having-being, as Nothing. But Nothing as that Nothing which pertains to the having-of-being is the keenest opponent of mere negating, Nothing is never

---

33   Adam Smith, *The Theory of Moral Sentiments* (Amherst, NY, Prometheus Books, 2000), 308.

nothing; it is just as little a something, in the sense of an object....it is Being itself, whose truth will be given over to man when he has overcome himself as subject, and as a means when he no longer represents that which is an object.[34]

Heidegger's philosophic detachment is more radical than Socrates'. What practical expectations does this idea of confrontation with nothing give us? How will this new revelation of Being influence us? True, we might develop a different view of the relationship between people and nature, but do we have to destroy Western Culture in order to change it? Are there not elements within Enlightenment philosophy that are open to alteration and change? For example, the environmental movement wants to protect the planet, not turn it into a standing reserve, and it is an outgrowth of Western metaphysics.

Leslie Paul Thiele argues that Heidegger does not long for a "millennial epiphany," but instead proposes "responsible dwelling in the world" while waiting to "attain...the outer border of the place where 'the God of gods' appears."[35] Thiele maintains that Heidegger hopes to inculcate "responsibility to otherness" and not "responsibility to act." Openness to the other precludes enforcing "Western patterns" on others in the age of globalization and democratization. As evidence of this point, Thiele offers a commentary on "Oxherding Pictures," meant to inspire people to be nonjudgmental. They should not esteem "particular doctrines or traditions" and cease "to differentiate between enlightenment and non-enlightenment."[36]

What kind of unenlightened people does Thiele want to encourage? Would he be tolerant of those without temperance, conscience, or virtue? For example, when I taught in Iraq, there were honor killings of women accused of infidelity. Iraqi students asked me what I thought. According to Thiele's principles (or lack of principles), I should have been open to the ways of the other. As much as it is unfair to claim to know more about an author than he does, I doubt whether Thiele means what he says. He, like me, would not be open to the other and would deem such practices barbaric.

---

34 Martin Heidegger, "The Age of World Picture," in *The Question Concerning Technology and Other Essays*, trans. William Lovit (New York: Harper & Row, 1977), 154.

35 Martin Heidegger, *Elucidation of Hölderin's Poetry*, trans. Keith Hoeller (Amherst. NY: Humanity Books, 2000), 224.

36 Leslie Paul Thiele, *Timely Meditations: Martin Heidegger and Postmodern Politics* (Princeton, NJ: Princeton University Press, 1995), 248–250.

Before we applaud Heidegger for his openness or Thiele for his acceptance of non-Western ways, we might ask, as Edmund Burke once did, how such ideas are to be:

> combined with government, with public force, with the discipline and obedience of armies, with the collection of an effective and well-distributed revenue, with morality and religion, with the solidity of property, with peace and order, with civil and social manners.[37]

As is seen in the *Apology*, Socrates' philosophic disengagement does not mean he dismisses civic responsibility. During his trial, Socrates refers to his role as a member of the jury at the trial of the generals accused of violating Athenian law by not recovering bodies of slain soldiers at the battle of Arginusae.[38] In that instance, Socrates faced a number of choices. He could have agreed with the people's pious outrage against the generals, protecting himself from their wrath. But to do so would have been unjust. In the middle of a storm, the intensity of which was unknown to the Athenians until after the danger passed, the generals behaved prudently. They acted according to the dictates of necessity to keep the fleet and Athens itself safe from disaster.

Socrates is not affected by religious sentiment and is aware that it is unwise for a country to kill its officer corps in the middle of a major war. It is also problematic to second-guess military leaders in critical situations. What general will act boldly for the good of Athens if he knows he might be put to death once the crisis has passed? Socrates could also have attacked religion and (given his considerable rhetorical skills and the sophomoric character of the Greek deities), he might have been able to challenge and undermine the religious enthusiasm that was threatening the generals.

Instead of attacking customary morality or abandoning his principles, Socrates finds another option. He defends the generals based on a legal technicality: precedent dictates that the defendants should be tried separately. The rule would not have saved the first general, but the bloodletting would have assuaged the people's fervor and might have saved the rest. Socrates did not attempt to undermine belief in the gods, because virtue is always

---

37 Edmund Burke, *Reflections on the Revolution in France*, Constitution Society, http://www.constitution.org/eb/rev_fran.htm.
38 Plato, Apology, 32a-d.

expressed within a particular community. For most people, belief in the gods is the source of virtue, civic or otherwise. Would Socrates have improved Athens if he had destroyed religion – the social bonds that kept it together?

Mansfield's analysis of Machiavelli's virtue makes us think of Aristotle's magnanimous man. He is unmoved by small matters, but rises for great occasions – in Machiavelli's case, redirecting the course of Western civilization. The magnanimous man seeks honor, and although he will accept it from anyone, he enjoys it only when it comes from the noble. He is generous, but distant, never making a show of his prowess. In fact, he almost conceals it to make it more extraordinary. He is reserved and remote from the concerns of ordinary people – a valuable perspective from which to examine and evaluate their actions. Yet this very remoteness from others, while providing a broader viewpoint, seems to have made the magnanimous Machiavelli ignore the longings, motivations, and perceptions of ordinary people. Aloofness can make people immune to contingency, weakness, and to the awareness that others are contingent and needy. Machiavelli's virtue places him beyond everyday social life that is so much a part of human existence.

It is a kind of philosophic blasphemy to judge someone with Machiavelli's power of mind. Yet there is something pathetic about Machiavelli's detachment. He was said to have dressed up in his finest cloths and, alone, converse with imaginary friends – the great philosophers of antiquity. The same distance that enables philosophy to judge practices without cultural bias can cause philosophers to forget the phenomena of social life – including its inevitable tendency for human beings to make judgments about the good and bad, the noble and base, and all the other virtues. Is the problematic nature of philosophic distance what made Socrates to go on a second sailing, a sailing that landed him in the midst of Athens and its ordinary people, which he refused to leave even at the cost of his life?

Leo Strauss reminds us that "to philosophize is to be conscious of the absolute transitoriness of *all* that is human, but at the same time as if one had all eternity at one's disposal, to search for the truth."[39] Those familiar with Strauss' work know that he sometimes writes in a manner intended to cause his readers wonder. Should Strauss' statement be read to indicate the transitory character of life, or of philosophy, or of Being, or of Strauss' statement? How can Strauss' observation be true if all things are transitory?

---

39   Quoted in Heinrich Meier, *Leo Strauss and the Theologico-Political Problem* (Cambridge: Cambridge University Press, 2006), 2.

Philosophers do not seem to present their ideas as transitory. Quite the opposite; they almost unanimously give advice about what is true and worth choosing. After all, even the anti-foundationalists argue that the truth is that there is no truth. Heidegger maintains that we *should* be open to Being giving us a sign of its meaning.

Is Strauss accusing some philosophers of not understanding the character of philosophy? Or is Strauss arguing that philosophers disguise their advice as the truth out of fear that ordinary people will discover how fleeting all human creations are? What would motivate so many philosophers to take this tack? Why do they employ the dangerous strategy of devaluing traditional morals by proposing higher, purer concepts of virtue? If they are concerned only for their safety, as Nietzsche argues in *The Genealogy*, would it not be wiser to act as the Stoics did – to seek a safe place and hide? Even if philosophers conceal their ideas using esoteric writing, they still expose themselves to the envy and distrust of defenders of custom.

The other alternative is that they seek a truth that is not transitory. Along with other human beings, they search for a connection with the infinite. They offer instruction on the virtues because the longing for these attributes is so common and the practice so noble, if rare. Perhaps truth and virtue are merely ideals, but they are principles so universal that they cannot be ignored.

Life is a constant tension between the poles of the transitory and the permanent – becoming and being. To trust that we can know with finality the truth can make us self-righteous and blind to life's complexities.[40] But surrender to Heidegger's no-thingness leads to apathy. Being discloses itself to us only partially. We get a hint of what is proper and fitting, but not a roadmap. If we were given too little, we might act like Hobbes' solitary combatants in the state of nature.

Virtues are human longings present in our lives exactly because they are not – in Heidegger's language – ready-at-hand. Virtues are ideals towards which we aspire. If life came with directions, we would lose our freedom – we would *know* what is right. However, if we knew exactly what to do, we would no longer have Dasein. We would be enveloped by the "thingness" that shrouds the rest of existence. If were given too much, there would be no choice and therefore no freedom or dignity. We would lose our consciousness and become like animals who act on instinct.[41]

40   Plato, *Meno* 100b.
41   Havel, *Letters to Olga*, 152. 342–43.

It is doubtless true that much of what we know as true is culturally determined. We live in a mediated reality because humans must create their societies. Nature dictates that we live together, but it does not provide regulations about *how* we should do that. In pushing us into life surrounded by other people, nature forces us to consider their views, needs, and concerns. Even the desire to promote our own interests within a group of equally self-interested beings compels us to think beyond our own narrow perspective and construct general rules of behavior. It is almost as natural for human beings to make value judgments about their own and other people's behavior as it is for them to eat. Those judgments are the foundation of nature's virtue.

Does nature command us to seek virtue? Command implies domination, but the diversity and complexity of human behavior indicates that we are not easily swayed. It might be better to say that nature beckons to us, and we are free to accept or reject the invitation. Nature's virtue does not call to us loudly, but it does call.

Bibliography

Acampora, Christa Davis, ed. *Nietzsche's On the Genealogy of Morals: Critical Essays*. Lanham, MD: Rowman & Littlefield, 2006 .

Achebe, Chinua. *Things Fall Apart*. London: Heinemann, 1958.

Al-Ghazali, Abu Hamid Muhammad. *The Incoherence of the Philosophers*. Translated by Michael E. Marmura. Provo, Utah: Brigham Young University, 2002.

Allison, David B. *Reading the New Nietzsche*. Lanham, MD: Rowman & Littlefield, 2000.

Antle, James. "Thanks to Rand Paul, libertarian politics is more popular than ever." *The Guardian*, March 18, 2013.

Antonio, Robert J. "Nietzsche's Antisociology: Subjectified Culture and the End of History." *The American Journal of Sociology* 101 (July 1995): 1–43.

Archdiocese. "What is virtue? Why is it important in the Christian life?" *Rediscover: Newsletter of The Archdiocese of Saint Paul and Minneapolis,*. Saint Paul and Minneapolis, MN, 2014.

Aristotle. *Metaphysics*.

—. *Nicomachean Ethics*. Translated by Joe Sachs. Newburyport, MA: Focus Publishing, 2002.

—. *The Politics*. Translated by Carnes Lord. Chicago: University of Chicago Press, 1984.

—. *The Rhetoric of Aristotle, an Expanded Translation with Supplementary Examples for Students of Composition and Public Speaking*. Translated by Lane Cooper. New York: D. Appleton and Company, 1932.

Arnhart, Larry. "Biopolitical Science." *Politics and Life Sciences* 29, no. 1 (March 2010): 24–47.

—. *Darwinian Conservatism*. Exeter: Imprint Academic, 2005.

—. *Darwinian Natural Right: The Biological Ethics of Human Nature*. Albany, NY: State University of New York Press, 1998.

Barber, Nigel. *Kindness in a Cruel World: The Evolution of Altruism*. Amherst, NY: Prometheus Books, 2004.

Benedict, XVI. "Three Stages in the Program of De-Hellenization." September 9, 2006. http://www.zenit.org/en/articles/papal-address-at-university-of-regensburg.

Blitz, Mark. "Reading Heidegger: A review of The Essence of Human Freedom and The Essence of Truth by Martin Heidegger." *Claremont Review of Books*, 2005 2005.

—. *Heidegger's Being and Time and the Possibility of Political Philosophy*. Ithaca, NY: Cornell University Press, 1981.

Blitz, Mark. "Virtue, Ancient and Modern." In *Educating the Prince: Essay in Honor of Harvey Mansfield*, edited by Mark Blitz and William Kristol, 3–17. Lanham, MD: Rowman & Littlefield, 2000.

Boethius. *The Consolation of Philosophy*. Translated by W. V. Cooper. Chicago: Regnery Gateway, 1981.

Boettke, Peter J. *Living Economics: Yesterday, Today, and Tomorrow*. Oakland, CA: The Independent Institute, 2012.

Bolotin, David. *Plato's Dialogue on Friendship: An Interpretation of the Lysis, with a New Translation*. Ithaca, NY: Cornell University Press, 1979.

Bowman, James. *Honor: A History*. New York: Encounter Books, 2006.

Brann, Eva. *Open Secrets/Inward Prospects: Reflections on World and Soul*. Philadelphia, PA: Paul Dry Books, 2004.

Brooks, David. *Bobos In Paradise: The New Upper Class and How They Got There*. New York: Simon & Schuster, 2001.

—. *The Social Animal: The Hidden Sources of Love, Character, and Achievement*. New York: Random House, 2011.

Brown, Donald E. *Human Universals*. Philadelphia, PA: Temple University Press, 1991.

Buchanan, James M. Jr. "The Constitution of Economic Policy." *Nobel Prize Lecture*. December 8, 1986.

Budziszewski, J. "A Vindication of the Politics of Virtues." *American Political Science Association*. New Orleans, 1985.

Burgin, Angus. *The Great Persuasion: Reinventing Free Markets since the Depression.* Cambridge, MA: Harvard University Press, 2012.

Burke, Edmund. *Reflections on the Revolution in France.* Edited by Jon Roland. Constitution Society. Austin, TX, 1790.

Burns, Jennifer. *Goddess of the Market: Ayn Rand and the American Right.* Oxford: Oxford University Press, 2011.

Busch, Michael. "Jeffrey Sachs's Metamorphosis From Neoliberal Shock Trooper to Bleeding Heart Hits a Snag." *Foreign Policy Focus*, January 22, 2012.

Bush, Jeb and Brian Yablonski. "Virtuous Reality: Character-Building in the Information Age." *Policy Review: The Journal of American Citizenship*, January-February 1996.

Campbell, David M. "Heidegger and Mind, Objects, and Virtue." *The Heythrop Journal* 50, no. 2 (February 2009): 271–83.

Campbell, David. "Nietzsche, Heidegger, and Meaning." *The Journal of Nietzsche Studies* 26 (Autumn 2003): 25–54.

Carter, Stephen L. *Civility: Manners, Morals, and the Etiquette of Democracy.* New York: Basic Books, 1998.

Chomsky, Noam. ""What We Know: On the Universals of Language and Rights"." *Boston Review* 30 (Summer 2005).

Cohen, Andrew Jason. "In Defense of Nietzschean Genealogy." *The Philosophic Forum* 30, no. 4 (December 1999): 269–288.

Cohen, Lenard J. "The Destruction of Yugoslavia." In *The National Idea in Eastern Europe*, edited by Gerasimos Augustinos. Lexington, MA: D.C. Heath, 1996.

"Conference on After Postmodernism." Chicago: University of Chicago, November 14–16, 1997.

Confucius. *Analects of Confucius.* Translated by James Legge. New York: Paragon Book Reprint Corp., [1893] 1966 .

Conly, Sarah. "Why Feminists Should Oppose Feminist Virtue Ethics." *Philosophy Now*, March/April 2014.

Conway, Daniel. *Nietzsche's 'On the Genealogy of Morals': A Reader's Guide .* New York: Continuum International Publishing Group, 2008.

Coyne, Christopher J. *Doing Bad by Doing Good: When Humanitarian Action Fails.* Stanford, CA: Stanford University Press, 2013.

Cropsey, Joseph. *Political Philosophy and the Issues of Politics.* Chicago: University of Chicago Press, 1977.

Danto, Arthur. *Nietzsche as Philosopher.* New York: MacMillan, 1965.

D'Aubigné, J. H. Merle. *History of the Great Reformation.* Vol. 1. Translated by Henry Beveridge. The Project Gutenberg EBook. London: R. Groombridge and Sons, [1845] 2012.

de Man, Paul. *Blindness and Insight: Essays in the Rhetoric of Contemporary Criticism.* Minneapolis, MN: University of Minnesota Press, 1983.

—. *The Resistance to Theory.* Minneapolis, MN: University of Minnesota Press, 1986.

Defoe, Daniel. *The Life and Strange Surprizing Adventures of Robinson Crusoe of York, Mariner.* London: Oxford University Press, (1719) 1972.

Derrida, Jacques. *Of Grammatology.* Translated by Gayatri Chakravorty Spivak. Baltimore, MD: Johns Hopkins University Press, 1976.

—. *Of Spirit: Heidegger and the Question.* Translated by Geoffery Bennington and Rachel Bowlby. Chicago: University of Chicago Press, 1989.

Dershowitz, Alan M. *Rights from Wrongs.* New York: Basic Books, 2005.

Dickens, Charles. *Bleak House.* An Electronic Classics Series Publication Classic. Edited by Jim Manis. Hazelton, PA: The Pennsylvania State University, 1999–2013.

Dostoyevsky, Fyodor. 1953. *The Devils (the Possessed).* Translated by David Magarshack. London: Penguin Books, 1953.

Drury, Shadia. *Alexandre Kojève: The Roots of Postmodern Politics.* New York: St. Martin's Press, 1994.

Esslin, Martin. *The Theatre of the Absurd.* London: Eyre & Spottiswoode, 1962.

Estrin, Saul, Kristy Hughes, and Sarah Todd. *Foreign Direct Investment in Central and Eastern Europe: Multinationals in Transition .* London: Pinter, 1997.

Farias, Victor. *Heidegger and Nazism.* Philadelphia: Temple University Press, 1989.

Ferguson, Adam. *An Essay on Civil Society.* Edited by Fania Oz-Salzberger. Cambridge: Cambridge University Press, 1995.

Foot, Philippa. *Natural Goodness.* Oxford: Oxford Univerity Press, 2001.

—. *Virtues and Vices and Other Essays in Moral Philosophy.* New York: Oxford University Press, 2002.

Ford, Paul Leicester, ed. *The New England Primer.* New York: Teachers College, Columbia University, 1962 [1683].

Foucault, Michel. *Discipline and Punish: The Birth of the Prison.* Translated by Alan Sheridan. New York: Michel Foucault, Discipline and Punish: The Birth of the Prison, trans. Alan Sheridan (New York: Vintage Books, 1995, 1995.

—. *Madness and Civilization: A History of Insanity in the Age of Reason.* Translated by Richard Howard. New York: Vintage Books, 1988.

—. *The Birth of the Clinic: An Archaeology of Medical Perception.* Translated by A. M. Sheridan Smith. New York: Vintage Books, 1994.

Frank, Erich. "The Fundamental Opposition of Plato and Aristotle." *The American Journal of Philology,* 1940: 166–185.

Friedrich, Carl J. "Justice: The Just Political Act." In *Justice, Nomos VI,* edited by Carl J. Friedrich and John William, 24–43. New York: Atherton Press, 1963.

Fukuyama, Francis. *The End of History and the Last Man.* New York: Free Press, 1992.

Fuller, Robert. *Spiritual but not Religious: Understanding Unchurched America* . New York: Oxford University Press, 2001.

Gallagher, Paul. "Martha Nussbaum on Compassion and Mercy." *American Journal of Economics and Sociology* 68, no. 1 (January 2009): 231–252.

Gay, John. *The Beggar's Opera.* Electronic Text Center, University of Virginia Library, 1765 [1728].

George, Robert P. *In Defense of Natural Law.* Oxford: Oxford University Press, 2001.

Gillespie, Michael Allen. *Hegel, Heidegger, and the Ground of History.* Chicago: University of Chicago Press, 1984.

Goldman, Minton. *Revolution and Change in Central and Eastern Europe.* Armonk, NY: M.E Sharpe, 1997.

Grant, Ruth. *Strings Attached: Untangling the Ethics of Incentives.* Princeton, NJ: Princeton University Press, 2011.

Greonhout, Ruth. "Aristotelian Virtue and the Contemporary Virtue of Care." In *Feminist Interpretations of Aristotle*, edited by Ruth Greonhout, 170–200. University Park, PA: The Pennsylvania University Press, 1998.

Guroian, Vigen. *Ethics after Christendom: Toward an Ecclesial Christian Ethic*. Grand Rapids, MI: Eerdmans Publishing Company, 1994.

Hamilton, Alexander. *The Papers of Alexander Hamilton*. Edited by Harold C. Syrett. Vol. 5. 26 vols. New York: Columbia University Press, 1961–1979.

Hamilton, Alexander, James Madison, John Jay. *The Federalist Papers*. Edited by George W. Carey and James McClellan. Indianapolis, IN: Liberty Fund, Inc., [1788] 2001.

Hansen, Victor Davis. *A War Like No Other.* New York: Random House, 2005.

Hartmann, Nicolai. *Moral Freedom*. Edited by S. Coit. Vol. 3. 3 vols. London: G. Allen & Unwin, 1932.

—. *Moral Phenomena*. Edited by S. Coit. Vol. 1. 3 vols. New York: Macmillan, 1932.

—. *Moral Values*. Edited by Andreas A.M. Kinneging. Vol. 2. 3 vols. New Brunswcik, NJ: Transaction Publishers, 2004.

Havel, Václav. "Address to the Senate and the House of Commons of the Parliament of Canada." Parliament Hill, Ottawa, April 29, 1999.

—. *Disturbing the Peace: A Conversation with Karel Hvíž ala*. Translated by Paul R. Wilson. New York: Knopf, 1990.

—. *Letters to Olga*. Translated by Paul R. Wilson. New York: H. Holt, 1989.

—. *Open Letters*. Translated by Paul Wison. New York: Knopf, 1991.

—. *Speech at Harvard University*. Cambridge, MA, June 8, 1995.

—. *The Beggar's Opera*. Translated by Paul R. Wilson. Ithaca, NY: Cornell University Press, 2001.

Hayek, Friedrich. *The Constitution of Liberty*. Chicago: University of Chicago Press, 1960.

—. "The Pretence of Knowledge." *Nobel Prize Lecture*. December 11, 1974.

—. *The Road to Serfdom: Text and Documents – The Definitive Edition*. Edited by Bruce Caldwell. Chicago: University of Chicago Press, 2007.

Hayes, Bernadette. "The Impact of Religious Identification on Political

Attitudes: An International Comparison." *Sociology of Religion* 56, no. 2 (1995): 177–94.

Heidegger, Martin. *Basic Concepts of Aristotelian Philosophy*. Translated by Robert D. Metcalf and Mark B. Tanzer. Bloomington, IN: University of Indiana Press, 2009.

—. *Being and Time*. Translated by John MacQuarrie and Edward Robinson. London: SCM Press, 1962.

—. *Contributions to Philosophy (From Enowning)*. Translated by Parvis Emad and Kenneth Maly. Bloomington, IN: Indiana University Press, 1999.

—. "Interview with Rudolf Augstein and Georg Wolff." *Der Spiegel*, May 31, 1976.

—. *Elucidation of Hölderin's Poetry*. Translated by Keith Hoeller. Amherst, NY: Humanity Books, 2000.

—. *Hegel's Concept of Experience*. Translated by Kenley Royce Dove. New York: Harper & Row, 1970.

—. *Identity and Difference*. Translated by Joan Stambaugh. Chicago: University of Chicago Press, 2002.

—. *Kant and the Problem of Metaphysics*. 5. Translated by Richard Taft. Bloomington, IN: Indiana University Press, 1997.

—. *Martin Heidegger: The Basic Writings*. Edited by David Farrell Krell. New York: Harper & Row, 1977.

—. *Nature, History, State:1933–1934*. Translated by Gregory Fried and Richard Polt. London: Bloomsbury, 2013.

—. *Nietzsche*. Translated by David Ferrell Krell. Vols. 1–2. 4 vols. San Francisco, CA: HarperSanFrancisco, 1991.

—. *Nietzsche*. Translated by David Ferrell Krell. Vols. 3–4. 4 vols. San Francisco, CA: HarperSanFrancisco, 1991.

—. *Ontology* . Translated by John van Buren. Bloomington, IN: University of Indiana Press, 1999.

—. *The Basic Problems of Phenomenology*. Translated by Albert Hofstadter. Bloomington, IN: Indiana University Press, 1982.

—. *The End of Philosophy*. Translated by Joan Stambbaugh. New York: Harper & Row, 1971.

—. *The Essence of Human Freedom*. Translated by Ted Sadler. London: Continuum, 2002.

—. *The Essence of Truth*. Translated by Ted Sadler. London: Continuum, 2002.

—. *The Fundamental Problems of Metaphysics: World, Finitude, Solitude*. Translated by iWilliam McNeill and Nicholas Walker. Blommington, IN: Indiana University Press, 1995.

—. *The Question Concerning Technology and Other Essays*. Translated by William Lovitt. New York: Harper & Row, 1977.

—. "The Way Back into the Ground of Metaphysics." In *Existentialism from Dostoevsky to Sartre*, edited by Walter Kaufmann, translated by Walter Kaufmann, 265–279. New York: New American Library, [1949] 1975.

Heims, Heinrich. *Monologe im Fuhrer-Hauptquartier 1941–1944*. Munich: Genehmigte Sonderausg, 2000.

Heller, Anne C. *Ayn Rand and the World She Made*. New York: Nan A. Talese, 2009.

Helm, Barbara. "Combating Misogyny? Responses to Nietzsche by Turn-of-the-Century German Feminists." *The Journal of Nietzsche Studies*, Spring 2004: 64–84.

Hinde, Robert A. *Why Goodness is Good: The Sources of Morality*. London: Routledge, 2002: Routledge, 2002.

Hobbes, Thomas. *Leviathan*. Edited by C. B. Macpherson. Baltimore, MD: Penguin Books, 1968.

Hoerber, Robert G. "Plato's Meno." *Phronesis*, 1960: 78–102.

Horace. *Satires, Epistles, and Ars Poetica*. Translated by Rushton Fairclough H. Cambridge, MA: Harvard University Press, 1970.

Horvath, Robert. "'The Solzhenitsyn Effect': East European Dissidents and the Demise of the Revolutionary Privilege." *Human Rights Quarterly* 29 (2007): 879–907.

Hösle, Vittorio. *Morality and Politics*. Translated by Steven Randall. Notre Dame, IN: University of Notre Dame Press, 2004.

Hout, Michael and Claude Fischer. "Why More Americans Have No Religious Preference: Politics and Generations." *American Sociological Review* 67, no. 2 (April 2002): 165–90.

Hume, David. *A Treatise of Human Nature*. Edited by L. A. Selby-Bigge. Oxford: Clarendon Press, 1739, 1896.

—. *An Enquiry Concerning the Principles of Morals*. Edited by J. B. Schneewind. Indianapolis, IN: Hackett Publishing Company, 1983.

—. *An Inquiry Concerning Human Understanding*. Edited by Charles William Hendel. Indianapolis, IN: Bobbs-Merrill, 1955.

—. *The Natural History of Religion*. Online Library of Liberty. London: A. and H. Bradlaugh Bonner, 1889.

Hutcheson, Francis. *An Inquiry into the Original of Our Ideas of Beauty and Virtue*. Edited by Wolfgang Leidhold. Indianapolis, IN: Liberty Fund, 2004.

Jaggar, Alison M. "Feminist Ethics." In *Encyclopedia of Ethics*, edited by L. Becker and C. Becker, 363–364. New York: Garland Press, 1992.

Johnson, William A. "Dramatic Frame and Philosophic Idea in Plato." *The American Journal of Philology*, Winter 1998: 577–598.

Jones, Daniel Stedman. *Masters of the Universe: Hayek, Friedman, and the Birth of Neoliberal Politics*. Princeton, NJ: Princeton University Press, 2012.

Kain, Philip J. "Nietzschean Genealogy and Hegelian History in 'The Genealogy of Morals'." *Canadian Journal of Philosophy* 26, no. 1 (March 1996): 123–48.

Kant, Immanuel. *Fundamental Principles of the Metaphysic of Morals*. Edited by Thomas Kingsmill Abbott. Translated by Thomas Kingsmill Abbott. EBook: The Project Gutenberg, [1785] 2004.

Katz, Leonard D. *Evolutionary Origins of Morality: Cross-Disciplinary Perspectives*. Thorverton: Imprint Academic, 2000.

Keane, John. *Václav Havel: A Political Tragedy in Six Acts*. New York: Basic Books, 2000.

Keynes, John Maynard. *Essays in Persuasion*. New York: The Norton Library, 1963.

Keysar, Ariela. "Who Are America's Atheists and Agnostics?" In *Secularism and Secularity: Contemporary International Perspectives*, edited by Barry Kosmin and Ariela Keysar, 33–39. Hartford, CT: Institute for the Study of Secularism in Society and Culture, 2007.

Kinneging, Andreas A.M. *Aristocracy, Antiquity & History*. New Brunswick, NJ: Transaction Publishers, 1997.

Klages, Mary. "Postmodernism." 2001. http://www.willamette.edu/~rloftus/postmod.htm (accessed April 29, 2014).

Kojève, Alexandre. *Introduction to the Reading of Hegel.* Edited by Allan Bloom Assembled Raymond Queneau. Translated by Jr. James H. Nichols. Ithaca, NY: Cornell University Press, 1980.

Kolnai, Aurel. *Privilege and Liberty and Other Essays in Political Philosophy.* Edited by Daniel J. Mahoney. Lanham, MD: Lexington Books, 1999.

Kosmin, Barry and Ariela Keysar. *Religion in a Free Market: Religion and Non-Religious Americans.* Ithaca, NY: Paramount Market Publishing, 2006.

Kraynak, Robert P. "John Locke, from Absolutism to Toleration." *American Political Science Review* 74 (March 1980): 53–69.

Kristol, Irving. "When Virtue Loses All Her Loveliness — Some Reflections on Capitalism and the 'Free Society'." *The Public Interest*, Fall 1970.

Lawler, Peter Augustine. *Aliens in America: The Strange Truth about Our Souls.* Wilmington, DE: Intercollegiate Studies Institute, 2002.

—. "American Nominalism and Our Need for the Science of Theology." *First Principles*, March 28, 2008.

—. *Stuck with Virtue.* Wilmington, DE: ISI Books, 2005.

Leiter, Brian. "Nietzsche and the Morality Critics." *Ethics* 107, no. 2 (January 1997): 250–85.

Lemke, J. L. "Semiotics and the Deconstruction of Conceptual Learning." *Journal of Accelerative Learning and Teaching*, January 1994: 67–110.

Lewis, Christopher Alan and Sharon Mary Cruise. "Religion and Happiness: Consensus, Contradictions, Comments and Concerns." *Mental Health, Religion & Culture* 9, no. 3 (June 2006): 213–225.

Lincoln, Abraham. "Lincoln on Slavery ." *Lincoln Home.* National Historic Site. July 1, 1854. www.nps.gov/liho/historyculture/slavery.htm (accessed 2 2011, June).

Lindstedt, David. "The Progression and Regression of Slave Morality in Nietzsche's Genealogy: The Moralization of Bad Conscience and Indebtedness." *Man and World* 23 (January 1997): 83–105.

Lowi, Theodore. *The End of Liberalism: The Second Republic of the United States.* New York: W.W. Norton, 2009.

Löwith, Karl. "Nietzsche's Doctrine of the Eternal Return." *Journal of the History of Ideas* 6, no. 3 (June 1945): 273–84.

Ludwig, Paul E. "Without Foundations: Plato's Lysis and Postmodern Friendship." *The American Political Science Review*, February 2010: 134–150 .

Lukács, Georg. *Marxism and Human Liberation: Essays on History, Culture and Revolution*. Translated by Henry F. Mins. New York: Dell Publishing Co., 1973.

Machiavelli, Niccolò. *The Prince*. Translated by W.K. Marriott. London: J.M. Dent, 1948.

—. *The Prince and the Discourses*. New York: Modern Library Edition, 1950.

MacIntyre, Alasdair C. *A Short History of Ethics: A History of Moral Philosophy from the Homeric Age to the Twentieth Century*. Vol. 2. Notre Dame, IN: University of Notre Dame Press, 1998.

—. *Whose Justice? Which Rationality?* Notre Dame, IN: University of Notre Dame Press, 1988.

MacIntyre, Alasdair C. *After Virtue: A Study in Moral Theory*. Vol. 2. Notre Dame, IN: University of Notre Dame Press, 1984.

—. *Against the Self-Images of the Age: Essays on Ideology and Philosophy*. Notre Dame, IN: University of Notre Dame Press, 1978.

—. *Dependent Rational Animals: Why Human Beings Need the Virtues*. Chicago: Open Court, 1999.

—. *Three Rival Versions of Moral Enquiry: Encyclopaedia, Genealogy, and Tradition*. Notre Dame, IN: University of Notre Dame Press, 1990.

Mackie, J. L. *Ethics: Inventing Right and Wrong*. New York: Penguin, 1977.

MacKinnon, Catharine A. *Women's Lives, Men's Laws*. Cambridge, MA: Belknap Press, 2005.

Mansfield, Harvey C. *America's Constitutional Soul*. Baltimore: Johns Hopkins University Press, 1991.

—. *Manliness*. New Haven, CT: Yale University Press, 2006.

Marcuse, Herbert. *One Demensional Man*. Boston: Beacon Press, 1964.

—. *Reason and Revolution*. Boston: Beacon Press, 1970.

Marx, Karl. *Capital Volume One*. Translated by Samuel Moore and Edward Aveling. Moscow: Progress Publishers, 1924.

McKinnon, Christine. *Character, Virtue Theories, and the Vices*. Toronto: Broadview Press, 1999.

McNeill, William. "Life Beyond the Organism: Animal Being in Heidegger's Freiburg Lectures." In *Animal Others: On Ethics, Ontology, and Animal Life*, edited by Peter H. Steeves, 197–248. Albany, NY: State University of New York Press, 1999.

—. *The Glance of an Eye: Heidegger, Aristotle, and the Ends of Theory.* Albany, NY: State University of New York Press, 1999.

McWhorter, John, "'Microaggression' Is the New Racism on Campus," *Time*, March 21, 2014, HYPERLINK "http://time.com/32618/microaggression-is-the-new-racism-on-campus/" http://time.com/32618/microaggression-is-the-new-racism-on-campus/.

Miles, Murray. "Plato on Suicide (Phaedo 60C-63C)." *Phoenix*, Autumn – Winter 2001: 244–258.

Miller, J. Hillis. *The Ethics of Reading* . New York: Columbia University Press, 1987.

Mises, Ludwig Von. *Human Action: A Treatise on Economics.* 4th Revised. San Francisco, CA: Fox & Wilkes, 1996.

Miyasaki, Donovan. "A Ground for Ethics in Heidegger's Being and Time." *Journal of the British Society for Phenomenology* 38, no. 3 (October 2007): 261–79.

Mulhall, Stephen. *Heidegger and Being and Time.* London: Routledge, 2005.

Murphy, James Bernard. "Nature, Custom, and Reason and the Explanation and Practical Principles of Aristotelian Political Science." *The Review of Politics*, Summer 2002: 468–495.

Murphy, John Patrick Michael. "Hitler Was not an Atheist." *Free Inquiry* 19 (Spring 1999): 1, 9.

Murray, Charles. *Coming Apart: The State of White America, 1960–2010.* New York: Crown Forum, 2012.

Myrdal, Gunnar. "The Equality Issue in World Development." *Nobel Prize Lecture* . March 17, 1975.

Niemeyer, Oscar. *Arch Daily.* December 5, 2012. http://vanessacorrea.com/here-then-wanted-architecture-created-courage-idealism-awareness-fact-important-life-friends-attempting-un-just-world-place-live/?utm_source=rss&utm_medium=rss&utm_campaign=here-then-wanted-architecture-created-courage-idealism-awa (accessed Janaury 20, 2014).

Nietzsche, Friedrich. *The Birth of Tragedy.* Translated by Ian Johnston. Prod. Blackmask Online. Nanaimo, BC, 2003.

Nozick, Robert. *State, Anarchy, and Utopia.* Oxford: Blackwell, 1974.

Nussbaum, Martha C. *The Fragility of Goodness: Luck and the Ethics of Greek Tragedy and Philosophy.* Cambridge: Cambridge University Press, 1986.

Owen, David. "Nietzsche's Event: Genealogy and the Death of God." *Theory & Event* 6, no. 3 (2002): 1–56.

Owen, David. "The Contest of Enlightenment An Essay on Critique and Genealogy." *The Journal of Nietzsche Studies* 25 (2003): 35–57.

Pangle, Thomas L. *Aristotle's Teaching in the Politics.* Chicago: University of Chicago Press, 2013.

Phillips, Derek L. "Authenticity or Morality?" In *The Virtues: Contemporary Essays on Moral Character*, edited by Robert B. Kruschwitz and Robert Campbell Roberts, 23–35. Belmont, CA: Wadsworth Publishing Co. , 1987.

Pinckaers, Servais. *Morality: the Catholic View.* South Bend, IN : St, Augustine Press, 2003.

Pinker, Steven. "The Moral Instinct." *New York Times Magazine*, January 13, 2008: 32–36, 52, 55–56.

—. *The Better Angels of Our Nature.* New York: Penquin Books, 2011.

Plato. "Critias ."

—. *Lysis.*

—. *Meno.*

—. *Republic.*

—. *Symposium.*

—. *Theaetetus.*

Pontuso, James F. *Civic Responsibility in the Postmodern Age.* Lanham, MD: Rowman & Littlefield, 2004.

Pontusson, Jonas. *Inequality and Prosperity: Social Europe vs. Liberal America.* Ithaca, NY: Cornell University Press, 2005.

Prichard, H. A. *Moral Obligation.* Oxford: Clarendon Press, 1949.

Putnam, Robert D. *Bowling Alone: The Collapse and Revival of American Community.* New York: Simon & Schuster, 2000.

Rahe, Paul A. *Republics Ancient and Modern: New Modes and Orders in Early Modern Political Thought.* Chapel Hill, NC: University of North Carolina Press, 1994.

Rand, Ayn. *Atlas Shrugged.* New York: Random House, 1957.

——. *The Fountainhead.* Indianapolis, IN: The Bobbs-Merrill Company, 1943.

Reginster, Bernard. "Nietzsche on Ressentiment and Valuation." *Philosophy and Phenomenology Research* 57, no. 2 (1977): 281–305.

Reno, R.R. "Nietzsche's Deeper Truth." *First Things: A Monthly Journal of Religion and Public Life* 179 (January 2008): 33–40.

Richards, Robert. "A Defense of Evolutionary Ethics." *Biology and Philosophy* 1 (1986): 293–297.

Ridley, Aaron. "Guilt Before God, or God Before Guilt? The Second Essay of Nietzsche's Genealogy." *The Journal of Nietzsche Studies* 29 (Spring 2005): 35–45.

Ridley, Matt. *The Origins of Virtue: Human Instincts and the Evolution of Cooperation.* New York: Viking, 1997.

Rorty, Richard. *Essays on Heidegger and Others.* Cambridge: Cambridge University Press, 1991.

——. *Objectivity, Relativism, and Truth.* Cambridge: Cambridge University Press, 1991.

——. *The Consequences of Pragmatism.* Minneapolis, MN: University of Minnesota Press, 1982.

Rosen, Stanley. *The Question of Being: A Reversal of Heidegger.* South Bend, IN: St. Augustine's Press, 2002.

Rothbard, Murray N. *The Ethics of Liberty.* New York: New York University Press, 1998.

Safranski, Rüdiger. *Martin Heidegger: Between Good and Evil.* Translated by Ewald Osers. Cambridge, MA: Harvard University Press, 1998.

Schacht, Richard, ed. *Nietzsche, Genealogy, Morality: Essays on Nietzsche's Genealogy of Morals.* Berkley, CA: University of California Press, 1994.

Schopenhauer, Arthur. *The World as Will and Representation.* Translated by E. F. J. Payne. Vol. 1. 2 vols. New York: Dover Publications, Inc, 1969.

Sharkey, Joe. "How Hitler's Forces Planned to Destroy German Christianity." *New York Times*, January 13, 2002: 4, 7.

Shell, Susan Meld. *The Embodiment of Reason*. Chicago: University of Chicago Press, 1996.

Shibley, Mark. "Secular But Spiritual in the Pacific Northwest." In *Pacific Northwest: The None Zone*, edited by Patricia O'Connell Killen and Mark Silk, 139–67. Walnut Creek, CA: Altamira, 2004.

Silver, Nate. "Poll Finds a Shift Toward More Libertarian Views." *New York Times*, June 20, 2011.

Slote, Michael A. *From Morality to Virtue*. New York: Oxford University Press, 1992.

Smith, Adam. *The Theory of Moral Sentiment*. Amherst, NY: Prometheus Books, [1854] 2000.

—. *The Wealth of Nations*. New York: Modern Library, (1776) 1994.

Sokal, Alan D. "A Physicist Experiments with Cultural Studies." *Lingua Franca*, May/June 1996: 62–64.

Sokal, Alan D. "Transgressing the Boundaries: Toward a Transformative Hermeneutics of Quantum Gravity." *Social Text*, no. 46/47 (spring/summer 1996): 217–252.

Sokolowski, Robert. *Introduction to Phenomenology*. Cambridge: Cambridge University Press, 2000.

—. *Phenomenology of the Human Person*. Cambridge: Cambridge University Press, 2008.

Solomon, Robert C. "Nietzsche on Fatalism and 'Free Will'." *The Journal of Nietzsche Studies* 23 (2002): 63–87.

Solomon, Robert C., and Mark C. Murphy. *What is Justice?* Vol. 2. New York: Oxford University Press, 2000.

Soloveichik, Meir Y. "The Virtue of Hate." *First Things*, February 2003.

Solzhenitsyn, Aleksandr. "Nobel Lecture." In *The Solzhenitsyn Reader: New and Essential Writings 1947–2005*, edited by Edward E. Ericson, Jr. and Daniel J. Mahoney 512–526. Wilmington, DE: ISI Books, 2006.

Stearns, Peter N. *Human Rights in World History*. New York: Routledge, 2012.

Steiner, George. *Martin Heidegger*. Chicago: University of Chicago Press, 1987.

Steiner, Lasse, Lisa Leinert, Bruno S. Frey. "Economics, Religion and Happiness." *Zeitschrift für Wirtschafts- und Unternehmensethik* 11, no. 1 (2010): 9–24.

Steiner, Peter. *The Deserts of Bohemia: Czech Fiction and Its Social Context.* Ithaca, NY: Cornell University Press, 2000.

Stern, Paul. "Anti-Foundationalism and Plato's Phaedo." *Review of Politics* 51, no. 2 (Spring 1989): 190–217.

Stern, Paul. "The Philosophic Importance of Political Life: On the 'Digression' in Plato's Theaetetus." *The American Political Science Review* 96, no. 2 (June 2002): 275–289.

Tarlton, Charles D. " Idealism and the Higher Morality versus Democracy: Using Nietzsche's Genealogy of Morals to Revisit Bradley's Ethical Studies." *Theory & Event* 8, no. 4 (2005): 1–64.

Tessitore, Aristide, ed. *Aristotle and Modern Politics: The Persistence of Political Philosophy.* Notre Dame, IN: Notre Dame University Press, 2002.

—. *Reading Aristotle's Ethics: Virtue, Rhetoric, and Political Philosophy.* Albany, NY: State University of New York Press, 1996.

The New Criterion. "Notes & Comments." November 2004.

Thiele, Leslie Paul. *Thinking Politics: Perspectives in Ancient, Modern, and Postmodern Political Theory.* Chatham, NJ: Chatham House, 1997.

—. *Timely Meditations: Martin Heidegger and Postmodern Politics.* Princeton, NJ: Princeton University Press, 1995.

Tierney, Brian. "Natural Law and Natural Rights: Old Problems and Recent Approaches." *The Review of Politics* 64, no. 3 (Summer 2002): 389–406.

Tinder, Glenn. "At the End of Pragmatism." *First Things*, September 2008: 43–46.

—. "Can We Be Good without God?" *The Atlantic Monthly*, December 1, 1989: 69, 72, 76–85.

Tocqueville, Alexis de. *Democracy in America.* Edited by Harvey C. Mansfield and Delba Winthrop. Translated by Harvey C. Mansfield and Delba Winthrop. Chicago: University of Chicago Press, 2000.

Toynbee, Arnold J. *The Disintegrations of Civilizations.* London: Oxford University Press, 1939.

Trevanian. *Shibumi.* New York: Ballantine Books, 1980 .

Van Steen, Gonda A. H. *Venom on Verse: Aristophanes in Modern Greece .* Princeton, NJ: Princeton University Press, 2000.

Visker, Rudi. "Can Genealogy Be Critical? A Somewhat Unromantic Look at Nietzsche and Foucault." *Man and World* 23 (October 1990): 441–452.

Walliman, Isidor. *Estrangement.* Westport, Conn.: Greenwood Press, 1981.

Ward, Keith. *Is Religion Dangerous?* Oxford: Lion, 2006.

Ward, Lee. *John Locke and Modern Life.* Cambridge: Cambridge University Press, 2010.

Weinberger, Jerry. "But Which Gods Will Save Us? The Political Legacy of Nietzsche and Heidegger." *Political Science Reviewer* 16, no. 1 (1986): 353–412.

White, Nicholas. "Harmonizing Plato." *Philosophy and Phenomenological Research,* June 1999: 497–512.

Wiggins, David. *Ethics: Twelve Lectures on the Philosophy of Morality.* Cambridge, MA: Harvard University Press, 2006.

Williams, Bernard. *Ethics and the Limits of Philosophy.* Cambridge, MA: Harvard University Press, 1985.

Williams, Walter E. "The Argument for Free Markets: Morality v. Efficiency." *Cato Journal* 15, no. 2/3 (Fall/Winter 1995/1996): 179–189.

Wilson, James Q. *The Moral Sense.* New York: Free Press, 1993.

Wininger, Kathleen J. "On Nietzsche, The Genealogy of Morals." *The Journal of Value Inquiry* 30 (September 1996): 453–470.

Winthrop, Delba. "Aristotle and Theories of Justice." *American Political Science Review* 72 (December 1978): 1201–16.

Wollstonecraft, Mary. *A Vindication of the Rights of Woman, with Strictures on Political and Moral Subjects.* Edited by Jr. Charles W. Hagelman. New York: Norton, 1967.

Young, Julain. *Heidegger's Later Philsophy.* Cambridge: Cambridge University Press, 2002.

Zuckerman, Phil. "Atheism, Secularity, and Well-Being: How the Findings of Social Science Counter Negative Stereotypes and Assumptions." *Sociology Compass* 3, no. 6 (December 2009): 949–971.

Zuckert, Catherine. "Nietzsche's Rereading of Plato." *Political Theory,* May 1985: 213–238.